Game of My Life
AUBURN
MEMORABLE STORIES OF
TIGERS FOOTBALL

MARK MURPHY

SportsPublishingLLC.com

ISBN 13: 978-1-59670-045-1

Publishers: Peter L. Bannon and Joseph J. Bannon Sr.
Senior managing editor: Susan M. Moyer
Acquisitions editor: John Humenik
Developmental editor: Laura Podeschi
Art director: Dustin J. Hubbart
Dust jacket design: Nic Mulvaney
Interior design: Nic Mulvaney
Photo editor: Erin Linden-Levy

Sports Publishing L.L.C.
804 North Neil Street
Champaign, IL 61820
Phone: 1-877-424-2665
Fax: 217-363-2073
SportsPublishingLLC.com

Printed in the United States of America

CIP data available upon request.

FOR CYNDE, ALICE, KEVIN, GEORGE, MARGARET,
BUDDY D., AND ALL OF THE PEOPLE WHO MAKE
AUBURN A SPECIAL PLACE

CONTENTS

FOREWORD

Auburn University football has a long and tradition-rich history featuring numerous outstanding players and many big games. Over the years, the offensive and defensive schemes used by Auburn and college football teams around the Southeastern Conference have changed many times. The same is true of the coaches on the sidelines and even the rules. However, one thing that remains constant at Auburn is a passion for the game of college football and a strong desire by the players, coaches, students, alumni, and fans to do it well and represent their university in a first-class manner.

Whatever the time period, playing college football is a challenge, something that was as true 50 years ago as it is today. Players who are successful at handling the demands of academics and athletics at the major college level are normally people who are successful after their collegiate days, something which is certainly true of the distinguished group of former players featured in *Game of My Life Auburn: Memorable Stories of Tigers Football.*

As head coach of the Tigers, I have had the opportunity to meet and get to know a large number of Auburn football players from a variety of periods. This book, written by Mark Murphy, the longtime editor of *Inside the Auburn Tigers* magazine, features some of the most interesting stories of those men, going back to the early days of the Shug Jordan era. Mark's knowledge of Auburn athletics and football in particular gives him the perspective to write in-depth about Auburn stars of different eras.

A common theme with these former Tigers is the great memories they have of their collegiate days at Auburn University. The fact that they still have a love for their alma mater says a great deal about the kind of place Auburn is and has been for many years.

As coach of the Tigers, my goal is to keep the tradition alive and make the Auburn football experience one worth remembering for players and fans for years to come. Our coaching staff has been fortunate to have been involved in our share of big games in recent years, including some of the memories shared by Auburn players who are featured in this book.

I hope you enjoy reading about this interesting group of Auburn players as they remember exciting days in AU football history.

War Eagle,

Tommy Tuberville

Chapter 1

KEN BERNICH

LOTS OF CHOICES FOR BIG LINEBACKER

Although college football is filled with countless stories of blue-chip, can't-miss prospects who couldn't make the transition from high school star to collegiate player, this isn't one of them. Ken Bernich was just as big a standout at Auburn as he was at Archbishop Shaw High in New Orleans, where he was considered a prize recruit by coaches around the country.

Even for a player as talented as Bernich, however, the transition to the rough-and-tumble world of college football in the early 1970s at an SEC power was far from easy. Bernich remembers questioning his own judgment a time or two as a freshman before settling into college life in a new location and different culture hundreds of miles from home.

"I grew up in suburban New Orleans in Gretna," Bernich says. "As an athlete I really started off in baseball, but I was always a pretty big kid. I gravitated towards football and found out that I was probably a little bit better at that than baseball. I was a typical kid who played all the sports. About my eighth grade year, I started to get pretty good at what I was doing. I attended an all-boys school and, with New Orleans being a big metropolitan area, it had good football. You were recruited in middle school and high school. It was a very competitive atmosphere."

Even though Archbishop Shaw didn't win a lot of games, Bernich made a lot of impressive plays and the college scouts soon knew his name. With a passion for the game featuring a style that included a love of contact, the 240-pound linebacker played like a man among the boys. Because of that, Bernich had his pick of about any college football program he wanted to join.

"Auburn and Georgia were my top two choices," Bernich remembers. "I escaped the clutches of LSU in the recruiting war, which was difficult to do because most of my family was in Louisiana at that time."

A visit to Auburn to check out the Tigers as they played a game against Georgia Tech in the fall of 1970 had a lot to do with Bernich signing with AU. "It was kind of hard to leave home, but my recruiting visit to Auburn was so good that on Sunday, when it was over, I didn't want to leave," he says. "Auburn is all about people—not that other places aren't, but Auburn is especially that way. That weekend I had a chance to find out what the people were like and I was really sold on Auburn."

However, despite his enthusiasm, the decision to attend the university wasn't easy. Bernich notes that he really liked Georgia, along with the program directed by former Auburn quarterback Vince Dooley and the defense managed by Auburn's last four-sport letterman, Erk Russell.

"The thing that really swayed me about Georgia was their defensive coach, Erk Russell," Bernich says. "I had seen them play twice and being a linebacker, I really gravitated towards him. It was tough to say no to him. I pretty much excluded LSU, which was kind of tough to pass, because 'Cholly Mac,' coach [Charlie] McClendon, was a real gentleman. It came down to LSU, Georgia, and the Auburn people. Coach [Ralph 'Shug'] Jordan and the other coaches are what swayed me."

A four-year starter in high school, Bernich played middle linebacker and tight end. He was also a college prospect in baseball as a first baseman and centerfielder, but football was his favorite.

A former Tiger, 1953-1955 offensive guard letterman Ernie Danjean, gave Jordan's staff an early heads up on Bernich's potential. In that era, unlike today, an alumni network actively helped with recruiting. "At that time, the Auburn coaches didn't do too much recruiting in Louisiana," notes Bernich, who says that Danjean helped cultivate his interest in Auburn.

"They called him The Hook," Bernich says. "I had a friendship with him and he was very, very influential in my decision. Paul Nix made initial contact with me from Auburn, and he was the baseball coach. Once they found out that I was really interested, [offensive coordinator] Gene Lorendo and [defensive coordinator] Paul Davis started recruiting me. When they came down to sign me, Coach Jordan was there."

However, before Bernich signed, LSU tried to use its home-field advantage. "There was definitely pressure to play for LSU," Bernich remembers. "Cholly Mac was a prince of a fellow and I really felt bad about it, but my visits to Baton Rouge were sub par. They knew I had visits to

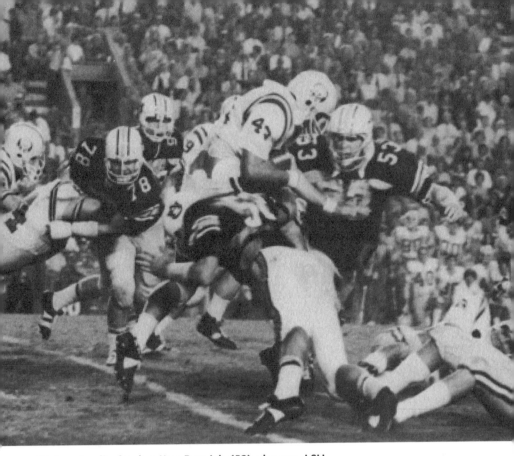

All-America linebacker Ken Bernich (53) plays vs. LSU.
Draughon Library Archives

other SEC schools and they couldn't understand why any other school was in the picture.

"We had a couple of incidents when we had gone up to Baton Rouge in a group from New Orleans," Bernich says. "It was kind of a sectional thing. The New Orleans guys were not well liked by guys from other areas, especially Baton Rouge, because New Orleans was a bigger area with more population and we had more press.

"I remember we got into a couple of fights. On Sunday morning on my recruiting visit there when they gave us the big push [to commit to LSU], I was sitting with a couple of prospects from metropolitan New Orleans and still getting over what happened the night before. It wasn't bad, but there was a lot of hell raising going on. I got a slap on my back and I turned around and it was Governor ['Big John'] McKeithen. He goes, 'You are going to be a Tiger, and not an orange and blue one, but a purple and gold one.' You talk about a salesman. I was ready to sign there, but that was an example of the kind of pressure that was put on you."

When Bernich signed in December, it was a regional letter of intent honored by SEC, ACC, and some others, but that didn't stop teams in other parts of the country from recruiting him prior to the national signing day in February. Bernich says he didn't have any intention to back out on his pledge to Auburn, but decided this recruiting business was too much fun to bypass free trips to see campuses. He visited several Big Eight and Big Ten schools before he realized he was getting behind academically. So he backed off, concentrated on school, and prepared to make his mark on SEC football.

LEARNING TO PLAY
WITH THE BIG BOYS

In the fall of 1971, freshmen were not allowed to play on the varsity. Prior to 1972, they had their own separate team that played a few games against other freshman teams, but most of the action took place on the practice field when the rookies served as scrimmage opposition for the varsity.

Bernich was a big linebacker at Archbishop Shaw. The SEC has always emphasized speed, so Auburn's coaches wanted him leaner and quicker when he reported. However, just the opposite happened. "When I got to campus I was 261 pounds, so the coaches were mad at me right away," he notes.

"The adjustment to college football was tough," Bernich admits. "My biggest problem coming into Auburn was that I was overweight. I had worked for Coca-Cola over the summer and I dropped a case on my foot. I had a broken big toe and had an ingrown toenail, which is not a good thing to happen in any sport.

"With Hub Waldrop and Kenny Howard as trainers, I will never forget I had to run a mile. And I was in bad shape. They were all over me. I was homesick and it was not a good experience. It was tough."

However, away from football, the adjustment was much smoother. "Coming out of the city, Auburn was a really good place for me," Bernich says. "I made a lot of friendships quickly and met a lot of good people who took me under their wings."

Bernich's talent soon became obvious to the coaches, who had big plans for his sophomore season, which would turn out to be a memorable year. The Tigers lost just one game despite the prediction they would be in major rebuilding mode after losing most of their stars from a team that was ranked fifth nationally. Few expected the Tigers to match the nine-win season led by Heisman Trophy recipient Pat Sullivan and his star receiver, Terry Beasley.

"As part of paying our dues, we were cannon fodder for the varsity," Bernich remembers. "When the freshman team finished, usually in October, they would bring up some of the freshmen to the varsity. I think they brought me up because of my size. This was 1971, which was Pat Sullivan's senior year. They immediately put my hand on the ground and made me rush the passer. This was a good team with great players. They just worked us over, so we really paid our dues. It was tough."

In the spring of 1972, Bernich was back at linebacker, where he would develop into a key player on one of the most physical and effective units in Auburn history. "I remember going 128 snaps in one particular scrimmage that spring," he says. "I started the scrimmage second team, but one of the inside backers got hurt, so I had to play the rest of the scrimmage with the number ones and number twos. It was really a transition year for us. A lot of the big-time players were gone and there was a lot going on with us on both sides of the ball in terms of finding some guys who could play and play quickly.

"That was an education for a lot of guys that spring, whether you were a sophomore, junior, or senior. I just kept my mouth shut and did what I could do and tried to hang on. I remember many times coming out of that stadium at 5:30, when [fullback] James Owens and I would try to hold each other up just trying to get across the street to Memorial Coliseum. That is how tough it was, but it set the precedent for that 1972 team.

"It was a team with a lot of character and, as a high school coach, I still try to teach those kind of things. Coach Jordan had always talked about dedication, determination, desire, and the rest of his seven 'Ds' of success, but that was a team that was expected to do nothing. It really had to find its identity."

It was a team that changed from a passing attack to a three yards and cloud of dust approach with heavy reliance on defense. The kicking game, always a point of emphasis with Jordan, would also be an even higher priority in 1972.

"I remember Coach Jordan sitting up in the stadium at 5:15 in the evening. Coach Davis and Coach Lorendo would turn around and look at him and he would just say, 'Keep going.' It always ended on the goal line. That was the start of a special team with a lot of camaraderie, with a lot of people finding out a lot about themselves."

The Tigers surprised virtually everybody by finishing 10-1. The only setback was a difficult-to-explain 35-7 loss to a good, but not great, LSU team in Baton Rouge on a night when everything seemed to go wrong. However, the Tigers recovered and handled the rest of the schedule with victories over Georgia Tech, FSU, Florida, Georgia, and Alabama before putting a 24-3 whipping on Colorado in the Gator Bowl.

That 1972 season featured a contest that is still recognized among fans more than three decades later as the "Punt Bama Punt" game. Auburn rallied from a 16-0 fourth-quarter deficit in the most unlikely fashion. On virtually identical plays, the same Auburn linebacker blocked punts by Alabama's Greg Gantt. Both times the ball bounced into the arms of the same defensive back, who returned them for touchdowns as the Tigers pulled out a 17-16 victory over their previously unbeaten archrival.

With many of its best players back, the 1973 team, featuring Bernich as a junior, was expected to be a powerful one, too. "That team had high expectations, which I think were justified, but injuries at key positions decimated the team, particularly at running back and quarterback," Bernich remembers. "Without a running offense, we stayed on the field a lot.

"We did get a big shutout win over Houston that year," Bernich says. "I believe that was the first shutout of Bill Yeoman's team in seven years."

To close the season, the Tigers went into the Sun Bowl with a disappointing 6-5 record and lost 34-17. "I remember we were winning the bowl game at halftime, but we just fell apart in the second half," Bernich says.

Auburn had better injury luck Bernich's senior season. "We were a good team in '74," he says. "Going into the Florida game we were 7-0, and we lost that one. If you look and are a statistics guy, you know that we traditionally beat Florida. That game really, really hurt because that was our shot at a major bowl. With victories over Georgia and Alabama, we would have had a shot at a national championship. That game and the loss to Alabama were really, really tough my senior year. It was a very good football team with great leadership with guys like [future NFL defensive back] Mike Fuller. There were players all over that field and it was a very close-knit team. There were a lot of guys who had started or backed up on the 1972 team who were now seniors, so we understood what it was like to lead and we knew what needed to be done."

The Tigers lost 25-14 at Florida in a game they had opportunities to win. They also dropped the regular-season finale 17-13 to Alabama. "Those two losses really dampened the season. Then we took it out on Texas in the Gator Bowl game and we beat them 27-3," Bernich says. That team featured running backs Earl Campbell and Roosevelt Leak, who took a pounding from Bernich and the rest of the defense. "To this day, Leak is the biggest human being I have ever run into," the linebacker says. "He was about 6-foot-4, 265 pounds. Campbell was big, too, about 6-foot-1, 230, but they didn't do too much against us at all. It was really a gratifying team thing. Our coaches were very, very pleased."

THE GAME OF MY LIFE
BY KEN BERNICH

I didn't really view football as me personally having a big game. I always viewed it as having satisfaction from a team perspective. I enjoyed it when we were all able to celebrate together. I do think that the 1972 Alabama game was interesting. That is the one that is obviously the most written about that I played in, but there are a lot of things that people don't know about that game, like the adjustment by [Alabama coach] Bear Bryant to move the punter up. That only intensified their problems. Their punter, Greg Gantt, was a three-step kicker. He was kicking the ball not from 14 or 15 yards behind the line of scrimmage. It was more like 12.

There was a tremendous amount of energy before that game walking onto the field. You could tell there was a lot of electricity in the air. During the game, there were a lot of heated matchups going on. I remember, in particular, [All-SEC defensive tackle] Benny Sivley battling with their right guard, [All-American] John Hannah. Benny and Hannah used to wrestle together in high school. They were very good and they were just jawing at each other after the plays and even during the TV timeouts. Benny was just yelling at Hannah, "Quit your damn holding, John. Quit your damn holding!" Hannah would yell back, "I ain't holding you!" That went on through the whole game, and John Hannah wasn't the kind of guy you wanted to get mad. But that was the kind of day it was. There were a lot of things going on all over the field, a lot of talking, and normally we weren't big talkers.

The sequence at the end of the game was really eerie. It was one of those destiny-type things. When they came back out with 1:22 left to try to get the lead after we went ahead 17-16, their quarterback was a Bogalusa boy [Terry Davis], who I knew. He was a very good option quarterback, so we Louisiana boys passed a few words.

After we won, we were obviously very excited. We were feeding off the crowd, which was just about in hysterics. We kind of knew we could pull it off. In our defensive huddle there was never any doubt we could win the game. I remember when Bill [Newton] got the call from Coach Davis for the punt block. He said, "I will get it." On the second one, he said,

"Somebody else is going to have to get it." We had really prepared well on special teams going into that game and knew we had a chance to block their punts.

It was a strange game because we were on the ropes. They were very good. They had trouble moving the ball and we had trouble moving the ball. Going into the fourth quarter, we were still hanging in there trying to win with turnovers and the kicking game. We stayed the course and the defense kept playing and playing. It just went back and forth. We had a very resilient group of guys.

Despite what [Auburn All-SEC tailback] Terry Henley says, that game was won with defense. I am going to plug the defense because we don't get enough credit. Off the field, we weren't much to look at when we were chewing gum and walking, but on the field, we were bold and we were very well trained by Coach Davis and his staff. We knew we were the backbone of the team. We knew we were going to have to carry the load. We knew that the offense needed to be on a short field to score, so we would give them the short field. We did that by stopping them and giving them great field position with our kicking game.

We really, really worked on our kicking game that season. We had a lot of memorable, physical games that season, like that Alabama game, which will always be a special one.

A COMEBACK FOR THE AGES

The true grit shown by Bernich and the defense was a major reason Jordan called the 1972 team his favorite. Auburn fans loved Jordan, but that day in Legion Field many of them let him know that they were unhappy with the decision that started the comeback early in the fourth quarter.

Trailing 16-0, the offense appeared overmatched against Bryant's 10-0 and second-ranked Tide. Once Auburn finally showed signs of snapping out of its offensive funk, Jordan's decision to go for a field goal with just under 10 minutes to play was met by groans and even boos from fans who wanted the Tigers to go for a first down on fourth and eight from the Tide 24. However, Jordan sent Gardner Jett onto the field and he nailed a field goal to cut the gap to 16-3 with 9:50 to play.

The fears of fans looked to be confirmed as the Tide's wishbone ground out three first downs after the kickoff before AU could force a punt. In preparations for the showdown with Alabama, blocking a punt was a high priority because the trained eyes of Davis had seen flaws in the protection schemes. Earlier in the game, the Tigers came very close to blocking a punt and had blocked a PAT after Bama's first TD in the second quarter. That point would prove to be a huge factor.

With time running out, the Tigers needed a big play and got it. With Roger Mitchell on one flank and David Langner on the other, both defensive backs raced toward the punter. Gantt's protector saw Mitchell coming and made the block, but that opened a path for Bill Newton, who was untouched and arrived to block the punt just ahead of Bernich. Langner grabbed the football on a hop and raced in for the score with 5:30 to play as the orange and blue half of the stadium went crazy.

Trailing 16-10 after Jett's PAT, Auburn's defense rose to the occasion and forced another punt. Everybody in the crowd of 72,386 knew that the Tigers were coming after Gantt with every ounce of energy they had left. Amazingly, lightning struck twice. Newton, the former walk-on, broke through untouched and blocked the punt. The ball again bounced into the awaiting arms of Langner, who raced in for the winning touchdown with 1:34 left.

With a one-point lead and a nasty Auburn defense on the field, this game was history. The Tigers got the ball back when Langner picked off a desperation pass thrown by Davis, and the celebration lasted all night.

LOVE FOR FOOTBALL AND AUBURN

Bernich played in an era that featured numerous talented players, but there is no doubt he was one of the most respected and most liked by the fans with his hard-nose, physical hustling style. Even the most casual Tiger fan knew about Bernich's toughness. Bernich notes he never really thought about being a favorite. "I was a gregarious guy," he says. "I liked to have a good time and was not a mean-spirited person. I was very close to my teammates. I just always wanted to be a team guy."

Bernich says his style was developed prior to college. "I think that goes back to high school. I was asked to play both ways and never came out of the game. At times I was triple-teamed and I just kept going at it. I didn't let that bother me. That was sort of born where I grew up playing high school ball. When I got to Auburn I was competing against a lot of very good players who made me better. The physical aspect of the game is something that always appealed to me. If we were going to play that type of game, I felt like I needed to be in there. I understood that you gave no quarter."

Although it has been a long time since he played for the Tigers, Bernich feels a bond with his alma mater. "The thing that stands out are the friendships and the camaraderie of the guys I played ball with," he says. "Auburn people have been fantastic."

Unless somebody asks, he doesn't mention his days as an All-American. "It is kind of a private thing," he says. "I don't go around talking about the fact that I played football at Auburn, but when I get back with my old teammates it is very special. There are fond, fond memories of playing football and getting a great education while doing it."

Although Bernich loves college football, he found out that he wasn't fond of playing the game professionally. After twice leading the Tigers in tackles, he was named captain of his team at the Senior Bowl, where he displayed his potential as an NFL prospect.

"The pro game is a very different game," he says. "I had a bad ankle my senior year, which turned out to be a chronic problem. I wasn't very healthy. I also had a turf toe injury that really didn't heal until about a year later. I was drafted by the Chargers [in the fourth round] and was traded to the Jets. I finished up with the Jets. They wanted me to come back to camp, but I said, 'No, things aren't going well here. I am going back to Auburn to get my degree.' That was it for me because it wasn't a good experience."

An education major, he finished his degree and then worked as a graduate assistant coach at Auburn before returning to New Orleans to coach high school football in 1980. He has been at it for 27 years, mostly in the Florida Panhandle area. "I love it and it never grows old," he says. "The good thing about high school is that it is a very hands-on affair. You aren't dealing with a polished athlete like you do at the collegiate and pro levels. There is an awful lot of teaching, which is what I like to do. You are also doing a lot of teaching off the field in terms of molding a young man's values.

"Coaching kids ages 15 through 18 in today's society, what we do as high school coaches is an integral part of their development," Bernich says. "The changes in education can get to be a little bothersome. In public education, you have got to do an even better job in the classroom than you do on the field. Not to say that you sacrifice one for the other, but the classroom part of it is very important."

Bernich says he still enjoys college football. "The SEC is a very special conference. I have a lot of appreciation for the guys we played against, because the league was just so competitive. You go through your life and you meet these guys from time to time and you have profound respect for them. The fans love the games so much it makes those Saturday afternoons real, real special."

Chapter 2

JACKIE BURKETT

A LOVE OF SPORTS

In the 1950s, Auburn had many strong teams and numerous standout players. One of the best of the best was a rangy, multisport athlete from the Florida Panhandle named Jackie Burkett. A high-energy personality both on and off the field, he was the type of player who would have been a star in any era. His excellent size, tremendous speed, and athleticism combined with a love of sports would lead him to a successful pro football career after his collegiate days and the opportunity to become part of NFL history.

"I came from an era if you had any athletic ability you just played everything," Burkett says of his childhood. "I played basketball, baseball, I ran track. I broke my leg when I was a sophomore in high school in a pickup football game we had before school. We would get to school an hour early so we could play. Sometimes when we would go into class we were so beat up I am surprised the teachers would let us in the room. We were dirty and sweaty after playing tackle football out on the field. I really liked it."

As a 6-foot-2, 165-pound junior, Burkett enrolled at Choctawhatchee High School, where he met a dynamic coach who would start him on the path to collegiate stardom. "I was a junior when I moved to Fort Walton Beach," he says. "I came down from Andalusia, Alabama. I had played some football up there, but not much. I was a halfback my junior year and I played defense. Then my senior year we got a new coach, a guy named Al 'The Hat' Wyatt. The reason he wore a hat is that he was going bald and he didn't want anybody to see it. He was a great guy who turned our program around. We had a pretty mediocre team my junior season. I think

11

we were about 4-6. When he came in he moved me to quarterback. He had seen me play in a pickup basketball game over at the school and said he wanted me as his quarterback, so that is what I played my senior year.

"We went undefeated except for one game we lost 14-13," Burkett remembers. "I hate to say this, but if there was ever a crooked game—if there have ever been a bad bunch of referees—that was it. All of the coaches, even the newspaper, said something about it being terrible. I think I scored four touchdowns that night and they were all called back. We had a great team. We ended up tied for the lead for our conference. Al Wyatt made a name for himself. Everybody liked him. He happened to be an Auburn graduate and he mentioned Auburn to me.

"After the season I was recruited by several schools. Alabama recruited me. Florida State was just getting started with its football program. It was 1955. For some reason the Panhandle area was not heavily recruited in that period. [The University of Florida in] Gainesville was a pretty good ways away, farther from Fort Walton Beach than Auburn was, and Gainesville was actually farther away than Alabama was. Bubba Nesbitt, who was the head recruiter for Alabama at the time, had come down to visit me. I basically told him I would sign with them even though Ears Whitworth was the coach and their program was not in great shape.

"Al Wyatt suggested that maybe I should visit Auburn before I signed. I said, 'Okay, if you will arrange it, I will be glad to go up there and spend the weekend.' The team was training at the time for its game in the Gator Bowl versus Baylor. I went up and stayed with M.L. Brackett and Joe Childress in their dormitory. They didn't do anything special for me. I ate with them in the chow hall. I think they brought me back home on Sunday and by then I had decided that was the place I wanted to go. I talked to the guys and they all seemed like good people. It was just a great place and a great school, with a lot of spirit and a program that was going in the right direction. I called up Bubba Nesbitt and told him I was sorry that I wasn't going to sign with Alabama. He got very upset, but I am sure that wasn't the first time it happened to him."

THREE-SPORT MAN AT AUBURN

Burkett arrived on the Auburn campus for preseason practices in the summer of 1955 with a recruiting class that would play a major role in one of the most successful eras in Auburn football history.

"I was fortunate to go up there at the time with a lot of other real good athletes like Tommy Lorino, Jerry Wilson, Mike Simmons, Ken Paduch, Lloyd Nix, Leo Sexton, Kenny Burrett, Zeke Smith—a bunch of good guys

Jackie Burkett was an All-American at Auburn. *Draughon Library Archives*

who came in that year," Burkett says. "We had a lot of people in training camp. We probably had around 70 freshmen. We had enough for several teams. I was able to win out the center position. At that time, two other guys were centers, but Zeke Smith moved to guard, and Ken Paduch moved to tackle. Both of them played a lot of ball for us."

It didn't take Burkett long to add size after he arrived at Auburn. "I went from the time I got up in the morning until I went to bed," he says of his days in high school. "My daddy died when I was a junior in high school so I had a job in addition to playing four sports and trying to keep my grades up. I probably didn't keep good hours. I am sure I didn't get enough sleep and I didn't eat right. When I got to Auburn they made me go to bed at a certain time and they fed me well. I went from 180 to 215 pounds in one year. By the time the spring was over that first year I weighed 215. That is basically where I stayed. I may have got up to 220 by the time I finished school, but I never got up to 225, which is what they had me listed at in the program."

Like all freshmen in that era, Burkett wasn't eligible for varsity competition until his sophomore season, and he was expected to contribute immediately that fall. "I played fullback my sophomore year," he remembers. "I got hurt right away in training camp. I hurt my knee. I don't know if it was in the plan or not, but they redshirted me my second year on the team. They redshirted me, Zeke, Teddy Foret, Ken Paduch—a bunch of guys. Just a couple of guys played as sophomores. As it turned out, it was a very fortunate thing for me because it gave me three more years of eligibility. We had a good team in 1956. I remember one game we lost was to Florida—the last time we lost to them in a long time. They beat us down in Gainesville, and Zeke and I both ended up almost having to go in that ball game, which would have ruined our redshirt year. Frank Reeves, the starting center, got hurt. Then they sent in the backup and he got hurt, too, a couple of plays later. They were going to send me or Zeke in, but they thought better of it and decided to move one of the guards over to play center because the score was 14-0 and the game was probably lost anyway."

The 1956 squad finished 7-3 and won its last four games. The Tigers entered 1957 with momentum and a strong group of redshirt sophomores ready to make a splash, including Burkett at middle linebacker and center. It didn't take long for that to happen. Coach Shug Jordan's team played a strong game on opening day, defeating eighth-ranked Tennessee 7-0 in Knoxville. The victory versus the Vols pushed the Tigers into the top 10 in the next poll at No. 7. After a 3-0 win at Georgia Tech in game four, the Tigers moved up to fifth. In game six they knocked off 19th-ranked Florida 13-0 before preparing to face a tough Mississippi State team that was ranked 17th and ready to give the Tigers one of their toughest tests.

THE GAME OF MY LIFE
BY JACKIE BURKETT

My most memorable game is probably one that wouldn't be brought up by a lot of people as a special game for Auburn football. It was a game against Mississippi State the year we were national champions. We were behind 7-0 at halftime. Shug made a good speech in there and we all talked and everything. It was like, "Hey, we have a lot on the line here. We are undefeated up to this point."

It was the seventh game of the season. I remember Coach Jordan's speech was about telling us that these guys weren't as good as we were. Let's go out there and kick their asses in the second half. It didn't take us long to get ahead of them in the third quarter.

We took the second-half kickoff and came out and just knocked them off the ball. We scored a touchdown to tie the game at 7-7. The first time they got the ball in the third quarter, we stopped them right away and forced them to punt. I didn't block the punt, but I got through the line so fast that I jumped up in the air and I was way up over the punter. I can still remember the picture of it. The punter saw where I was and he pulled the football down and tried to run. John Whatley tackled him in the end zone for a safety. That put us ahead 9-7. Then, later in the game we scored another touchdown that made the score 15-7, which is how the game ended.

I believe that game was the turning point of our national championship season. After that we said, "By golly, we can win every game." Mississippi State had a good team that year. They had Billy Stacy, who was an All-SEC quarterback, and I believe he made an All-America team. He ended up playing in the pros for a number of years as a defensive back. He was a good player and they had a good ball club, but we just manhandled them after the first half.

I would say that was my most memorable game at Auburn. I had a lot of good plays that day. It just seemed like it was one of those games that I was always in the right place at the right time. It was really exciting to me because it was also one of those games in which it looked like we were going to have a real problem winning, but we just took it to them and proved we were the best.

I won't say the coaches were really upset at us at halftime, but they were concerned because we were letting Mississippi State get a lead on us and we weren't playing very good football. We came out in the second half and drove right down the field against them and then we got the safety. We scored nine points on them before they even got off the ground. That was the game I really remember from my college days. Of course, that 40-0 victory over Alabama to finish the season wasn't too bad, either. I had a touchdown run in that game. After that we knew we had a chance at the national championship, because we were second going into that game behind Ohio State and then the AP voted us No. 1. That whole year was sort of a magical season for us. We had a lot of luck that year and then we had no luck the next couple of years. I guess it all evens out.

REFLECTING ON AUBURN
AND THE PROS

Burkett says his time as an Auburn student was special. He showed just how much the school, his teammates, and coaching staff meant to him when he turned down an offer from the NFL's Baltimore Colts to go pro after his redshirt junior season. With his wife, Jacqueline, by his side, he finished his engineering degree and moved on to a 10-year career in the NFL.

"Jackie and I met in high school," the Auburn star notes. "We got married when I was in college and she had just graduated from high school. She got one of those PHT degrees, pushing hubby through, making sure I graduated so I could earn a good living. It worked out really well. She spent the last two years up at Auburn with me. We had a good time. We raised three sons. They are all not very wealthy, but they are healthy."

Burkett notes that the training he received at Auburn helped him both as a pro football player and after he put away the pads for good. "I was very fortunate to be able to play at Auburn. I was very fortunate to be voted captain my senior year. I have always considered it one of the real honors I have had—when you have been voted captain after being with your teammates for four years, practicing with them, and going through the hardships we had. That is real special. I will never forget any of those guys who did that."

Burkett played more than just football at Auburn. He was an excellent basketball player and competed for coach Joel Eaves' freshman team in what was a very strong era for the sport at Auburn. "I loved basketball," he says. "I even enjoyed practice, but at that time it interfered with spring training, which was winter quarter. I played basketball as a freshman, but after [the football coaches] saw I was going to be a football player, they didn't want me to play basketball any more. So I had to quit that. I did play baseball. I played three years of baseball. We won the SEC one year and I really enjoyed my baseball career. We had three different coaches. Erskine Russell was the coach one year, Joe Connally was the coach one year, and Dick McGowen was the coach one year."

Burkett's basketball teammates still remember him as an excellent player, and Burkett was good enough in baseball to be drafted by the Boston Red Sox while at Auburn. He remembers a Red Sox scout visiting him in Fort Walton Beach, where he was working a summer job as a lifeguard. "A guy stayed down here for several days trying to get me to go with him to Boston and visit up there," Burkett remembers. "He said that Ted Williams wanted to talk to me, although I am sure Ted Williams didn't know who the heck I was. But he tried to make it sound like that. Although they wanted me to sign, I didn't feel confident in my ability to make anything in baseball, but I felt like I had something going in football. I turned them down and I am glad I did because I never could hit a good curveball. I could hit a fastball and I could hit a curveball if a pitcher let me know it was coming."

The NFL's Colts also drafted Burkett after the 1958 season, when he was voted the top linebacker and center in the SEC by the league's coaches while earning the first of back-to-back All-America awards. "Zeke [Smith] and I both got drafted by Baltimore after our junior years since we both got redshirted, but we didn't really consider signing with the pros because we felt like Auburn had invested in us and was good to us," Burkett says. "We didn't consider it. I told Baltimore it was great that they drafted me, but they would have to be willing to wait to sign me. We thought we had a great team and we could come back and win a national championship our senior year. It didn't happen. We had some missing links and the team didn't gel exactly right. We had a good team and we beat some people badly. We had a good defense, but for some reason we couldn't score when we needed to and we couldn't move the ball when we needed to, particularly in that first game against Tennessee."

The Tigers finished 7-3 Burkett's senior season. "We didn't have a lot of luck that year," he says. "We didn't have as good a team as we did in 1957, but we could have won all of our games in 1959. We lost three ballgames by a total of 14 points.

"The 1958 team was probably our most talented," Burkett says of a squad that finished fourth nationally with a 9-0-1 record. The only game the Tigers didn't win was at Georgia Tech. "I really believe that was our best team," he says. "Georgia Tech cost us the national championship on a fluke play. We beat them up and down the field that day in Atlanta. It rained up there all day long. We had like 300-and-something yards of total offense and they had around 100, but they ended up tying us at 7-7. It was just a shame because we would have won back-to-back national championships."

Even though he was a linebacker and center, Burkett was probably the fastest on the team and a player the pro scouts coveted. He was the Colts' first-round pick, the 12th player taken overall, and he signed with the NFL club for what today would likely seem a ridiculously low amount of money.

"Guys ask me all the time if I feel bad that I played in an era before football players made the big money, but I always say, 'Hell, no,' I was doing what I wanted to do and I was making three times what other guys coming out of college were making in engineering jobs," Burkett says. "I would have signed for probably $6,000 or something. Instead, I signed for $12,000 and got a bonus, plus I was able to work in the off-season. I made another $5,000 working during the off-season. I was making more money than I needed at the time. Don't feel sorry for me because the guys are making big money now. I don't harbor any grudges."

Burkett, who played through the 1970 season, says his biggest contract was for $30,000 while playing for the New Orleans Saints his final year. "I probably made more money my last year in Dallas with the playoff bonuses," he notes.

Burkett played linebacker for the Colts through the 1966 season and was outstanding. He went to the Saints in the 1967 expansion draft. He played there for one season before being traded to the Dallas Cowboys, where he played two years for coach Tom Landry's team before finishing in New Orleans. In addition to playing outside linebacker, he was a deep snapper. Two of his most memorable moments as a pro came in that capacity his final season with the Saints.

"My whole game against the Lions, my last year in football, was sort of a magical thing," Burkett points out. "I had a great game and Tom Dempsey kicked that field goal. I had a bunch of tackles, plus I had two interceptions, and we won the game on a world-record field goal. It was 63 yards and I snapped the ball. I got a game ball that day along with Dempsey. I tell people the one I have could be the ball that was used for the record field goal, because it got back in the ballgame. The field goal didn't go into the stands. It just barely went over the goal posts."

Burkett also remembers his final game in 1970 against the Chicago Bears and legendary tough-guy linebacker Dick Butkus. "Going into the game, we always watched film of the other team," Burkett notes. "Every week we would do that. Butkus was on the punt return team and he would line up right over the center, but he wouldn't get down in a three-point stance. He could get there in a two-point stance. Butkus was a big guy with big arms. When the center would raise his head up, he would forearm the guy right across the facemask. He did it time and time again. It was like a forearm, which he could legally throw, and he was trying to hit the guy in the jaw with his elbow, which wasn't supposed to be legal. I saw all of that stuff going on, and going into that game, I was seriously thinking about having a sore hand or something and not being able to snap for punts.

"I said to myself, 'Nah, I can't live with myself knowing I did that, although nobody else would know.' I just decided to take my punishment. I figured this was my last game ever. I said it would be just like me to get my jaw broken or my neck broken by Butkus, who was a big, mean son of a bitch. We got the ball and, like what usually happens, we had a three and out. I got over the ball and fully expected to see Butkus, but instead there was a guy lined up in a three-point stance, and it was No. 74. It was some rookie. I snapped the ball, ran down the field, and everybody was happy."

BUSY AFTER PRO FOOTBALL

During his first stint with the Saints in 1967, Burkett and two teammates ran a business they called Saints Pest Control. With Burkett as president, they quickly signed up enough customers to get started after forming the company. "I guess we were playing on the Saints being everybody's heroes down there, even though we didn't win many ball games," says Burkett. "I figured out why everybody loved us so much. Of the 16 games that year we beat the point spread something like 13 times, so the people of New Orleans loved us." However, while the pest control business had lots of customers, it wasn't a big moneymaker. "People signed up with us to do their houses, which back then was five dollars a month," Burkett notes. "I didn't really like that business. We ended up with more than 1,000 customers and they were all paying five dollars a month, so it wasn't a good business."

By the time he decided to say goodbye to football after the 1970 season, Burkett was out of the pest control business, but had another business going strong. He owned a sidewalk restaurant in the French Quarter near Jackson Square. "I announced my retirement and retired," he says. "I was just tickled to death to be one of the few guys who was able to do that and say I was through. I had a retirement party after my last game. I had the mayor come to it. It was just a real, real thrill to be able to do that."

However, the Saints weren't finished with Burkett. They tried to lure him back to the team during 1971 as a deep snapper. "Jerry Sturm, he was the center who was also the backup long snapper to me," Burkett says. "He became starting snapper after I retired and he snapped two balls over the punter's head in the first three ball games. John Meachem, who was the owner of the Saints, came to see me at my restaurant and said, 'Jackie, you have got to come back.' I said, 'If you give me five weeks to get in shape and pay me $30,000, I'll come back.' He said, 'That's crazy, come back next week.' I said, 'There ain't no way. Those guys hit hard out there.'

"It was fun playing in the NFL," Burkett adds. "I wouldn't take anything for that experience. It was just wonderful. It opened doors for me in all of the things I have done since then. I was a sales manager for a pipe company for 17 years because of somebody I met through my restaurant, which was popular because I was a ballplayer." That job led to his current position as an engineer for PBS&J. When he decided to run for public office back home in Fort Walton Beach, his notoriety as a former college and pro star probably helped him get elected as a county commissioner. He served for one term before deciding politics wasn't his cup of tea. "I am glad I did it and had the experience, but I wouldn't do it again for three times the money," he says. He now spends his spare time with his wife or on the golf course, where, not surprisingly, the natural athlete excels.

Burkett still keeps up with Auburn football and is excited about the success his alma mater has had on the gridiron. The Tigers have produced many great players in the 50 years since Burkett graduated from Auburn, but few have played the game as well as the two-way star from the 1950s.

Chapter 3

DAVID
CAMPBELL

FROM TUBA TO TACKLE

For Auburn teams in the 1960s, it's a good thing that the mother of future All-American David Campbell had a change of heart.

Growing up in the little town of Sumiton, about 30 miles north of Birmingham, Campbell played baseball and marched in the Dora High School band. "My dream was always baseball, and that was what I was best at," Campbell remembers. "Of course, I was a big guy. In the eighth grade I was playing tuba in the band, but during the season I slipped off and went out for football against my mother's wishes. My mom came to a game to see me play my tuba, but after she got there I had two older sisters and they said, 'Mom, Dave is not in the band. He's over there on the sidelines.'

"She saw me standing there, and I was playing on the varsity team as an eighth grader. I remember when they put me in the game that night, the band cheered for me because their ex-tuba player got into the game. My mom realized it was kind of a done deal, so she didn't get mad at me."

The band's loss was Auburn's gain, although it took some heavy lobbying to make that happen, especially for a prospect who turned out to be a college All-American.

"I happened to have a coach who was an ex-Auburn football player, a guy named Joe Baughn, who was a great player at Auburn himself," Campbell says. "My senior year in high school he carried me to Auburn three or four times, and every time we would go he would take me in to talk to coach [Shug] Jordan. The last trip we made, he begged Coach Jordan to give me a scholarship. I think we were playing Mississippi State that day and he just kept begging and begging and begging. Finally Coach

Jordan said, 'We are going to give that boy a chance.' I could feel my heart leaping in my chest because I was so excited to have a chance to play college football."

Campbell was a four-year starter in high school and an all-county and honorable mention All-State pick, but college recruiters weren't exactly lining up to sign him. "We didn't get a lot of credit at Dora because we just didn't have a good team my last two years of high school," Campbell notes. "I played every position on the field, from quarterback to fullback to defensive tackle. You name it, I played it. It was kind of crazy, but I could run, and back then a big guy who could run a 4.7 or a 4.75 40 was very unusual. There weren't many around."

Campbell's coach was the brother of Georgia Tech All-American Maxie Baughn. "Joe was a big influence on me," Campbell notes. "I am thankful I had him as my high school coach, because without him I don't think I would have ever had the chance to go to Auburn."

A GROWING EXPERIENCE

Campbell reported to Auburn prior to the 1966 season. Although not considered big by today's standards, at 6-foot-4 and around 195 pounds he was immediately groomed to be a defensive lineman.

"The thing that was amazing to me when I got there was how everybody could run and how everybody had pretty good size," he remembers. "The first day I was there I looked around at all of the guys who were big and I was amazed at the level of athletes. We did have some guys who weren't very good, but they didn't stick around. Back then you could sign 40 [per year]. We usually had a lot of walk-ons and a lot of times the walk-ons were better than some of the signees. The adjustment to college really began for me as a sophomore. That is when I realized what it was really all about. Freshmen back then had to play on the freshman team."

The SEC has always been known for its rough-and-tumble style of football. That was particularly true in the 1960s, as Campbell found out the first time he scrimmaged against the varsity as a freshman. "I remember going up against a guy named Bill Braswell, who is a friend of mine now," he says. "Bill liked to kill me. They had been practicing for about two hours already. I was fired up and I was in the backfield the first few plays. Braswell comes up to the line and said, 'All right, freshman.' Then he hit me in the chin with an elbow and it felt like it drove my jawbone through my left ear. I said to myself, 'I can't let this slow me down.' The next play I was in the backfield and here he comes. He hit me on my left side and drove my

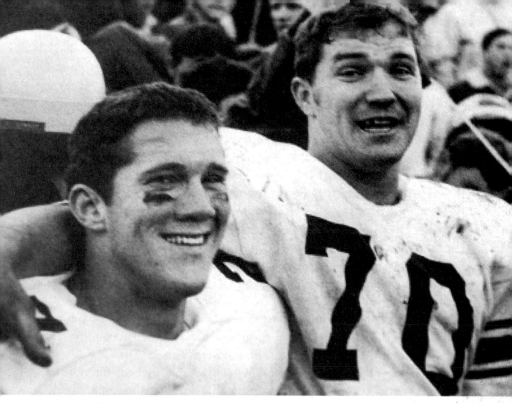

Buddy McClinton and David Campbell (70) enjoy a victory.
Draughon Library Archives

jawbone through my right ear. The next time I said, 'I got the message, okay?' It was tough.

"The next real experience was in the off-season when they put us in the padded room. George Atkins, who recruited me, was a coach I loved and respected. I was always afraid they were going to move me to the offensive line, and he was tough—and boy, do I mean tough. Coach Atkins was in the padded room with us and just about anything was allowed except for biting, pulling hair, and closed fists. I think the coaches closed their eyes to the closed fists.

"The first guy I wrestled was Gusty Yearout. Of course, he wore my tail out. I was a young freshman and didn't know what was going on. The second guy I wrestled was [All-America center] Forrest Blue, and Forrest wore me out. They left me out there and then they called Ron Yarbrough, who was a year ahead of me. He was a guy full of fire and vinegar, as Coach Jordan used to say."

Campbell won that showdown and proved to the coaches he was tough enough to play SEC football. "That was the day I grew up at Auburn University. A lot of guys who played at Auburn in that period grew up in that padded room. It helped make them the men they were looking for when they stepped on the football field. They were some of my toughest memories, but also some of my favorite memories."

Auburn's coaches wanted Campbell to add muscle and weight. It didn't take long for that to happen when he arrived at college. "I think I started gaining weight the first day I moved to campus," he says. "It was unbelievable. I couldn't believe how they fed us. When I found out you could eat all of the chicken you wanted, man, I got excited! I would sit down and eat two or three chickens at a meal."

By his sophomore year, Campbell was up to 235 pounds and kept getting bigger. He weighed 265 as a junior and played at 270 as a senior. "When I graduated I weighed 299 pounds and I was 6-foot-5 1/2. I had grown an inch and a half and put on 104 pounds while I was at Auburn eating in the dining hall."

Campbell and teammate Richard Cheek, who later played for the Buffalo Bills, were known for their huge appetites. "Richard and I loved to eat," Campbell says. "We always had those jumbo shrimp. One day I ate four dozen of them and I was thinking, 'How could anybody eat more than that?' And Cheek did. He ate 50-something of them. I remember coming in from a game after we played Georgia Tech over there and I ate seven T-bone steaks in the chow hall."

While he enjoyed the cuisine, the on-field experience was less pleasant his first year in college. "I had a pinched nerve and it was terrible," he says. "It felt like somebody was sticking a hot knife down through my collarbone. It was a terrible, terrible feeling."

Campbell's sophomore season was much better. He didn't start, but saw significant playing behind tackles Charles Collins and Roy Tatum. "I played in every game and probably played in every quarter my sophomore year," he notes. "It was a great experience. Charlie Collins was a good influence on me while I was at Auburn. In fact, Charlie [a minister in Atlanta] is a great leader of men now. I learned a lot from him. They just don't get any better than Charlie in my book.

"There were some guys who I was really close to on the team. It was unbelievable. It was like a brotherhood with people like Mike Kolen, Tom Banks, Don Bristow, and Buddy McClinton, John Riley and Sonny Ferguson, and more. That sophomore year we all stuck together. My freshman year we were supposed to be one of the poorest signing classes Auburn had ever had, but I think something like seven of us ended up making All-SEC. We had a good bunch of sophomores that year who went on through to graduate.

"My junior season was actually my best year," he says. "I remember going into practice. I had a bad Achilles tendon, and when I say it was bad, it was so bad that I limped. About four days before the first game, Dr. [Jack] Hughston from the Hughston Clinic and [trainer] Kenny Howard came to me and said, 'Dave, we have something that is going to make you well.' I said, 'What is it?' They said, 'It is Decadron, a type of cortisone, and we are going to shoot it in your heel. We just have got to find the sore spot and then you will be okay.' I remember Dr. Hughston telling me there in my dorm room, 'This is going to hurt a lot, Dave.' When he found the sore spot, I thought I was going to die. It was worse than any pain I have ever had. The next morning I got up to go to the dining hall and I felt so good that I ran in place in front of everybody. My teammates couldn't believe it, because I had looked pitiful all fall. I felt like I had a new lease on life and had a really good junior year.

"I was SEC Lineman of the Week against Tennessee and Miami that year, and I was National Lineman of the Week against Miami. I made All-America on two or three teams. The only bad thing I remember about my junior year is we ended up losing to Georgia and Alabama when we weren't supposed to. We were supposed to beat both of them and that kind of put a damper on things, but we went out to the Sun Bowl and had a great time in El Paso and in Juarez, Mexico. I remember in the Sun Bowl I was the most valuable lineman. That was a great experience because we won the game. It was a lot of fun."

THE GAME OF MY LIFE
BY DAVID CAMPBELL

The game that I will probably never forget is the Miami game my junior year. We were playing them for homecoming. They were ranked [ninth] in the top 20 and we weren't even ranked. They were supposed to kill us. I have the clipping to prove this and I don't know if it has ever been matched, but we held them to minus-89 yards that day. It was unheard of to hold a team ranked that high to minus-89 yards. I had five sacks in that game, and one of those was one of the longest sacks I can ever remember. Sonny Ferguson, the outside linebacker, and I had a screen play covered. Miami's quarterback was an ol' boy named David Olivo who played for the Cardinals for a while. He just turned and ran straight back. I didn't tackle him until he decided he was going to make a turn, and when he did that, I got him. It was just a great game for us and it is one a lot of us will remember.

Miami had a lot of good players. Ted Hendricks was playing, and they had another defensive end who played with the Raiders for a long time, too. They had a good team. They had a running back named Vince Opalsky. It was one of those games when everything went great for us on defense. Coach Paul Davis, our defensive coordinator, and the rest of the coaches had a great game plan that day and we just wore them out.

About the third play from the end of the game I made a tackle on Opalsky and ended up spending the night in the infirmary with a concussion. I didn't remember a whole lot about the game until we got to see the film. In fact, my wife got the film out of the archives at Auburn. It is always fun to watch that. A bunch of us starters were still in there late in the ball game because when you are playing a team ranked in the country, you want to beat them as badly as you can.

MANY MORE YEARS OF FOOTBALL

Many fans remember the 1969 season as the start of the Pat Sullivan and Terry Beasley era. The Tigers improved from 7-4 Campbell's junior year to 8-3. "We had a good year," he says. "We went to the Bluebonnet Bowl in Houston. We finished up the year beating Georgia and Alabama, and that was a great way to finish. I had some injuries that really hurt me my senior year. I broke my big toe the week before we played Tennessee in the second game. I think Pat threw five interceptions and Tennessee ended up beating us badly in the fourth quarter. We lost 45-19 that day.

"The week before we played LSU, I broke my arch in practice and I remember talking to the trainer. Kenny [Howard] told me it was a terrible injury; it was probably going to hurt a lot. I was able to go back to practice and I could hardly walk. I missed two or three games, but I came back and started the LSU game. They had deadened my foot, but it was dead all the way up to my knee, so they could see I couldn't play that day. I felt like I was on a stub playing with a wooden leg. I didn't play at all in the Florida game. I came back and had real good games against Georgia and Alabama. I didn't play well in the bowl game against Houston. They wore us out. They were coming off probation and were hungry. We went out to Houston and had a good time out there. We really didn't have our mind on the ball game and kind of got embarrassed, but it was a good year, mainly because we beat Georgia and Alabama."

After suffering narrow losses to Alabama his sophomore and junior years, Campbell notes that he is thankful to go out a winner versus Auburn's in-state rival. "That loss to Alabama my junior year was heartbreaking," he says. "I will be honest with you. If we had never beaten

Alabama while I was at Auburn, it would have had a bad impact on me. It would have been something that would have stuck in my craw throughout my coaching career all of the way up to today. I will tell you one thing, buddy, anybody who thinks that the Auburn-Alabama game isn't big better think again. Those guys who have beaten Alabama all four years, I feel wonderful for those guys. In a way I kind of feel sorry for those Alabama guys ... no, what am I saying? I don't feel sorry for those Alabama guys. I can't do it. Those guys will find in the years to come it is a bad thing they won't even want to talk about. They don't even want to remember it.

"That Alabama game [Auburn 49, Alabama 26] my senior year was great," Campbell notes. "Seeing Connie Frederick pull that punt down and run it for a touchdown, it was one of the most joyous moments I ever had. I remember the Alabama quarterback, Scott Hunter, had a great day. I think he threw for over 400 yards, but we almost beat that boy to death. Scott just kept on throwing the football. I bet I hit Scott 12 times that day—I just killed him—but he kept on throwing that football. We had a guy throwing the ball pretty good named Sullivan. We also had a guy named Beasley. Those two guys were something else, too."

A pro prospect, Campbell played in the All-American Bowl all-star game in New Orleans and the Coaches All-American Game after his senior season. The spring before his senior year, he made the 1969 Playboy All-America team. "I got to go to Chicago to spend a weekend as part of the Playboy All-American team and I had a good time up there," he says. "That was quite an experience for an ol' country boy, and I got to know a lot of people that I played against."

Although Campbell's senior year didn't go as well as he hoped due to the injuries, unlike when he was ready to make the jump from high school to college, the NFL had plenty of interest. Campbell was drafted in the sixth round as the fourth overall pick by the Miami Dolphins. "I went to Miami and things were going good there," he notes. "They had a strike that year and the veterans didn't come in for five or six weeks, but while I was there, my Achilles tendon injury flared up again. I ended up being cut, but was put on the cab squad. I stayed on it for a while. Then, at the end of the season, I got cut from the cab squad mainly because of my Achilles tendon and because my big toe flared up on me. They wouldn't give me cortisone shots because they would have had to pay me for all of the things they promised.

"The next year I went down to New Orleans to play for the Saints. Although things were going good there, I got up one morning and I could hardly walk to the bathroom. I decided it was time to finish playing football. I moved to Jasper and began coaching. I worked in Birmingham for a year and then [current Troy University head coach] Larry Blakeney and I, who were teammates for four years, and another Auburn guy, Scotty Long, went to Walker High School. I stayed at Walker High for 20 years. Larry left and went to Vestavia and I stayed at Walker until I retired from public education. I was the head coach at Walker for 13 years and got out of coaching. I went into the real estate business for myself and got where I could retire. I am totally retired now. I am doing a lot of traveling and enjoying life. Larry and I are good friends. Larry was a great influence on me in coaching. I took the head coaching job at Walker behind him and had a lot of great years in coaching."

After Walker and before he retired, Campbell decided to take one more coaching challenge. This was a daunting one. He accepted the job as head coach of a private school in his childhood hometown. When he arrived, the Sumiton Christian team was the Bad News Bears of that area. Campbell took over a team with an all-time record of one win and 49 losses. "When I went there, it was a private school. I got them into the public school league and we ended up having some really good teams," Campbell says. "The first year we went 9-1, the next year we went 12-2. I was the head coach there for seven years and we went to the playoffs all of the years I was there. We grew to a 3A school and then I turned it over to my nephew. He is coaching there now."

Campbell still follows the football fortunes of his alma mater and says he has fond memories of his time as an Auburn athlete. "The greatest thing that happened to me at Auburn is that is where I met my wife, Glenda Burton. I met her at the end of my sophomore year and we got married at the end of my senior year. She was from Jasper, but I never met her until I was at Auburn." The couple raised a daughter named Amy, and the former Tiger star notes he is a proud grandfather.

He also notes that he has lots of great memories of his days on campus. "I am like a lot of guys. I can't tell you how dear Auburn is to my heart. There were so many great people there, like Brownie Flournoy, the dorm coach. I loved him like I love my father. Joe Connally, our defensive line coach, I loved him too, even though I could never do anything right for Coach Connally. He never accepted anything except perfection and there is no way to do anything perfect. You can always find something wrong with your performance. He would have me do things over and over and I appreciated that. He was a great coach and he turned out some great football players the years he was at Auburn.

"I remember our defensive coordinator, coach Paul Davis, called me over to the sideline my sophomore year and said, 'Let me tell you something, you are going to be an All-American at Auburn.' I remember coming home that weekend, telling all of my friends that I was going to be an All-American. Coach Davis told me that and I believed it. He had a very big influence on me while I was there, along with Coach Atkins, Sam Mitchell, and Bill Oliver. They were just great influences. When I say Bill Oliver, a lot of people will say they don't think of him as an Auburn man, but I will tell you, the four years I was at Auburn, those guys on the team will tell you he had a great impact on our football team.

"To this day, Coach Jordan still is having an impact on my life. I think about the things he talked about when I played at Auburn. I made one of his speeches to every football team I have ever coached. It was called the 'Big D' speech—about dedication, determination, discipline, desire. He would always get down to the last big D and he would say, 'Fellows, when you try all of those things and they don't work, you have got to remember to damn it anyway and start all over.' There have been hundreds and hundreds of kids who have heard that speech from me, and it is the way I have tried to live my life. I have always remembered those Big D's and sometimes when things get you real down, you remember what he said and you go back to determination, discipline, and desire and make it happen."

Chapter 4

JASON CAMPBELL

DECIDING ON FOOTBALL

Many kids dream of becoming a star athlete in more than one sport, but few are legitimately good enough to be top-level, major college prospects in both football and basketball. However, when Jason Campbell was leading little Taylorsville High School to championship seasons, he was one of those rare athletes with the ability to be a college star in either sport.

Growing up the son of a respected high school coach, Campbell notes that he always enjoyed being the quarterback, the only position he ever played. A two-time Mississippi All-State selection in football, he was even more passionate about basketball, the sport in which his dad worked as head coach at Taylorsville High.

"I liked playing quarterback, but throughout high school, basketball was always my favorite," says Campbell, who was also a two-time All-State pick in hoops. "When I was a senior I had a decision to make, and I decided I had a better opportunity in football because there aren't that many 6-foot-5 quarterbacks. I thought football would give me the best opportunity."

After committing to football, the next order of business was to find the right college. "That was a tough decision," Campbell admits. "The SEC schools were recruiting me along with schools from the Big 10 and a couple of schools out west, but I always wanted to play in the SEC because that is where I felt the top competition was. Those games are always tough and that is how you want it to be. I felt when it came down to the end of recruiting it was Auburn, Georgia, and LSU."

After finishing his senior football season, Campbell was ready to make his choice. He announced at his church in front of family and friends that he was headed to Auburn, an exciting development for Don Dunn, the assistant coach who recruited Campbell, and head coach Tommy Tuberville, who had instructed his staff to find a big-time quarterback prospect to help rebuild the program he had taken over a year earlier.

"I made my commitment early in December of my senior year so I could focus on my senior basketball season," Campbell says. "LSU was going through a coaching change. Georgia was a nice school, but at the same time, it was three or four hours farther away from my parents and family to come to the games. At Auburn, it was the right time for me to have the opportunity to play early and for my people to get back and forth to the games with no problem."

Family is a big deal to Campbell. Growing up with athletic siblings helped to develop his passion for sports. Older sister Melody was an outstanding basketball player and hurdler whose athletic career ended early due to a knee injury. Larry, who is six years older than Jason, played linebacker at Mississippi State.

"I grew up around sports with my brother and my sister, who were involved in sports at a young age," the quarterback remembers. "I was always involved, too. The main thing that got me going was playing yard football with the older guys. We wouldn't play touch football; we would play tackle football. When you have those big guys in the yard with you, it makes you tougher and you learn how to earn what you want to get.

"That is the same way it was in basketball, playing in the yard with the older guys like my brother. I was always competing against him. He helped me get to the point where I am now.

"Also, being around my dad all of the time, who is a coach in both football and basketball, really helped me. I was always involved in camps at a very early age and got to travel around and compete against a lot of different guys. It let me see what my skill level was and what I needed to do to improve."

By the time he was a ninth grader, Campbell was a starter at guard on the varsity basketball team. He also played varsity football as a freshman and took over the starting assignment as a sophomore. As a junior he led the team to the state championship, throwing for 2,719 yards and 33 TDs. As a senior he totaled nearly 3,400 yards of offense on a team that reached the state semifinals.

Jason Campbell led the Tigers to a 13-0 season in 2004.
Inside the Auburn Tigers magazine

Campbell's basketball stats were impressive, too, but after he committed to Auburn, he put all of his energy into becoming a great quarterback.

FULL-TIME FOOTBALL

Even for an athlete as talented as Campbell, the adjustment to college wasn't easy. "From high school to college I think was a bigger jump than from college to the NFL because you are moving out of your parents' house to live by yourself," he says. "You basically have to teach yourself how to study and do it on time and have the responsibility of going to class, along with playing football the same day and making sure you have everything in order. It is a challenge.

"I was in college for four or five years, and I saw a lot of guys come and go because they weren't dedicated to what they were supposed to be doing," Campbell points out. "The tough guys are the ones who would stick it out and stay. It takes a lot of dedication. To me, once I started playing in the SEC I think it really prepared me for the NFL because I played against a lot of guys who are in the league now.

"SEC football is a fast game. Guys are competitive. You see all kinds of defenses and blitzes week in and week out. You are also playing in front of the big crowds, and it is so fun to have an opportunity to play in front of crowds like that week in and week out."

Campbell was redshirted his first fall on campus, which meant he was a spectator on game days, but got plenty of exercise as he joined the other redshirts for Coach Kevin Yoxall's strength and conditioning classes.

"I remember those 5:30 morning drills with Coach Yox and seeing guys throwing up left and right," he says. "I think that is when you develop the toughness to play.

"February is the toughest month of the year for college football players. That is when you have your early mornings and mat drills. You have to get up early and basically work out for three hours and then you have to go to class the rest of the day. If you have a test the next day, you have to stay up late to study and then get yourself up and be ready for class. It is tough. You learn a lot in college. I think men are built when they go to college.

"I think Coach Tuberville and our staff did a good job of making good, young men out of us," says Campbell. He notes it was reassuring that the Tigers had an excellent counselor, former Auburn player Chette Williams, who also directed the campus Fellowship of Christian Athletes program. "I think Brother Chette played a major role in helping us, because any time we had any problems we could go to him. He is someone I still call and talk to from time to time, just to talk to him."

In 2001 as a redshirt freshman, Campbell shared playing time with senior Daniel Cobb, a former high school All-American who had transferred to Auburn from junior college after originally attending Georgia. Cobb would later be granted a rare sixth year of eligibility for the 2002 season after missing two years of football to rehab from a serious medical problem.

Campbell got the call to start on opening day as a redshirt freshman in 2001 when the Tigers defeated Ball State 30-0. He completed 16-28 passes for 218 yards with one touchdown and no interceptions. In his first SEC game a week later, he completed 15-19 passes as the Tigers defeated Ole Miss 27-21.

He started eight games and played in two others. Campbell finished with 1,117 passing yards with four TDs and four interceptions. It was a solid start, but those aren't the kind of numbers a player with Campbell's ability hopes to produce.

"My redshirt freshman year, I was still learning the game and wasn't ready to make that next step," he says. "I would probably say I got comfortable playing college football my sophomore year. I got a chance to know guys. My sophomore season, Daniel Cobb came back for his sixth year. Coach decided to start him early, and that whole time he started I was watching and learning. I was still playing in most of the games and I ended up starting six games that year. I was 5-1 as the starter, so I feel like my career really took off that season.

"I feel like it really took off after the Syracuse and Florida games that year," he notes. Both matchups went to overtime. AU defeated Syracuse and lost at Florida, but came on strong down the stretch. Campbell led the Tigers to nine wins, including victories over three top 10 opponents.

In 2003, Campbell became the full-time starter and passed for 2,267 yards as he adjusted to his third QB coach/offensive coordinator once Bobby Petrino left to become head coach at Louisville. Despite very high preseason expectations, the Tigers finished 8-5, but did close the year with momentum from a victory over Alabama and a bowl win versus Wisconsin.

Those wins solidified support for Tuberville, who was in jeopardy of losing his job to Petrino. At the urging of university president William Walker, a group of Auburn officials had secretly met with Petrino concerning Tuberville's job. When that meeting was exposed, the Auburn Family was outraged, and it was the beginning of the end for Walker as president. Tuberville emerged stronger than ever, winning National Coach of the Year honors just one season later.

Campbell had a lot to do with Tuberville's success in 2004. He stepped up his level of play, leading the Tigers to a 13-0 record with one of the best all-around performances by a quarterback in Auburn history. The offense got a boost that year when Tuberville brought in veteran coach Al Borges to direct the offense. The season's only disappointment came with the Tigers' final BCS ranking. The team finished third behind unbeaten Southern Cal and Oklahoma, which meant they wouldn't get a chance to play in the national championship game.

On his way to being named SEC Player of the Year, Campbell passed for 2,700 yards, second most in Auburn history, while completing just under 70 percent of his throws, also the second-best average for an Auburn quarterback. He set a school record with 10.0 yards per pass attempt while tying Pat Sullivan's single-season mark of 20 TD passes. Campbell's 172.89 passing efficiency rating that season remains the best in school history.

Borges saw Campbell as a major talent waiting to have a breakout season. "He let me be myself and have control when I was on the field," the quarterback says. "I will always appreciate him. From day one he came in and told me that he had already watched a lot of film, and we were going to do amazing things together."

Campbell points out that with Carnell Williams and Ronnie Brown lined up behind him, everything was in place for a strong offense in 2004. "It helped to have some great running backs," he says. "Our senior year we were 50-50 run or throw. I think that kept a lot of people from beating us, because they didn't know what we were going to do. I think Coach Borges did a good job of mixing Ronnie, Carnell, and my abilities together. We also had a veteran offensive line, and that is always important."

Campbell says a hard-fought 10-9 victory over fifth-ranked LSU jumpstarted the Tigers toward their unbeaten season, and a 34-10 win at No. 10 Tennessee two weeks later increased the momentum. The LSU game was in jeopardy of being postponed by an approaching hurricane, but the storm was gone by game time, and the SEC showdown went on as scheduled. Campbell's pass to Courtney Taylor with 1:14 to play gave Auburn the victory.

"Going to Tennessee also stands out to me," Campbell says. "There is nothing like playing in front of 110,000 people on the road. The way we played as a unit—as a team that night—we were together. I think a lot of teams have talent, but the ones who are together are the ones who win championships. I remember no one gave us a chance going into that game and we just really showed the heart of our team."

The rematch with Tennessee in the SEC Championship Game is another favorite. "We were up early 21-7, and Tennessee fights back and ties it up going into the fourth quarter," Campbell says. "Looking down the sideline and seeing the guys staying focused and the way we finished up that game was special. I wish we would have had the opportunity to play in the national championship game."

THE GAME OF MY LIFE
BY JASON CAMPBELL

One that sticks out is the LSU game when we played them at home my senior season. Each year the Auburn-LSU game stands out. A lot of them have names like the "Hurricane Game" my senior year and, before that, names like the "Earthquake Game" and the "Fire Game." Every year it seems like something strange happens when Auburn and LSU play. I can remember the game as well as yesterday. I feel like it was the starting point for our season. Also, driving down the field for the winning touchdown was special.

Seeing Courtney Taylor get open and make a huge catch on fourth down and 12 to keep the drive alive stands out. Then he turned around and made a big touchdown catch on third down from 16 yards out, and it really put our team over the top.

On the fourth-down pass that "C.T." caught, I remember rolling out and I remember LSU bringing an all-out blitz. I just knew I was about to get hit and about to get creamed.

I remember Courtney running an excellent route going past the yardstick, and I remember throwing the ball and then hearing the crowd go wild. I wasn't able to see the throw. When that happened and we scored the winning touchdown a few plays later, it showed that all of the hard work you put in over the summer throwing to your receivers paid off at that moment.

Our defense played an extraordinary game that day. On offense we were driving the ball, but we could never put points on the board. As long as you score when it really counts, I guess that is what really matters.

LSU had a great team. There are a lot of great athletes in the SEC. You play against them week in and week out and you see a lot of them on every team in the NFL. We all remember each other and we wish each other luck.

ON THE PROS

Week after week during Campbell's senior season, NFL scouts attended games to study Auburn's backfield, featuring Campbell, Williams, and

Brown. They also watched another senior, cornerback Carlos Rogers. All four would become first-round NFL draft picks in 2005.

Brown was the first of the quartet selected and the second player chosen, going to the Miami Dolphins. He was picked just ahead of Williams, the fifth player taken overall and brought on board by Tampa Bay. The Washington Redskins, who had spent a good deal of time on campus checking out Campbell, had two first-round draft picks. They used their first to take Rogers ninth, then added Campbell as the 25th pick.

The other three broke into the starting lineup as rookies. Playing the most challenging position, Campbell moved into the starting lineup for the first time a year later, after one season as an understudy.

"I have enjoyed pro football a lot," the quarterback says. "The only thing you miss is that it is not like college. Once you leave practice, guys have families to go home to or go to other places. It's not like college where you might go to a friend's house.

"In pros it is a job that requires true dedication. It is grown men you are dealing with. If you aren't dedicated and don't have a true passion for the game, you won't make it. You see a lot of guys come and go, and a lot of times what separates the ones who make it from the ones who don't isn't ability—it is passion and dedication."

Campbell is doing his best to stay dedicated. He lives near the team's headquarters and works out with teammates year-round. In his spare time he does community service work, a holdover from his time at Auburn.

Looking back on his college days, Campbell notes he is proud he earned his degree in communications before heading off to the NFL. "I think [counselors] Troy Smith and Virgil Starks did a great job of making sure guys were committed to excellence in the classroom and earning degrees as well as playing football," he says. "I respect Coach Tuberville a lot because if you didn't get your grades and were not serious about getting your education, he wasn't going to play you. I saw that happen a number of times.

"I think the FCA program was important, too. Those meetings that we had on Wednesday nights are memorable. I think those got a lot of guys through college. You never know what is going on in a person's life until those nights when we had those meetings and would talk about things going on in our lives. You have an opportunity to listen to a lot of guys' stories about where they came from and how they grew up. That meant a lot." The big quarterback is quite fond of his alma mater. "I had a lot of fun at Auburn," he says. "I met a lot of different people and I have a lot of friends from my time there."

Chapter 5

DAMEYUNE CRAIG

OVERCOMING HURDLES

Although it's difficult for anybody who watched him play at Auburn to believe, when Dameyune Craig was a youngster he wasn't allowed to compete in organized sports for health reasons. Growing up in perhaps the roughest neighborhood in the state of Alabama in the Mobile suburb of Prichard, he dreamed of one day playing quarterback for the Auburn Tigers. At the time, however, that seemed improbable.

"When I was a young kid my two older brothers always played sports, but my mom wouldn't let me play because I had asthma," Craig remembers. "It was pretty bad. It was so bad that my mom used to rush me to the emergency room quite often. It was to the point that I used to get so many shots I became immune to needles. They don't even bother me now. I was on medication a lot and my mom was worried I would have an attack."

Despite his ailment, Craig grew up with a love of sports, particularly football. "I always played in the yard with friends, but they didn't really think I was going to be a good football player because I was so sick all of the time," he says. "I think that really drove me throughout my career, because I wasn't able to play when I was young and I was always trying to prove to people I could do it."

As he entered his teens the asthma condition improved, and by the time he was an eighth grader he was able to talk his parents into letting him go out for the school football team. "I played running back that year at Scarborough Middle School," he remembers. "I had a pretty good year. My dad didn't know I was that talented at the time.

"Coach Ben Harris had just got the job at Blount High School and he was going into his second year. [In-town rival] Vigor High had just come off back-to-back state championships. I decided I wanted to go and make my own name for myself and help the Blount team win. At the time, nobody was going to Blount. They hadn't had much success except for the year before when Coach Harris took the team to the playoffs, which was the first time that had happened in about 20 years."

Craig was always able to throw a football well, but when he began playing he wasn't interested in being a quarterback. "I wanted to be a running back because that is what my older brother played," he says. "At that time when I was on the freshman team at Blount, I was playing about everything but running back because we didn't have enough players on the team. I had to go out and recruit some more guys to play. When we finally got some, I was such a good athlete they played me at receiver, running back, defensive back, and defensive end. My best friend played quarterback. One game we were losing, so they put me there. I brought us back and we ended up losing by two points, but from that point on, I was a quarterback. I ended up starting the last game of the season against LeFlore. We lost that game 16-9 or something like that."

Craig was also a good basketball player and spent plenty of time on the court. "One of the reasons we would work out in the summertime is that Coach Harris would open the gym and let us play basketball after we lifted weights," he says. "That was a good motivation to go to the gym every day." However, Craig played just one more season of hoops after leading the Leopards to the state 5A title championship as a sophomore quarterback. "I decided to concentrate on football because I figured that was the best sport for my future."

He was right about that. Craig developed into a star, thanks to a strong work ethic and improved health. "My asthma problem got a lot better when I was in high school," he notes. "It really didn't affect me a lot again until I got into the NFL and then I started having to get medication. Through high school and college every now and then when the seasons changed I may have had to get a shot, but it really didn't bother me much. Once I moved to North Carolina for pro football, all of the pollen there really affected me."

A broken bone in his arm ruined Craig's junior season, but he bounced back ready to play as a senior and again led Blount to the state title.

Dameyune Craig launches a pass against the Florida Gators.
Inside the Auburn Tigers magazine

Because he was injured as a junior, the quarterback didn't receive as much attention from recruiters as some less talented prospects, but he refused to let that bother him.

"I didn't think about going to college until my senior year," he admits. "I loved playing so much that coming from where I came from, it was my way of venting my frustration and relaxing. Playing sports kept us out of trouble. Coach Harris was a savior for us down there in Prichard. He gave us something to do. He also gave that community something to be proud of, because everybody was down on that community when I was growing up. If you went to that high school, people looked down on you. When we started winning football games, Blount started getting a lot of positive attention.

"It never dawned on me that I would be going to college until my senior year. I knew I didn't want to stop playing football because I loved it. My junior year I broke my arm in the third game of the season and I was out for the rest of the year. My senior year I came back and we had another big year and won the state championship again. I started getting a lot of attention during the playoffs from colleges because that is when the coaches could be out watching you and recruiting you. We were fortunate to be able to go to the state championships and I had a lot of colleges look at me during that time."

When Auburn assistant coach Joe Whitt began seriously recruiting Craig, the other colleges didn't have much of a chance.

"I grew up an Auburn fan," the quarterback points out. "I remember watching my first Auburn game on TV. When you are from the state of Alabama, you automatically have to pick a side. Everybody in my house was for Alabama, but I wanted to make my own name and do things my own way, so I kind of gravitated toward Auburn. I liked their colors. I was a big fan of Reggie Slack, Bo Jackson, Lawyer Tillman—all of those guys.

"I said to myself, 'When I grow up, I am going to be the quarterback at Auburn University.' At that time I wasn't even playing organized football. I could throw a football pretty hard then, but I didn't have any formal training. By my 10th grade year, I had it all planned out. When Stan White would leave, I was going to be ready to take over. It was a far-fetched dream for somebody coming from where I came from, but I believed it would happen someday.

"Anybody who knows anything about Prichard knows that especially during that time when crack cocaine came on the scene, it pretty much ravished the neighborhood," Craig says. "You would see drug addicts, people selling drugs, and things I just can't even talk about that you had to witness. You heard about people being killed and then friends started getting killed. People dropped out of school and started selling drugs and using drugs.

"Football probably saved that community from being worse than it was, because Coach Harris took a lot of kids off the street and got them interested in football. They could have been out there doing those same types of things. I think Coach Harris saved the whole community by coming down there and spending so much time with us. He took kids to church and he became a father figure for so many people. I am thankful for that, and I will always be indebted to him for what he did for me."

Harris gave a high recommendation of Craig to Whitt, who recruited the Mobile area for the Tigers from 1981-2005. When Terry Bowden took over for Pat Dye as head coach before the 1993 season, Craig became a player of major interest to the Tigers. "I want to thank Coach Bowden because he gave me a scholarship and a chance to play at Auburn," he says. "When I was in high school, he was the coach at Samford and he was recruiting me and my best friend, but they didn't think they had a shot at me then. Auburn wasn't really recruiting me until Coach Bowden was hired. I wasn't even on their radar. That kind of hurt me because Auburn was the school I always wanted to go to, although that is understandable because I was hurt my junior year. I was told when Coach Bowden got the Auburn job I was the first person he called, and he started recruiting me. I appreciate him for giving me a chance to go to a great university. I have a lot of respect for Coach Dye. I grew up a Coach Dye fan. I love the way they played football in the 1980s and early 1990s when he was there.

"Alabama came in recruiting me on the back end after they found out Auburn was going to offer me a scholarship, but Auburn was where I wanted to be. Auburn won a lot of games when Coach Bowden was there. Coach Tommy Bowden was a big influence on me, too. I learned a lot from him. I was influenced by his religious beliefs and what he would talk about with his kids. I respect all of them."

A MAJOR ADJUSTMENT

Adjusting to college is normally a challenge for any freshman, especially one who has to cope with the demands of being a scholarship athlete. For Craig, the adjustment was even greater than most face.

"Coming from the community I came from that was 100 percent black, I was fortunate that when I was growing up there was an elementary school less than a mile from my house. But I was shipped out about 10 to 15 miles away to go to a mixed school. It was a chance for me to grow up around other races and learn about them because when you came home all you saw were black people. From elementary to middle school, I was around other races. Once I got to high school, it was 100 percent black. When I got to college I had to adjust again.

"I think the biggest culture shock was my first day in class. I was the only black kid in the classroom. My professor was President [William] Muse's daughter. I had to write an essay—something I had never done in high school. I was pretty afraid of that. That was worse than any game I ever played in. I thought, 'If I can get through this first class at eight o'clock in the morning, I think I will be okay for the rest of my college career.' I ended up making up a C in the class, and I was fine after that."

Craig arrived at Auburn in the summer of 1994. Terry Bowden had taken over the program from Pat Dye, who retired after the 1992 season. The Tigers had just finished an undefeated season with senior Stan White at quarterback. Patrick Nix, his understudy, took over the starting assignment for the next two seasons, while Craig was a backup. As a junior in 1996, Craig was the man at quarterback and developed into one of the most exciting SEC football players of the 1990s.

THE GAME OF MY LIFE
BY DAMEYUNE CRAIG

There was a lot of stuff leading up to the game at LSU. A big thing I remember is the interception game [in 1994, Auburn had a 30-26 comeback victory]. They put me in that game late in the fourth quarter to try to get a spark going with our team. I remember that game very clearly because I really didn't do anything. It was my chance to go out there and take advantage of an opportunity to perform, and I went out there and laid an egg. That stuck with me throughout my career. After the game, my coach [Jimbo Fisher] told me that you may only get one chance to go out and do things and you may never get another chance. You never know.

The team I disliked more than any team was LSU. I hated LSU with a passion. It was a good rivalry while I was in school. The next year we only scored six points at LSU [in a 12-6 Auburn loss]. The following season, 1996, was my first year starting. We were playing them in Auburn, and I got knocked out of the game with a concussion and a sprained ligament in my left leg. When that happened in that game, a lot of people thought I had lost my composure, but they didn't know I had a concussion. Coach Bowden was trying to make me come off the field. He kept sending the second-string quarterback in to get me, but I wouldn't come out. I thought I tore my knee up and I was out there limping around. He made me come to the sideline. By the time we played them my senior year, I hadn't really done anything against LSU and we had only scored like 12 points [offensively] on them in three years. They had our number.

It was the third game of my senior season when we played LSU again. Really, a game is not big until you lose it. We had played Virginia and Ole Miss and they were big games before we played them, but after we won those I heard that they weren't really big games, and that Dameyune Craig hadn't proven yet he could win a big game. So we were ready to go out there. It was hot that day. They had a really good team. We went down there to LSU and it was a dogfight. It was like a PlayStation game. They had Rondel Mealey, they had [Kevin] Faulk, and Cecil "The Diesel" Collins—the kid who went to jail. It seemed like every time he got the ball he would rip off a 20-yard gain. We would score; they would score. It seems like Cecil had 200 yards rushing and the other back had around 150.

I remember the fourth quarter. I think we were down by four points. They were about to kick the ball to us. I looked at my teammates and the only thing I could think about was that we used to do a winter workout program we called "The Bubble," which was designed to make you mentally tough. I said, "If we can make it through The Bubble, we can make it through anything." I told the guys around me, "We are going out there and we are going to score a touchdown and win the game." There were three minutes left and we drove downfield and scored the winning touchdown. It was a big game for my career, establishing myself not as a great quarterback, but I would say one of the good quarterbacks in Auburn University history. That is the game that a lot of people questioned whether or not we could go down there and win at LSU. I think the coaches were a little uptight. [All-America linebacker] Takeo Spikes and I called a team meeting the night before the game. He addressed the team and I addressed the team, and we had everybody fired up. I told them, "Listen, we are going out the first drive and we are going to drive it down their throats and score. Then the defense is going to stop them with a three and out, and we are going to get the ball back and score again."

The chances are probably 15 to 20 percent that we were going to score on LSU two times in a row to start the game because they had a really good defense that year. But that is exactly what happened, and after we did it the team had so much confidence we were going to win. That was one of the most memorable games I ever had.

BIG FINISH

The victory over LSU set the stage for a run to the SEC West title. Craig led the charge with one of the best all-around seasons ever by an Auburn quarterback. He passed for a school-record 3,277 yards and 18 touchdowns, up from 2,296 yards and 16 touchdowns as a junior. Craig's 24 TDs in 1997 are the second most in school history for one season, two behind the record set by Heisman Trophy winner Pat Sullivan in 1970.

In a tremendous performance in the SEC Championship Game, Craig gave his Tigers a great chance to defeat Tennessee, but errors by teammates helped Peyton Manning's Tennessee team escape the Georgia Dome with a 30-29 victory.

The All-SEC quarterback finished his AU career with school records for total yards in one game (445 vs. Army), most completions in a season (216), most career 300-yard passing games (six), and most consecutive games with a touchdown pass (13).

Although short for a quarterback by NFL standards, Craig's ability earned him a shot at pro football. "After college I played in the NFL for four years with the Carolina Panthers," he says. "I played a half season of Arena Football in Indiana and I had a little short stint with the Washington Redskins while coach [Steve] Spurrier was there. It was short-lived, but I had a great time with him. Some of the great things he said about Auburn University you would never believe. He has a great deal of respect for Auburn. He told me it was his favorite place to play. He even had plays named after our school and some of our players. It was amazing to talk to him about the respect he had for the place.

"After that I coached a season at my high school and then I was a graduate assistant at LSU for coach [Nick] Saban. He took me to Miami when he became head coach of the Dolphins and I spent a season as a special teams assistant coach. Now I am at Tuskegee University as a quarterback coach."

The highlight of Craig's pro career came in NFL Europe the summer after his rookie year. While playing for the Scottish Claymores, he passed for 611 yards in one game, setting the all-time record for passing yards in a single NFL or NFL Europe contest. The performance received recognition with a display in the NFL Hall of Fame. "I had a great time over there playing football in Europe," Craig remembers. "They always treated me with respect and I enjoyed the fans."

While at Auburn, Craig had a very close relationship with his quarterback coach, Jimbo Fisher. "He taught me a lot about football and a lot about life," Craig says. "The first thing he established with me is that you aren't going to be able to beat everybody with your legs. He said you have to be a student of the game. You have to out-think people to become the complete quarterback. We spent a lot of time watching film in the off-season, and I think that is when I became a better quarterback. His door was always open for me. He taught me a lot. It was a joy playing under him. I think he will be a great head coach one day. He is a great coach, but a demanding coach. If you can't handle being critiqued in a different way, you can't play for him. He makes you mentally tough as a player."

As a football coach, Craig is following in Fisher's footsteps. "I have coached on every level and I have played on every level," he notes. "My ultimate goal is to become a head coach at the college level. I think this opportunity to be at Tuskegee University is something for me to give back. I have learned a lot from a lot of great coaches like George Seifert and I feel there is a lot I can give back, helping out black quarterbacks. I feel good about it. I feel like Auburn is my home. It feels great to be back here with my family. Being at Tuskegee is as close as I can be to Auburn without working for Auburn."

Craig met his wife, Nek, at Auburn, and they have two sons, seven-year-old Devin and four year old Drake. "Hopefully we can send our kids to Auburn," says Craig. "I had the time of my life at Auburn," says Craig. "I will always be proud to be an Auburn Tiger."

Chapter 6

JOE CRIBBS

NEVER ANY DOUBTS

Even when he was a young child growing up in the small West Alabama town of Sulligent, Joe Cribbs believed he was destined to be a football star. However, unlike countless other little boys who harbored the same dream, as the talented athlete grew into a poised and polished running back at Sulligent High School, he had plenty of reasons to believe his dream could come true.

In more than 100 years of Auburn football, the Tigers have developed a tradition of great running backs. Although it has been more than three decades since he was darting past defensive linemen and eluding linebackers and safeties, few who came before or after Cribbs did it as well as the 1970s star.

"Playing college football was never my goal growing up," Cribbs notes. "My goal was to play in the NFL. When I first started playing ball, I idolized some of the professional guys. Playing at that level was always my dream. When I was in high school I felt that I would realistically have the talent to play at the highest level of football, which was in the pros. Maybe I was a little full of myself, but I believed it. I never boasted about it, but internally I always felt confident in my abilities."

Growing up with his cousin James McKinney as his running mate, Cribbs began playing football about the time he started school. "I can't even remember when I first started playing, but I know I was young," he says. "It was probably in the first or second grade, and that was playing with the kids in school. I didn't play organized football until I got in the sixth grade."

Always the running back while McKinney played quarterback, both were stars, something the coach of a rival Pee Wee League figured out right away. "Except for one half of one game, the only position I ever played was running back," Cribbs notes. "I remember we played this team in a league that had a weight limit. You couldn't weigh over 105 pounds or something like that. I played the first half and I had scored like three touchdowns. The coach from the opposing team protested and wanted me weighed. They weighed me at halftime and I was one pound over, so for the rest of the game they decided I couldn't play in the backfield. I had to play on the line. Our coach put me at tight end. I don't know how he worked it out, but he petitioned the league and got me back in the backfield for the rest of the season."

That opposing coach was the first of many who tried to find ways to stop a talented tailback who had the ability to make would-be tacklers look silly as they reached for him and came away with nothing but air.

In the winters Cribbs played basketball, and in the springs he ran track and played baseball. He also played baseball in the summer, but there was no doubt that football was his favorite.

There was also no doubt that Cribbs was Auburn's favorite running back recruit. Head coach Doug Barfield assigned two assistants, Mike Neel and Dave Beck, the task of convincing the tailback to sign with the Tigers.

"Coach Neel probably spent more time in Sulligent than anybody else," says Cribbs, who was a Parade All-American his junior and senior years. "He got to know my family very well. Almost every time I turned around Coach Neel was there. They did a real good job of recruiting me. Even at that age, I understood that they would be putting on their best faces. A lot of my decision was going to be based on what I thought after I visited the school and saw the facilities and the underbelly of the school. I had the opportunity to spend time with the players and talk to them. Coaches are usually going to tell you all of the positives, but I had a chance to sit down with some of the guys who were at Auburn during that time, like Secdrick McIntyre, Jimmy Brock, and Reese McCall, and talk to them about the situation—what was positive, what was negative. You could talk to those guys a little more openly.

"I knew that going to Auburn I had an opportunity to do something unique, because at that time the program was down. I had a chance to go in as part of a group who could turn the program around, which was

Joe Cribbs was a star at Auburn and in pro football.
Auburn University Media Relations

challenging because I was never really lacking in self-confidence. I felt like I could go down there and make all of the difference in the world. I felt like I could go there and instantly we would win."

Auburn and other colleges were also recruiting McKinney, who decided to join Cribbs at Auburn. He became a star for the Tigers too, as a two-time All-SEC safety.

"I guess the primary reason why I decided to go to Auburn after looking at some other schools and considering everything, I felt like it was better for me to stay in the state," Cribbs says. "I really eliminated Alabama kind of early from consideration. I didn't even take an official trip to Tuscaloosa when I was being recruited. When I was at Sulligent, I remember we always had scouts coming in to look at me. One of those was from Alabama and he talked to my high school coach. Coach [Ralph Ferguson] and I were very close—very good friends. There really weren't many secrets between us. He told me the coach had made the comment if I wanted to play at Alabama that I needed to make a lot of improvement and various things. That didn't sit well with me and I decided then they weren't going to be on my list."

The fact that McKinney would be going to Auburn helped make the transition easier. "We grew up together," Cribbs says. "We always played sports together. If you stopped one, you couldn't stop the other in football, basketball, or whatever. James was also recruited by a lot of schools. He was a great high school quarterback. Tennessee wanted him to play that position, and there were some other schools that wanted him at quarterback. He decided to go to Auburn because I decided to go there. At Auburn, the coaches put him at defensive back right away. We were roommates when we first got there. It was nice having somebody with you that you could count on and trust. I think it enabled us both to grow and we had comfort."

A SLOW START

Cribbs arrived at Auburn in a period of transition. Ralph "Shug" Jordan had hoped to end his 25-year tenure as head coach with a big finish in 1975, but his Tigers slumped to a 4-6-1 mark, Auburn's first losing record since 1966. Doug Barfield, who had been promoted from Jordan's staff to take over, was in his rookie year as head coach when Cribbs arrived.

The tailback expected to be an immediate star when the Tigers opened the 1976 season. After dominating in high school, he assumed that would carry over to college. "I remember my freshman year being totally dejected and upset because I wasn't starting," Cribbs says. "I didn't even make the travel squad for the first game when we played at Arizona. I had to deal with a lot of things that are normal that as a young man I didn't realize. I felt like I was the best player on the team and should be playing—the normal thing most good players feel. I didn't even make the travel team and my cousin James did. I was back home in Sulligent for the weekend and I was totally dejected. I was talking to my uncle, who has always been a big supporter of me even though he wanted me to go to Alabama. He was telling me that I had the ability. I just had to stay focused, believe in myself, and go back down there and show them that I could play.

"It was not an easy job cracking that lineup," notes Cribbs, who was playing behind several veteran running backs, including a talented senior named Secdrick McIntyre. However, McIntyre had injury problems and that eventually opened the door. "Midway through the season they finally realized they needed to give me an opportunity to play," Cribbs says. "The first game I played in was against Florida State. I was returning kickoffs. I remember the first time I touched the ball in a game was on a kickoff and I almost scored a touchdown. I ran 62 yards and then ran into an official. He got credit for the tackle. It was kind of the start of my career at Auburn."

Cribbs says he realizes that his coaches knew what they were doing. "I look back on it and I know now that I still had a lot of maturing to do," he says. "You can't just throw somebody in there, although I wanted to be in there."

The freshman showed he was a star in the making and was one of the bright spots in a disappointing season for the Tigers, who broke even in the SEC at 3-3 and finished 4-7 overall. He led the team in all-purpose yardage with 171 rushing, 59 as a receiver, 490 as a kickoff returner, and 80 as a punt returner. As a sophomore he led the team in rushing with 872 yards while averaging 5.4 per carry, despite sharing playing time with a highly regarded freshman named James Brooks, who would also become a star at Auburn and in the NFL.

Going into his junior year, Cribbs was primed to have a big season. However, an injury limited his mobility and put him behind Brooks on the depth chart. With Brooks rushing for 226 yards, Auburn opened with a victory at Kansas State, won at Virginia Tech, and beat Tennessee in Birmingham. Then, in week four, the Tigers fell 17-15 at home to Miami. Brooks was injured that day, setting the stage for Cribbs to become the main man and put together one of the more productive seasons in school history.

The next game was an SEC road trip to Vanderbilt. Cribbs set an Auburn record that day with five touchdown runs. In the first quarter he scored on plays of nine, 20, and four yards. Number four came in the second quarter on a 23-yard run. The junior added a fifth touchdown from five yards out in the third quarter when his backups came in to mop up.

He finished the year with 16 rushing touchdowns and 1,205 net yards, breaking the old mark of 1,006 set by All-American Jimmy Sidle in 1963. In game nine that season, a wild 22-22 tie vs. Georgia, Cribbs rushed for 250 yards, which at that time was the second highest total in school history. Currently, it is still fourth behind a 307-yard game from Curtis Kuykendall in 1944 versus Miami and totals of 290 and 256 by Bo Jackson in 1985 and '83.

THE GAME OF MY LIFE
BY JOE CRIBBS

It is very difficult to pick out one game. The game against Georgia when we came out in the orange jerseys and I had a record-setting day when I rushed for 250 yards, that was one of my most memorable ones because of the numbers and the fact we tied the game. If I had to pick the game that really set the tone for me as a player, it was the one against Vanderbilt my junior year because I scored five touchdowns that day. The reason I say it was probably the most significant game is that earlier that summer I had been injured. I stretched a ligament in my knee a little bit. It was not severe, but it was enough to get me out of the starting lineup.

At the time we had another running back named James Brooks, who was also an exceptional player. No matter how you looked at it, we were playing the same position, so we were competing against each other. I was first team and he was second team and then I got hurt and he was elevated to number one.

The opening game was against Kansas State. James exploded. He had a great game, rushing for over 200 yards. It was just an awesome performance and I was injured. My thinking was, "I have got to get back out there on the field." The next week we played Virginia Tech. I was trying to get back out there, but I was not 100 percent. I didn't feel like I had a glowing performance. I was still trying to get my position back.

By the time we played Miami, I was getting healthier. In that game, James hurt his foot. I think he broke a small bone and we ended up losing that day. O.J. Anderson scored the winning touchdown at the very end. The next game we played at Vanderbilt. James was out and I was back. Although I was still not 100 percent, I was close, but I still didn't have the confidence that a player needs to be really successful. I was concerned about my knee. I did not really want to let it go full speed. You are apprehensive about cutting in that situation. The first couple of plays against Vanderbilt that day, things just opened up. It seemed like every time I touched the ball things just opened up and I was in the secondary.

I remember my mom was there that day. It was one of the few road games she ever came to see me play. Back then we had the old tearaway jerseys. My mom had tickets in one of the end zones. On one particular play I was running the ball and there is a photo of me where I am actually coming out of my jersey. I have nothing on but my shoulder pads as I am going into the end zone. In the background my family and friends are in the picture.

Because I had such a good game that day, it restored my confidence. I felt like I was back, and from then on I played football. From that point on I think I averaged 120-something yards per game the rest of the way out. I think the junior year solidified my opportunities to play professionally. Even though my senior year I had to share some of the limelight with James and I did a lot more blocking, we both went on to rush for more than 1,000 yards. The fact that I was able to play fullback my senior year and block a little more actually enhanced my numbers for the NFL scouts.

ON TO PRO FOOTBALL FAME

The following season in 1979, the Tigers posted an 8-3 record and were 4-2 in the league as the senior tailback earned All-SEC honors for the second time. Cribbs rushed for 1,120 yards, which still ranks 10th in Auburn history for a season. He averaged 5.6 yards per carry, up from 4.76 the previous year. Playing tailback and fullback, he still knew how to find the end zone. He scored 13 touchdowns, which ties him for fourth in a single season.

Unlike his freshman year in college, he didn't have to wait to become an impact player his rookie season of pro football. Selected with a pick the Buffalo Bills had obtained for trading O.J. Simpson, Cribbs was chosen in the second round of the NFL Draft and immediately broke into the starting lineup. He rushed for 1,185 yards and 11 touchdowns and caught 52 passes for 415 yards and another score. He was named the American Football Conference Rookie of the Year and was the only rookie to earn a starting spot in the Pro Bowl.

In 10 seasons he was a three-time selection to the Pro Bowl. He played for the Bills through 1983 and was a star each year. However, he wasn't happy with his contract and became one of a large group of players to jump to the new United States Football League. Cribbs signed with the Birmingham Stallions. He was a star there for two seasons, but the USFL folded and he returned to the Bills in 1985. He was traded to San Francisco in 1986 and spent two seasons with the '49ers before finishing his career with the Indianapolis Colts and Miami Dolphins in 1988. He scored 42 career NFL touchdowns, netted 5,356 rushing yards, and added 2,199 more as a receiver. Cribbs led the USFL in rushing yards in 1984 with 1,467 and caught 39 passes for 500 yards. He added 1,047 rushing yards and caught 41 passes for 287 in his second year with the Stallions.

"Playing 10 years professionally, I got to play in a lot of significant games," he says. "I feel like I had a pretty good career. I don't think I could have a better year than I had my first season when I won Rookie of the Year playing for the Bills. It was just a great year. The only thing about professional football, the more you play it and get familiar with it as a player, the more you understand it is a business. The more you realize it is a business, the less fun it is to play."

Cribbs and his wife Vernessa live in Birmingham. They have a daughter and two sons. The former Tiger star is now in the insurance business. His firm provides supplemental insurance to employers. A member of the Alabama Sports Hall of Fame, Cribbs was one of those players with exceptional talent who would have been a star in any Auburn football era.

Chapter 7

MARK DORMINEY

THE YOUNG LIFE OF MARK DORMINEY

As a youngster in South Florida, Mark Dorminey grew up with a passion for sports—football in particular. Before he would put away the pads for good, the hard-hitting defensive back's love of the game would be tested in a way that few before or after him have been on their way to becoming standout performers at Auburn University.

"My brother is a little short of two years younger than me, and I remember as soon as we could walk we would always have a football with us," Dorminey says. "If you see photographs with us as kids, we always had a ball in our hands. Whatever season was in, that was what we were outside playing. Football and basketball were the ones that I ended up liking the best."

Dorminey began competing in organized football when he was around 10 years old, playing in Hialeah against a variety of teams from the Miami area. "All the way up through Little League to my 10th grade year in high school, I always played running back and free safety," he remembers. But all sports activity had to be put on hold his sophomore year, when Dorminey was diagnosed as suffering from Osgood-Schlatter Disease, a condition found in young, growing athletes who put heavy stresses on their knees due to large amounts of athletic activity.

Although he was sidelined his first year at Hialeah High, Dorminey was able to bounce back impressively from his first major medical setback. However, even bigger hurdles would be placed in his path to success in years to come.

Back on the field for opening night of his junior season, Dorminey was full speed and played a terrific game at free safety. He put together a strong season that attracted the attention of college coaches from a variety of major programs.

"Ironically, the first game I ever played my junior year—my very first game—was probably the best one I had my whole high school football career," he says. "Auburn was looking at somebody else in that game, saw that tape, and started recruiting me. Then we sent that tape out and whenever the colleges we sent the tape to saw it, they would start recruiting me, too. We went all the way up the ladder to a scholarship offer from Notre Dame, which, at that time in 1978, was the number-one team in the country. So I was recruited by them, Penn State, Florida State, Miami, Auburn, and others."

Dorminey planned to play basketball after his junior football season, but missed out while recuperating from surgery to remove a calcium deposit from his knee. The future Tiger was ready in plenty of time to play football his senior year and helped Hialeah to a 7-3 record, its best season in many years. Everything was going well for the safety until he suffered an injury—the kind that needed major surgery. "When I tore up my knee in the last game of my senior year, a lot of the schools backed off," Dorminey notes. "It turned out that Auburn was the southernmost school that was still recruiting me."

Dorminey grew up an SEC football fan. He notes that he was more familiar with Florida, where his younger brother would play college football, but decided he would check out Doug Barfield's Tigers, who were trying to get back to the top of the league. "When I went there on my recruiting trip I liked it a lot," says Dorminey, who accepted the offer to play at Auburn. He didn't know it at the time, but he wouldn't be playing for the Tigers for a while.

A TRYING TRANSITION

Before he could even put on his first pair of shoulder pads as a Tiger, Dorminey received some really bad news from Dr. Jack Hughston, the world-famous surgeon from Columbus, Georgia, who also served as Auburn's orthopedic doctor when Dorminey began his college days in the summer of 1978.

Mark Dorminey was known as a big-play safety.
Auburn University Media Relations

"My freshman year was pretty tough because of what happened with me," he notes. "I didn't have surgery when I hurt my knee my senior year. They just put it in a cast. When I was ready to come up to college for my freshman year, they asked me to come up a little early and I went to see Dr. Hughston. He looked at my knee and he told me after just having a physical exam that I needed to have major reconstructive surgery. They ended up having me stay up there and I had the surgery before anybody else even reported for the season.

"I was at Auburn for two weeks by myself in a dorm room after I had surgery. I didn't have a roommate or anything. I had the trainers coming in and checking up on me, so it was really a weird start to college football. I was isolated and trying to get through a major operation. Up to that point I hadn't gone through a major surgery, so that was pretty traumatic. I was also away from home for the first time and that was a little traumatic. I got really close to [team trainer Hub] Waldrop at that time. He did a good job of checking on me and taking care of me."

Dorminey had torn ligaments that had to be rebuilt. That meant he would be redshirted. "It was such a big surgery I couldn't do anything with the team," he says. "It was almost like I wasn't even a part of the team. I spent most of my time working with the trainers. I didn't even go to practice.

"They had to make new ligaments," Dorminey points out. "It was a major reconstruction deal. They didn't have the technology they do today. I had to wear the full leg cast for eight weeks, and after that I had to wear what looked like a polio brace for another eight weeks with one of those orthopedic shoes on the end of it. Just going to class and walking around campus, people almost looked at me like I was handicapped. It sure wasn't the way I would have wrote it up to start college football."

Nobody was going to outwork Dorminey on a football field or in rehab, so by the time spring practice started in 1979 he was ready for some football. "I am sure the surgery caused me to lose a little speed, but I could do everything," he remembers. "There were no limitations. I didn't have blazing speed to begin with anyway."

Dorminey wasn't big, but his physical style of play, hustle, and willingness to be aggressive on every down had a big impact. The coaches noticed and had high hopes for the young defensive back, even though he wasn't 6 feet tall or much heavier than his high school weight of 165 pounds. However, his play in practice didn't translate into a chance to become an impact player on Saturdays in the fall of '79 or again in 1980.

"Every time I would make a move or start catching the coaches' eyes, I would end up getting hurt," Dorminey says. "I had three surgeries before my junior year, which was the season I finally earned a starting job. Up until then I would do something good, move up the depth chart and get ready to play, and then I would get an injury."

Dorminey's redshirt freshman year was ruined by shoulder surgery, and in the 1980 season, Barfield's last at Auburn, it was a no-go after a spring training injury required another surgery to the knee—the same one that had been operated on his freshman year. "It was sort of getting to the point where I spent more time working with trainers trying to get back to square one than actually being out there on the field playing football," he remembers. "When you are hurt and you aren't out there practicing with everybody, it is almost like you are a second-class citizen. You don't really feel a part of the team."

While football was frustrating, Dorminey didn't let the injuries sidetrack him in the classroom. He chose a demanding major, building science, and made academic All-SEC his first three years on campus before establishing himself as an All-SEC candidate on the field.

As a redshirt junior in 1981, Dorminey was finally able to show what he could do on the football field, but he had to impress a new staff. Auburn had hired former Georgia star Pat Dye to take over after Dye had been impressive in coaching assignments at East Carolina and Wyoming.

"It was an interesting time to be a football player at Auburn," Dorminey says. He notes that at first he didn't think it was going to be a major change, because he and his teammates were told they would continue to do what they had always done with their winter workouts, preparing for the preseason with off-season weight lifting and conditioning. However, it soon became apparent that Dye was an unusual coach.

"You noticed a difference in that Coach Dye really looked like he had a plan for us," Dorminey says. "A major part of his plan is that he was so strong on us being more physical. He wanted us to be one of the most physical teams in the SEC, and he was so big on all-out effort on every play. You really noticed the difference when we were training, whether it was winter workouts, spring practice, or whatever. The physical requirements were a lot more demanding. The coaches were all amped up and they wanted all-out hustle every play, physical contact every play, and really wanted us to bring it every play. It really worked to some of our guys' benefit. That was my strong point and that is the way I liked to play—a physical game. Guys like Bob Harris and Tim Drinkard, that suited their style. It worked well for us to be able to fit into Coach Dye's style. I don't know if we would have been playing back in Coach Barfield's era, because they didn't put as much emphasis on that."

Auburn opened the Dye era with a 24-16 win over TCU before taking on Wake Forest in game two. It was a disappointing day for the Tigers as they lost 24-21, but the game proved to be memorable for the safety. "I wasn't a starter to start the season," Dorminey notes. "When we played Wake Forest at Auburn I was playing second string. They put me in and I had a good game. I intercepted a pass and made some tackles and that won me the starting job."

With his brains and tough demeanor, Dorminey proved to be a great fit in the secondary. He was almost always in the right place at the right time and delighted coaches with his physical style. Once he moved up to first team on a squad that was short of talent but played with tremendous intensity, he was a fixture there the rest of the 1981 season.

THE GAME OF MY LIFE
BY MARK DORMINEY

For me the most memorable game was in my junior year against Nebraska, when we played them out at Nebraska. It was the best game I ever had at Auburn. I had just played a couple of games and I really feel like that was the one that really gave the coaches confidence that I could be the starter. There really wasn't any doubt about it after that. That is always a great feeling as a player, when you know the coaches are confident in you to be the starter and you don't have the pressure hanging over your head wondering, "Am I going to get yanked out?" To actually be a starter makes such a big difference in your all-around career as a football player. You see a lot of guys who don't get to play, and the experience is just not the same.

We had ideal conditions that day in that Nebraska was mainly a running football team. That played into our hands and into my strength. I was better against the run than the pass and it was drizzling out there all day. They had a great running back, Roger Craig, and the conditions made it tough for him to cut. It was a perfect situation for our defense that was playing good football and playing physical football.

I think we had something like seven turnovers that day. That kept putting them down close to our goal line. Nebraska's touchdown drives ended up being less than 20 yards [nine yards and eight yards]. I remember we were winning 3-0 at the half. What I also remember is that I hit Roger Craig on the sidelines and knocked him out of the game. We were all excited that we had knocked out their number-one running back, but his backup was Mike Rozier. We thought there would be a big drop-off, but there wasn't.

The game was just a dogfight. I remember how well everybody played on defense and how into the game everybody was. Sometimes there are games you get into and people talk about being flat or you look into guys' eyes and you can tell they aren't all there that day. This was not one of those games. This was one of those games in which everybody seemed to be into it. We were just having fun out there and it was one of those things you will remember for all time because everybody was flying to the ball and just having fun.

In a normal game when the offense would turn the ball over, on the sideline the defense would groan or be mad at the offense. On this day, it was like, "Let's go, man!" Everybody on defense was happy to get back out there on the field and play some more. I had 21 tackles that day. The coaches gave out bonus points for tackles, caused fumbles, and other big plays. I know I caused a fumble that day, and I had an interception that ricocheted off my hands that [cornerback] David King caught. Our coaches told me I had the most bonus points anybody had ever had on defense for the first half of that game.

After that game was done, I was treated differently from that point on. The coaches looked at me differently. It was just like I was accepted as a bona fide player after that. We didn't win the game, but we sure played hard and had a great game on defense. When we came off the field, the Nebraska fans gave us a standing ovation because they appreciated our effort. That gave us a lot of confidence we could play with anyone, because at that time Nebraska was a national title contender almost every year.

ONE LAST HURDLE

Although Auburn finished the 1981 season just 5-6, the excitement level was high because knowledgeable fans could see better days were on the horizon.

Dorminey notes the players were excited, too. "When you are that age you don't understand if a coach is a good coach from just them going over their Xs and Os, because we weren't that smart knowing all of the strategies. The difference we noticed was in the results, especially on defense. I think everybody noticed we were a lot more physical and we played a lot harder."

Dorminey's senior season was 1982, the year the Tigers would get back onto the bowl scene after an absence since 1974. The safety says it was no surprise that the Tigers won nine games and defeated a Doug Flutie-led Boston College team in Orlando to set the stage for an SEC title the following year. "You could tell we were going to be better by the players we were getting," he notes. "Bo Jackson came on the scene that year. When we were working out, we could really tell that we had upgraded our team athletically. We went into that year confident that we could have a great season."

Dorminey was one of Dye's favorite players, and the feeling was mutual. "He was just a player's coach," the safety says. "The things that he talked about and believed in are the things that I believed in as a player. I never articulated them like he did or had a formalized plan like he did, but when he talked about outworking people, the intangibles, out-hustling them, and all of the things you can do off the field to get better, those are the things that I and a bunch of guys on our defense had to do to be able to play at that level.

"When I went through all of those years of rehabbing and training, those are the kind of thoughts I had in my mind. I was thinking, 'Hey, I am outworking the next guy. I know they aren't doing these things I am doing.' You are just hoping that one day it pays off. To have it pay off and to be able to play for a coach who you felt was right in lock step with you and laid it out perfectly for you, and then had everybody else believing and working that hard, was just the perfect fit for me."

Dorminey was a preseason All-SEC pick going into his senior season, along with his buddy and fellow safety Bob Harris. The duo was collectively known as "The Bruise Brothers" for their physical style. Defensive tackle Donnie Humphrey, another holdover from the Barfield era, was expected to be All-SEC, too. "We went into that 1982 season with a lot of publicity," Dorminey remembers. "Me, Bob, and Donnie got a lot of publicity. We were really excited and we worked super hard over the summer."

The Tigers won six of their first seven games with the only setback a home-field loss to Nebraska. In the game seven win at Mississippi State, Dorminey was injured again. He hit a Bulldog player so hard on the sideline that he knocked himself out. When he woke up, he was experiencing sharp pain in his knee.

"I tore up my knee, so it was a bit of a downer for me even though the team was doing great," he says. "I faced being finished about the time my senior season was halfway through. They wanted to operate on my knee, but I asked if there was any way I could put off the surgery until the end of the season, and they said I could.

"They flew me up to Tennessee to get a special brace made for my knee. They got the brace ready, but I couldn't play with it because it pinched my knee and made it sore. I just kept working out and I got to the point where I could run and cut, so I was able to just tape my knee from my thigh all the way to my ankle and the tape held my knee in place. I didn't have any ligaments because they were torn on the inside of my knee. I was able to come back and play in the Alabama game and the bowl game versus Boston College."

While the bowl game win was memorable for ending Auburn's postseason drought, the victory over Alabama was even bigger because the Tigers at last halted their all-time worst losing streak that had begun against the archrival in 1973.

"The Alabama game that year was special for a bunch of reasons," Dorminey notes. "The previous year we were beating Alabama and had them on the ropes and I ended up getting burned for a long touchdown that turned the whole momentum of the ball game. Thinking that my senior year was over, to be able to get back on the field and play them again and get redemption, that was super big for me.

"It was also a big thing to go to our first bowl game, to play against Flutie, to go out there and win that one, and have a good game," he says. Dorminey played a starring role in the bowl game and was named defensive MVP. "I think it set Auburn on a new level. We finished 14th in the nation and let everybody know what was to come. You couldn't write a better ending to a career."

Before finishing his degree in the spring of 1983, Dorminey had another knee surgery after the season. He immediately went to work with a general building contractor near home in West Palm Beach, Florida. He made a major change in his professional career 10 years later, going into the childcare and schooling business. In 1993 he bought Tiny Tikes and now runs three schools—two in West Palm Beach and one in Boynton Beach. Dorminey and his wife, Robin, are parents of a 12-year-old son and a 10-year-old daughter.

Although it has been more than two decades since Dorminey finished at Auburn, Waldrop, the longtime Auburn trainer, says that he remembers the defensive back's tough times and good times at AU as if they had happened yesterday. "Mark's one of the toughest guys who ever played football at Auburn and is just a remarkable person," Waldrop says. "He has a terrific sense of humor and was a great influence on the other players. He is just an outstanding person, and I am glad to have him as a friend. He told me that despite all he had to go through at Auburn, he would do the same thing if he had it to do over again."

The former Auburn standout tries to return to campus every season to watch the Tigers play and notes that he is excited to see the program's continued success as a nationally prominent power. Dorminey can look back in pride, knowing he did his part to help make Auburn football what it is today.

Chapter 8

TUCKER FREDERICKSON

BIG, FAST, AND GOOD

Any informed discussion about the greatest football players in Auburn history is not complete without the inclusion of 1960s star Tucker Frederickson, who was unquestionably one of the best defensive backs to play for the Tigers. He was also the first Tiger running back selected as the No. 1 player in an NFL Draft.

Teammates and coaches from his years at Auburn point out that they had never seen a player quite like Frederickson when he arrived on campus. He featured every attribute to become a standout, with excellent size, speed, intelligence, maturity, confidence, toughness, and a feel for the game.

A number of stories convey just how impressive he was, even as a freshman. One of the best is from longtime Auburn administrator Buddy Davidson, who worked as a student manager for the football team when the big back arrived on campus.

Davidson remembers Frederickson's first practice. Playing linebacker, Frederickson hit offensive players so hard on three consecutive plays that each had to be taken to the campus infirmary. For the rest of the offense's protection, Davidson says the coaches immediately moved Frederickson farther away from the line of scrimmage to safety, the position he would play throughout college.

A telling sign of his ability, Frederickson had played organized football for only three seasons prior to arriving for fall classes in 1961. Even though neither of his parents nor his three sisters were athletes, Frederickson had a lot of natural ability and lived in a great environment to develop as an athlete. "Growing up in South Florida is what made it easy," he says. "Sports were part of my life on a daily basis, outside running around the neighborhood and down at the local public parks."

Frederickson notes the weather allowed him to compete outside in sports on a year-round basis. "I played football, basketball, baseball, track, golf—everything."

He became so good at football he received scholarship offers from colleges around the country. "I don't think I had a favorite sport growing up," Frederickson says. "I just had a better natural ability in football. I excelled in it even though I didn't work any harder in it than I did at basketball or track or baseball. I just played it a little better."

Frederickson notes that he didn't give the idea of playing college football a lot of thought until his final year in high school. "I heard that I had a chance to play," he says. "We had a pretty good football team my senior year, but I didn't get heavily recruited at all. Recruiting then wasn't like it is these days. I got a lot of letters which I did not respond to."

However, no matter what the era, he was so impressive during his senior season that recruiting intensity would inevitably pick up—and it did. "Towards the end of my senior year I started getting real strong interest from the University of Florida, Florida State, and Miami," he remembers. "Then, after the football season was over, I got letters from every big school in the country because I made All-America. That is when I had to make a decision.

"I had an uncle who was a veterinarian, a father who was a veterinarian, and I didn't know any better, so I figured I wanted to be a veterinarian. So I sort of narrowed my choices to the University of Florida, which did not have a vet school, or to a college with a vet school that played pretty good football. Georgia, Auburn, and Purdue were the three that I looked at."

Dick McGowen was the assistant coach who helped convince Frederickson to sign with the Tigers. Auburn's head coach, Shug Jordan, made McGowen's assignment easier, as Frederickson recalls. "Let's give Shug a plug, too," he says. "I went to see Georgia and [head coach] Wally Butts scared the hell out of me. He was about 5-foot-8 or 5-foot-9 and 280 pounds. He was about as wide as he was tall. He was rough and that scared me.

"I took a trip to Auburn and Coach Jordan was just the opposite. He certainly made a better impression than Wally did. I also went to Purdue, to Florida State, to Miami, and to Florida. Florida is where I would have gone if they had a vet school, but they didn't have one at the time."

Tucker Frederickson (20) goes airborne while running for the Tigers.
Draughon Library Archives

Auburn's star quarterback and future NFL player, Bobby Hunt, remembers he was assigned to be Frederickson's host when he came to Auburn for a recruiting trip. "I was asked to show him around, but he didn't get in until 9:30 because his plane got delayed coming in from Miami," Hunt says. "They brought him into Graves Center around a quarter 'til 10. I was in the KA fraternity and we were having a party that night. After we got him in the room, I asked him if he wanted to go to a fraternity party and he said, 'No, I don't think so,' so I took him out to the bowling alley on Opelika Road. We bowled one game, went up town and got a hamburger and a milk shake, and then we went back to Graves

Center. The next morning he signed. I guess that is probably the best thing I did for Auburn.

"Tucker was the best looking high school athlete I have ever seen," Hunt adds. "You just didn't see guys that big 215 or 220 pounds playing running back in those days. He was a freshman when I was a senior. He was an excellent football player."

OFF TO COLLEGE

Except for the few people he had met on his recruiting trip, Frederickson says he "didn't know a soul" at Auburn when he arrived as a freshman.

"It was pretty scary," he recalls. "You just wonder if you can compete. It is sort of the same transition you have when you go to pro football. You want to come in and sit back a little bit and become one of the guys as quickly as possible. That's how I transitioned. I sort of went slow, met a few guys, and became part of the guys. I made a few quick friends and hung with them and started participating in football."

Frederickson remembers being part of a talented freshman squad. "We had a really good team with Jimmy Sidle and myself. We tied Alabama, who had [Joe] Namath, and then we beat Florida and we beat Georgia. You only had three games then and you didn't practice with the varsity. We had a real good freshman team."

Frederickson adjusted to college off the field, too. "I enjoyed it," he says. "I am not so sure I studied as hard as I should have. My first year I thought I was going to be a veterinarian, so I was taking some pretty tough courses. As I got into it, I slacked up a bit.

"Auburn was fun. It was a nice atmosphere with nice people, and I had great friends. Looking back, it was a great place to be. I got a degree in bio science, sort of a pre-vet type of degree, but I never went on with it."

When he moved to varsity in 1962, colleges were still playing one-platoon football. This meant limited substitution, so players saw action on both offense and defense. Jordan kept fresh players on the field by replacing his entire starting lineup with 11 different individuals.

"We had three different teams, and I got to play as they alternated teams," Frederickson says. "We had a good second team, which had me and the Rawson brothers [Lamar and David]. We started off real well my sophomore year. I think we won our first six games and then we hit the wall and lost three of our last four games. It was a transition year for me trying to get to realize I could play with the big boys. I didn't think I played all that well my sophomore year.

"My junior year we had a really good team. Jimmy had a great year. We won every game except the Mississippi State game, and then we got beat in the Orange Bowl. We had the chemistry and everything clicked. We played really well together. We weren't big, but we were fast and we played great defense. We were well coached on defense. I think we were ranked number one or two in the country on defense, but on offense we weren't very creative. Jimmy would roll out and pretend like he was going to pass and then he would run the ball.

"Looking back on Jimmy Sidle, he could have been as good or better than Namath because he was such a good athlete," Frederickson says of the All-America quarterback whose career was cut short by injuries. "We didn't throw the football at all. We won with defense as our strong suit. We played Nebraska in the Orange Bowl, and they were huge and we were tiny. I was one of the biggest guys on our team. There were some big tackles on the Nebraska team. They killed us the first half and we killed them the second half and they beat us 13-7. My junior year was a great experience."

The Tigers graced the cover of *Sports Illustrated's* preseason football issue in 1964. With Frederickson and Sidle leading the team, Auburn was picked to be number one that year. However, Sidle injured his shoulder in a 30-0 opening-day victory over Houston and couldn't pass the ball after that. With little offense, AU squeaked by Tennessee 3-0 in week two. "Then we got beat by Kentucky and everything came apart," Frederickson notes. "We finished 6-4 and it was a disappointing senior season."

However, a star at both running back and safety, Frederickson did everything he could for the team. On defense, he covered a tremendous amount of territory. On offense, he started the season at halfback but finished as a fullback who put up big numbers for a player at that position.

"I really enjoyed that and the light went on," Frederickson says of the new position. "[Coach Jordan] switched me over to fullback in the seventh game when things were really going bad and I had a couple of 100-yard games in a row.

"Looking back I should have played fullback all along, because it is a much more natural position for me. It was a disappointing season in that we didn't do what everybody expected us to do. All good things happened to me, but it was a disappointing year for the team."

Frederickson, who won the Jacobs Trophy as the SEC's top blocker his junior and senior seasons, was a consensus All-American in 1964 and finished sixth in the voting for the Heisman Trophy, even though AU's sports information director, Norm Carlson, had left for another job. Still a student at the time, Davidson handled the sports publicity assignment that fall. He later took over as the full-time sports information director and says had he known then what he would know after several years on the job, he believes he could have helped Frederickson become the university's first Heisman winner 17 years before Pat Sullivan won the trophy.

THE GAME OF MY LIFE
BY TUCKER FREDERICKSON

The Nebraska game was a memorable experience because they were huge, and it was fun because I was from South Florida. It was fun to go back and play in the Orange Bowl, so that game certainly stands out.

The Alabama game, when we beat them 10-8 that year, certainly stands out when I caught the touchdown pass from Mailon Kent that won the game. But the defense really won the game. The 10-8 game over Alabama is the obvious one because we won that. I played pretty well on defense and I was all alone in the flat for the touchdown. It wasn't as if I did anything spectacular.

Just beating them to go to the Orange Bowl was memorable. I guess that was the game. We got off the snide and beat Alabama. Going to the Orange Bowl was the icing on the cake. Winning that game had to mean a lot to Coach Jordan. They had beaten him five times in a row.

Hal Herring was our defensive coordinator that year and he had a great defensive mind. He went on to be a defensive coordinator for the Falcons. He knew how to get us to play. I played like a linebacker when I was at safety. I came up so quickly that they could have thrown over me all day, I suspect, but they didn't try it very often. Thinking back, I just reacted. I think he just let me do what I wanted to do and I reacted most of the time pretty well. Our defenses were very good all of the way through. I related to that. I was a big part of our defenses and I sort of had a free hand from Coach Herring to do anything I wanted to do my junior and senior years when I substituted myself. I went in when I wanted to. I didn't come out very often.

IN HIGH DEMAND

After wrapping up his collegiate playing days on the 1964 team, Frederickson finished his degree in '65 and began playing pro football for the NFL's New York Giants. "I had not heard from the Giants," he remembers. "I knew I was going to be drafted in the first round, but I figured it was going to be the Lions or one of the AFL teams I had heard from.

"We had played Alabama the last game of the season and the draft was the next day. We were staying in Birmingham for Jimmy Sidle's wedding. I got a call the day after the game from the head scout of the Giants, and he told me they were going to draft me number one if I had an interest in playing in New York.

"Looking back I should have said 'maybe' instead of saying, 'Okay, great!' It probably cost me some money, but I will never second-guess myself, because New York was fantastic for me. So anyway, I was there for Jimmy Sidle's wedding. We had gotten beat by Alabama. We should have killed them. We just physically beat them all day and they beat us with a kickoff return and they had one long pass, but the rest of the game we beat them up and down the field.

"After not hearing from the Giants, they called and I said, 'Yes, I will play for you.' The next day they had a guy who called and talked about money. I said that sounded great and that was it. The Denver Broncos called about that time and said they were going to draft me No. 1 in the AFL Draft. I told them, 'Don't waste the pick, I want to go to New York. I am just being honest with you.' I am sure I cost myself some money, but that is just the way I am. I didn't have an agent. I didn't have anything. New York is where I wanted to go. It turned out great for me, although maybe not for the Giants, because I got hurt the next year."

While the NFL Draft has turned into a major production with several months of build-up, when Frederickson was the top pick it was different. "It was nonchalant, no big deal," he notes. "There was no big hoopla, nothing. There were a few calls from the press and that was it, and I was too busy going to Sidle's wedding."

Frederickson was a hit in New York City with the organization and fans after leading the team in rushing as a rookie. "Pro football was great fun," he says. "To be able to do something you like to do and get paid for it, especially in New York City, was great. New York City turned out to be beyond my expectations in terms of the networking and what the Giants organization is all about. I had a real good first year. I made the Pro Bowl and it was really going well and then I got hurt in practice the next year. I hung on for six more years, but it never was the same."

Playing in an era before arthroscopic surgery, it is amazing that he was able to play running back after missing the 1966 season with what was then considered a career-ending surgery on his left knee. He bounced back from that, but then had to endure the same surgical procedure on his right knee in 1967. "I am told those are the operations that kids come back from better than ever now," Frederickson notes. "I wore a cast for six months on my leg for two years in a row. Now they walk out after surgery.

"Even though I played another six years, I had my knees taped for every game, every practice from that point on. I am going to have to get knee replacements for both of them in the near future."

Before he retired from the Giants, Frederickson was preparing for the next stage of his life. "I realized my career in professional football was going to end sooner than I wanted it to, so I got into Wall Street and I became a registered broker in 1968," he says. "I was in different areas of Wall Street until 1983 and then I came back home [to Florida]. I got into the real estate business and that is what I am still doing."

The former Tiger star satisfies his competitive urges on the golf course these days and rides a bike to stay in shape. The father of three girls who aren't athletes, Frederickson's son, Jon Erik, is a good one who plays wide receiver for the University of New Hampshire, one of the country's top I-AA teams.

Frederickson says that he has positive memories of his days as an Auburn student and athlete. "I haven't been back in a while. Auburn was a lot more small, college-town oriented relative to what I hear it is now. The stadium held about 30,000 when I played there. I hear it is about 90,000 now.

"It was a great experience for me. There were a lot of nice people at Auburn, and I still have some great friends from Auburn. I joined a fraternity and became a KA and I still keep in touch with those guys. I keep in touch with Mickey Sutton, Mike Alford, and those guys. It was just a good time for me. It worked out. It was hard playing football, don't get me wrong. Auburn was tough, but it was certainly the vehicle for the next level and all of the good things that happened."

Chapter 9

PHIL GARGIS

ONE TOUGH TIGER

Longtime observers of Auburn football can tell you that few tougher players ever lined up for the Tigers than Phil Gargis. He wasn't the biggest, the fastest, or the best quarterback in Auburn history, but he was one of the most productive. He was a leader and took a backseat to nobody when it came to showing the physical and mental toughness needed to succeed as a QB who was equally adept as a runner and passer.

It surprised nobody who knew Gargis that, when he entered a campus-wide boxing tournament after his senior season, he emerged as the heavyweight division champ. Tough-guy defensive players who say that overprotected quarterbacks need to dress in skirts on game day never had Phil Gargis in mind.

As the youngest of five brothers growing up in the tiny community of Ford City on the outskirts of Leighton, a small town in Northwest Alabama, Gargis says he had no choice but to grow up tough, an attribute that would serve him well on the gridiron. "I grew up fighting all of my life out of necessity at home."

Organized football did not exist in the area until he got into junior high school, but Gargis played with the bigger boys and developed an early love for the game. By the time he was a sophomore at Colbert County High, he was the starting quarterback and safety on a team loaded with talent. By the time he was a junior it was obvious he was a college prospect, and by his senior season he had developed into an SEC-caliber prospect.

Gargis notes that it took him a while to figure out he would be good enough to play at the collegiate level. "Where we grew up there wasn't a lot of exposure to colleges," he says. "There wasn't the media and the TV like there is now. We always watched pro football on Sundays and that was always a dream to play at that level.

"As far as realizing I might have a chance to play in college, I don't think that happened until maybe my junior year," he says. "I really didn't have anything to measure to because I had never been on a college campus and I had never seen college players other than watching them on TV. You thought you were good enough, but you really weren't sure."

Gargis was good enough, and he had quality athletes all around him. Tight end Ozzie Newsome, who would play at Alabama and in the NFL, was a teammate, along with Thad Flanagan, a receiver who later played for the Tide. Gargis was also a member of the Colbert County basketball team, which won the state title his senior season. Center Leon Douglas, who would become a star at Alabama and eventually play in the NBA, was the big name on the court.

"I was the hatchet man in basketball," Gargis jokes. "When you have guys like Leon Douglas and Ozzie Newsome on the team, you have a pretty good core of basketball players. We had a lot of talent that came through our school. In a period of eight or 10 years, there was a lot of talent that came out of that whole part of the state—that includes Leighton, Town Creek, Courtland, and those areas.

"We won the football, baseball, and basketball state titles my senior year," says Gargis, who directed the football team's wishbone triple-option offense. "We went to the semi finals in football my junior year."

Auburn was one of the colleges to express an early interest in the athlete, and Gargis committed to the Tigers. "There was a lot for me to learn about being recruited," he says. "Thad Flanagan and I went on a lot of recruiting trips together. I was just in awe of everything. The schools were so big. The programs were so big. We had never seen anything like that. It was a great experience to go through it. I also really liked Mississippi State. It was one of my three choices, along with Auburn and Alabama."

Although Gargis decided on Auburn, a complication almost kept him from playing for the Tigers. "I was told going into the last week before signing day that I did not have a scholarship at Auburn," he remembers. "What had happened was that there was a guy named Calvin Culliver, who later played at Alabama. We had played against him my junior year in high school. He was at W.S. Neal High in Brewton. Culliver had committed to

Quarterback Phil Gargis was known for his toughness.
Draughon Library Archives

Auburn, and I was told Auburn was overcommitted with more promises than they had scholarships available, so I committed to Alabama the week of signing day. Danny Ford was recruiting me for Alabama along with coach [Pat] Dye, who was actually an assistant coach at Alabama in those days.

"Friday night before the signing day, which was on Saturday, we had a basketball game," Gargis remembers. "Where I grew up we didn't have a phone, and I got a message to be by the phone at my girlfriend's house after the basketball game at 10:30. I did, and [Auburn coach Shug] Jordan called me directly and told me that they wanted me. He explained to me what happened. They had overcommitted, but Culliver had backed out and was now going to Alabama. They had a scholarship available for me.

"Coach [Alabama's Bear] Bryant had told me, 'You will never see the offensive side of the ball,'" Gargis notes. "He said, 'You will be a defensive back and you will be a good one.' Coach Jordan, during the process of recruiting, told me, 'We will give you a chance to play offense,' which is what I wanted to do. I liked Auburn, and Coach Jordan convinced me that they really wanted me. I recommitted back to Auburn that Friday night about 11 o'clock or midnight.

"Saturday morning, both teams showed up at my house to sign me. It got to be kind of hairy that day. Alabama would take me into a room and try to convince me to go their way, and Auburn would take me into a room and try to convince me to go that way. One of my brothers came in and asked me what I wanted to do and I told him that I wanted to go to Auburn. I couldn't make the decision with everybody there. He went in and told the coaches I was going to Auburn, and that is it."

FROM A TINY TOWN TO A BIG COLLEGE

Gargis arrived on campus in the summer of 1973 with three years of starting experience at Colbert County High. His older brother, David, was scheduled to be the starter Gargis' sophomore year, but injured both of his ankles in spring practice. Gargis was such a natural at the position the coaches decided to keep him there when David returned that fall, so his brother, who would later play college football for the University of North Alabama, was moved to receiver.

The quarterback found his path to the starting assignment in college was a lot more difficult both on and off the field. Although Auburn isn't a big city, the bustling campus was a big adjustment for Gargis. "Athletically, yes, the players were a lot better, but we didn't know any more than to just go hard on the football field," he notes. "That is all we were ever taught by our coaches growing up. The physical part of adjusting to college wasn't as big a hurdle as getting adjusted to college life and being away from home. It turned out that it was the grandest thing that could have happened—getting a chance to play college football. There is nothing like it."

However, Gargis admits that was almost nipped in the bud. "I packed my stuff two or three times and I was headed home. If I had gas money, I would have probably done it. I got extremely homesick. I think that is part of growing up in a small town. We didn't travel a lot, so I hadn't been away from home for any length of time.

"It was pretty tough at first as a freshman, but you get into what is going on and meet people. Going down there and not knowing anybody except for two or three people I had met in the high school all-star game made it tough. It got a little better when classes started, and you got to know people and started moving around campus a bit. Also, I had my girlfriend from high school, Scarlotte [Hall], who became a majorette at Auburn. When school started, at least she was there. That helped me tremendously."

Gargis arrived at Auburn near the end of Jordan's 25-year tenure as head coach. "I got to know Coach Jordan really well, and there is not a better person that I have ever met as far as leadership and the qualities he had as a coach," Gargis says. "We kind of bonded together. He kind of took me in."

Like almost all freshmen, Gargis wasn't ready to contribute at the SEC level when he arrived on campus, but he was a lot closer than most. "My freshman year was a tough one, but it was the best thing that could have happened that we had a freshman team. That is something they have taken away, but it sure was wonderful for me. We had a pretty good freshman team. We played against the Georgias and all of those people. It helped you adjust to college and made you feel like you could play at the varsity level, and it was extremely fun."

Gargis didn't even mind the assignment of scout team quarterback when he and the entire freshman squad would prepare the varsity for its next opponent. "Getting to go against the number-one defense in practice every day was a lot of fun," he says. "I enjoyed trying to move the offense with a lot less talent than the varsity defense had. You have to compensate for that and you learn how to make your yardage; you learn to make your passes. It was a great learning experience."

While Gargis had fun with the freshmen, the 1973 campaign was not going well, even though the Tigers had finished 10-1 the previous season. The Tigers opened the season with wins over Oregon State and Chattanooga, but were blanked 21-0 in the SEC opener at Tennessee. They finished just 2-5 in the conference, but despite posting a 6-5 record, the team managed to receive an invitation to play Missouri at the Sun Bowl in El Paso, Texas.

The quarterback had spent his season on freshman and scout teams, but that would change. "One of my most memorable games was my freshman year when I got to make the trip to the Sun Bowl," he says. "I had gone through bowl practice with the feeling that I might get a lot of playing time and maybe I might even get to start. When we got out there, for whatever reason, I didn't get in the game for a little while. We got behind and I got put in and actually had a real good game. We came back, but we didn't win that game. But I went into the following spring thinking I had a chance to win the starting job. That was exciting going into my sophomore season establishing myself, at least as someone they could kind of count on. It was a fun year to be going into."

Gargis' play in 1974 helped to make the season fun. With the hard-nosed quarterback surrounded by quality veterans, the Tigers bounced back and posted a 10-win campaign. "The 1974 season was unreal for a lot of reasons," Gargis remembers. "I really looked up to the players on that team. There were a lot of seniors who kind of took care of me and carried me all the way through the season.

"We went into the season with a lot of talent and a lot of expectations," he notes. "We had a new offense. We were running the veer, so there was just a lot of excitement. One game just kind of fed on the next one. We kept getting better and better and it was the most fun year anyone could ever have. We ended up going 10-2 and our two losses were games we were right there into the end. With a play or two going differently, we could have won. It was a very good year, a very exciting year, and a huge learning year."

Making it more fun for the quarterback was the talented line in front of him, featuring All-SEC center Lee Gross and two future All-SEC players, tackle Chuck Fletcher and guard Lynn Johnson. "We had a really good line and the receivers and the running backs were great, too," Gargis says. "Also, you couldn't ask for a better group of people to have for teammates."

Auburn won seven straight before falling 25-14 at Florida. The second loss was a 17-13 setback in Birmingham to second-ranked Alabama to close the regular season. The Tigers bounced back with a 27-3 victory over Texas in the Gator Bowl to finish sixth and seventh in the major polls. In the bowl, Gargis threw a pair of touchdowns to tight end Ed Butler versus coach Darrell Royal's Longhorns. He also passed for a two-point conversion to tight end Dan Nugent, a future NFL player, and netted 51 rushing yards.

THE GAME OF MY LIFE
BY PHIL GARGIS

The Gator Bowl in 1974 is one that really stands out. We were a big underdog going into that game against a University of Texas team that had star players like Earl Campbell, Doug English, and people like that. Even though we were underdogs, we felt confident that we could play with anybody that year.

We went in there and got off to a good start and basically manhandled them. That is a game that will stand out for years. At that point we didn't know that Earl Campbell was going to be the great player that he became. Our defense stepped up that day and played tremendous football, stopping him and the rest of the Texas offense.

The festivities at the Gator Bowl also stand out to me, along with a lot of our alumni being down there. Our fans had high expectations for us going into that game. It was just so exciting going in as the underdog and getting off to a great start. Our fans were really into the game and it was just a great experience. I know that our running backs, Mitzi [Jackson] and Secdrick [McIntyre], had big games, and I think I threw it to our tight ends a good bit.

The Texas players were very arrogant going into the game. We could tell that from all of the functions we had together before we played them. Even the Texas band was arrogant to our band. It was the typical underdog game. It didn't do anything but fire us up and I think they felt like they already had the game won. They were more or less laughing at us before the game.

Coach Jordan really enjoyed winning that game versus Texas. Some of the speeches that he gave before games and at halftime were really good. Being around him a lot, you wouldn't think he was a fiery type of guy, but he had great motivational talks and the way he could get you prepared to play was unreal. He had us ready for that game.

Coach Jordan could cut up with us and laugh at himself, but he was a forceful guy, too, and everybody respected him tremendously. Our offensive line just totally dominated Texas. I believe Doug English was supposed to be one of the top players in the country as a defensive tackle, but he was just a non-factor the whole game.

DOING HIS PART

Unfortunately for Gargis, his junior and senior seasons at Auburn weren't nearly as fun and successful on the playing field. "I remember 1975 was a tough year. Because we lost so many good seniors, we were kind of rebuilding," he says. "For some reason, things just didn't click in '75. We had some good games and we had games we lost to teams we shouldn't have lost to, like Memphis State. It was the year Coach Jordan was retiring. It was a hard year and it was the same thing my senior year [1976]. I don't think we lived up to what we were expected to do my junior year. It was one of the seasons if anything could bounce the other way, it did."

The Tigers slipped to 4-6-1 in 1975 and finished 4-7 the following year with Doug Barfield promoted to head coach. Gargis was an effective quarterback, but the SEC's top teams overmatched the Tigers physically.

"Coach Barfield was a great individual coach and he was always my quarterback coach," Gargis notes. "It was a huge step for him and for everybody else to have him take over the team. He had his coaching philosophies. With the people he brought in, it was an adjustment period. I thought he did a good job with what he did, but it was just a lot different. The schemes weren't the same and there was a lot of learning. It was going to take a few years for him to get things the way they needed to be. It was another tough year for us."

Although rule changes meant to help the offense have altered the game of football since Gargis played, he is still on the Auburn All-Time Top 10 list at number eight in touchdowns with 31. He is ninth in total offense with 3,920 yards—1,884 on the ground and 2,036 passing. He is also seventh in yards per completion at 13.88.

Pro scouts were interested in Gargis, but not as a quarterback, because nobody was running the veer option in the NFL. "I actually got drafted [12th round] by the New York Jets," he says. "I went up to preseason camp and they put me at running back. I felt very good about my chances, and then when we came back for the regular season they moved me to defensive back. They put me on the corner and I wasn't good enough to play it. They gave me a lot of opportunities, but without playing it in college, it is a tough deal to break into unless you have blazing speed, which I didn't have.

"It was a great experience," he remembers. "I wouldn't take anything for it. I was able to let football go after that. I was able to see there were people out there who were a lot better football-wise than I was. I was able to enjoy everything I did in football and not regret not doing something.

"I went back to my hometown and got into the insurance business for a while, but living in Leighton after being exposed to a lot of things … there just wasn't enough going on," Gargis adds. "I found a job in Birmingham and I have lived in Homewood since 1979. I work with a company called EHS [Electronic Healthcare Systems]. We do billing systems for doctors."

Gargis married his high school and college sweetheart, Scarlotte, and they have three kids. His oldest, Phillip, was a star quarterback at Homewood High and signed a football scholarship with Auburn. Although Gargis says his son enjoyed attending AU, Phillip didn't see any game action for the Tigers. Gargis' younger son, Parker, developed into a football and baseball star at Homewood and played at Samford University in Birmingham. Their daughter, Kathryn, just finished her sophomore year at Auburn. "It is much more rewarding to see my kids do well than anything I did," the quarterback says.

Gargis also notes that he and his family are still close friends with many of his teammates. "About 25 of us from the 1974 team get together every year and go deer hunting," he says. "Our kids have grown up with their kids, and we still do that to this day. We get together for three days early in the year and have a great time. It is a real close-knit group. I loved my time at Auburn. I loved playing football there and I can never repay Auburn for all of the opportunities it gave me. It was a great experience."

Chapter 10

BOBBY HUNT

TOUGH ENOUGH

Hall of Fame high school coach Mal Morgan sent many of his star players on to college football. Bobby Hunt, one of the best of the best to come from Morgan's Lanett High teams, made the short trip down old U.S. Highway 29 to Auburn, where he became a two-way standout during the Shug Jordan era.

Even though it has been 50 years since Hunt played for Morgan, he still has great respect for the high school coach who set him on a path that would lead to success in college and pro football.

"Coach Morgan was so tough," notes Hunt. "Everybody on our team was scared of him. I don't care if it was me, Richard Wood, Mailon Kent, or David Hill—we were scared of him. You did it one way and it was his way. Everybody knew that." Wood, Kent, and Hill also became prominent players at Auburn, and both Wood and Hill played pro football with Hunt.

"We worked and worked and worked," Hunt says of his high school days in a small textile mill town on the Alabama-Georgia state line. "During the summer we would go up to the swimming pool and practice football. The assistant football coach was the head of the pool. They would have the shoes and the balls up there and we would work out."

No matter what time of year, playing football—or any sport, for that matter—was just fine with Hunt. "Since I was five or six years old, I was playing something," he says. "Growing up in Lanett, everybody played sports. We started midget football and then we played basketball and baseball. Playing sports is pretty much what we did year-round."

Hunt was also a standout in basketball and baseball. "When basketball would come, just about everybody who played football would play basketball," he says. "We didn't have a [high school] baseball team, but each textile mill would have one and we all played on those teams."

Although he could have signed a pro baseball contract, Hunt opted for football and college, both of which proved to be wise decisions. He signed with the Tigers after a standout senior season in 1957 at Lanett High, where he played quarterback and defensive back. His team seldom lost, something Hunt says is a direct result of the coaching.

"Coach Morgan was probably the smartest football coach I ever met," Hunt says. "We would make adjustments. He would look at some films and then away we would go. We tied one game my junior and senior years and we won the state championship our junior and senior years. We worked hard and we thought we were going to win. He was a super football coach.

"Looking back on it, he was really an influence on me," Hunt notes. "He took me to Auburn once to watch spring training. We got in the car, and you never said anything until he asked you something. He finally asked me, 'You think you are tough enough to play down here at Auburn?' I said, 'Yes sir, I think so.' Coach Morgan is 92 now and is just as sharp as ever. He has mellowed a lot, though, over the years."

Although Auburn was close to home, Hunt wasn't certain if he would sign with the Tigers. He grew up a Georgia Tech fan and strongly considered the Yellow Jackets. His father had attended the University of Alabama; however, the Tide fell out of the picture when the university's basketball coach reneged on a scholarship offer to Hunt's older brother, Jim. "You can imagine what that did to the household, especially my mother," Hunt says. "That just turned her against anything from Alabama. Until the day she died, if they were playing Russia, she would be for Russia."

Hunt's interest in Tech went back to seventh grade, when a family friend invited him to attend a Tech-Alabama game in Birmingham. "My daddy's friend was a big Georgia Tech fan and I thought that was the greatest thing in the world," Hunt says. "It really came down to Georgia Tech and Auburn on where I decided to go. I went to Georgia Tech to watch them more during recruiting, but I think it came down to convenience for my mother and daddy. Auburn was only about 20 miles

Bobby Hunt was a two-way star for the Tigers.
Draughon Library Archives

from Lanett. [Auburn assistant Hal] Herring went to high school with my mother and Coach Morgan went to Auburn. We had guys before me sign with Auburn, although not a lot of them stayed."

Hunt played on the freshman team in 1958. As a sophomore, he didn't have to wait long to see prime-time action on the varsity. "We played Tennessee the first game in Knoxville. I was standing on the sideline, and in the middle of the first quarter they called, 'Hunt.' I went up there and they said, 'Go in.' I didn't do that well, but later on everything kind of fell into place and I had a good sophomore year.

"I was scared to death eating that pregame meal going into the Tennessee game," says Hunt. "I didn't even know I was going to play. Once I got over that first game, I did pretty well, to tell you the truth."

Playing quarterback and left cornerback, one of Hunt's most memorable games was his first against Georgia Tech, a game the Tigers won 7-6. "We beat Tech up in Atlanta and I scored a touchdown there," he says. "That game stands out, and the one we played against Mississippi State when I had like 214 yards stands out, too. I had a good year."

Buoyed by his success, Hunt trained hard for his next season—probably too hard. "I think during the summer going into my junior year I overdid it," he says. "I played baseball and played catcher and I was always sweating. Back then we wore those old wool uniforms, so you can imagine how hot it was down there. Once I got through playing baseball I would go run steps and do sit-ups the same day. I was working out seven days a week. After that I just didn't have the same pep I did as a sophomore and I didn't have a good junior year."

The Tigers, who were 7-3 Hunt's sophomore year, improved to 8-2 as the junior again started at quarterback and cornerback. In his final college season, 1961, the Tigers slumped to 6-4. "My senior year was tough," he says. "We didn't have a good year and Alabama just beat us like a drum. We had a better team than the way we played. I don't know what happened to us. We started off pretty good. It was a nightmare."

THE GAME OF MY LIFE
BY BOBBY HUNT

It would have to be from my sophomore year. Beating Georgia Tech in Atlanta would be most memorable, because back then that was really a big rivalry. It wasn't as big as the Alabama rivalry, but it was close.

With me being from Lanett, it was all textile up there. The home office for [WestPoint Pepperell] was there and there were a lot of Georgia Tech people who worked up there. We beat them 7-6. It was a packed crowd. We would ride the train in the morning and we would ride it back that night. We never did stay overnight in Atlanta.

I think that touchdown was in *Sports Illustrated*. I guess scoring that touchdown was probably the main thing, along with a couple of other plays that kept drives going. We used to run the belly series. I remember the touchdown was like a six-yard run. Ed Dyas was our fullback. I would fake it to him and carry the ball around end. If the defense tried to tackle me I would pitch the ball to the halfback.

On the touchdown, the other guy took the halfback and it was just wide open for me to run through. Tech had good football teams and coach [Bobby] Dodd was a well-respected coach. He was one of the top football coaches in the South and probably the nation. Anytime you could beat him it was a big deal.

ON TO THE SUPER BOWL

After finishing college, Hunt was courted by the rival pro football leagues. He had also been to a pro baseball tryout camp. The athlete could have signed in that sport; however, football was his favorite.

"Ever since I was a kid I had dreamed about being a pro football player," he says. "I thought if I could just get off the team bus and go into a hotel lobby as a pro football player, that would be the greatest thing in the world. I didn't know if I would ever make it, but I knew in football if I was drafted I would know in six weeks whether I was going to make it or not. I knew if I tried pro baseball I could be riding around the minor leagues for five years and never make it."

It didn't take Hunt long after his final college game to sign a pro contract. "Back then they would take guys and hide them," he says of the competing leagues. "The NFL would hide them from the AFL and the AFL would hide them from the NFL. You could sign with them anytime then after the season was over. Sometimes they would sign guys under the goal posts after a game.

"After the Alabama game, the Monday when I came back, I was over at the chow hall and somebody told me there was a guy to see me. He told me he was a representative of the Dallas Texans and said, 'Bobby, we would like you to go to Dallas with us and talk about signing.'

"I called my daddy and I asked him what he thought, and he said, 'Son, do what you think is right.' I went to Atlanta with him and we flew to

Dallas. When I got to Atlanta we saw Gil Brandt [of the NFL's Dallas Cowboys], who was on his way to Auburn. He changed his ticket and flew back to Dallas.

"We were walking through the Dallas airport and the guy I was with said, 'Lamar, I would like you to meet somebody.' It was Lamar Hunt, who was the owner of the Texans, so I talked to him for a while. I was like 21 and he was like 29.

"The Cowboys had told me, 'Don't do anything until you talk to us.' I went in and talked with the Texans and they said, 'This is what we will give you to play for us.' I said, 'Let me think about it.' I called my dad and he said, 'Son, it sounds good to me. You do what you want to.'

"I called the Cowboys and told them I was going to sign with the Texans. I went out there and made the team, even though I was worried I wasn't going to make it."

Hunt had one class left to graduate in business administration. He opted to start his pro career and finished his degree by correspondence course. The Texans, who would move the following year to Kansas City and become the Chiefs, wanted Hunt as a safety.

The former Tiger can still remember his first pro training camp in detail. "There were a ton of people there," he says. "The guy who played ahead of me had been the starter for the last two seasons, so I knew I had an uphill battle. They started playing me more and more during the exhibition season, and then the guy ahead of me broke his leg. I found out that they had a trade worked out. They were going to send him to San Diego and I was going to become the starting safety.

"We were in training camp from July to September and we didn't get any per diem money. We stayed on SMU's campus in Dallas. We lived in the dorms and they fed us. We played five exhibition games and got $50 per game. By the time they took out taxes, my pay was $36.

"On Tuesday mornings they had someone who was like a ball boy come to the locker room. Coach [Hank] Stram and the other coaches would send him down with a list of who had been cut and he would walk up to them, tap them on the shoulder, and say, 'Get your playbook.' He was a little ol' boy, about 15 or 16 years old.

"That training camp was tough, but once the season began it was great," Hunt recalls. "I started, and Johnny Robinson from LSU was the other starting safety. We got to be great friends."

Hunt had a long and successful pro career before retiring after the 1971 season. He played his final two years with Cincinnati.

"Playing in the first Super Bowl would probably be the highlight," he notes. "Of course, it was nothing like it is now. To win the American Football League Championship and go against the Green Bay Packers was memorable. Looking back now, if you tell somebody you played in the first Super Bowl they say, 'Wow!' But it wasn't as big a deal then as it is now."

Hunt played in an era before large salaries. His rookie contract was worth $15,000. "It was enough to buy a car and pair of black and brown alligator shoes," he recalls. "I was in the service in the off-season, so I didn't spend anything, although I did buy a car after my first season. Back then just about all of the players worked in the off-season. I was in the Air Force reserves."

Although he retired from playing in 1971, Hunt wasn't finished with football. "I was in Cincinnati and a guy called me and said, 'I would like you to come up here and interview for the defensive backfield coaching job for the Buffalo Bills.' I had played eight years. I wasn't getting any faster and the tight ends were, so I flew up there and talked to the guy, John Rausch. When I got ready to leave he said, 'You can have the job as my defensive backfield coach.' I thought I wanted to get into coaching and I told him, 'I am going back to talk to my wife and I will let you know tomorrow.' I decided to take the job and I stayed there for two years."

Hunt's football connections helped him move into another career after the entire Buffalo coaching staff was fired. "Coach Stram was big friends of the Haggar Clothing Company," Hunt notes. "He got to know them at SMU when he was coaching there and he really got to know them at Notre Dame when he was an assistant coach there. We had a couple of other guys who played in Kansas City who went to work with them.

"I called Coach Stram and he called the Haggars. They flew me to New York City to talk to the national sales manager. He said, 'Bobby, I would like to hire you, but you have got to go to Dallas first and talk to the people there.' I went to Dallas. They offered me a job and I said, 'I will take it.' The guy in New York, who was a big football fan, said, 'Bobby, if we give you this job, I don't want you to take it and then six weeks later get back into coaching. I said, 'Yeah, I understand that.'

"At Haggar, they had me on a training program. Then Abe Gibron of the Chicago Bears called me and he said, 'I would like you to come up here and be my defensive backfield coach for the Bears.' I told him, 'Coach, let me think about it and I will call you back.' I called Coach Stram and asked him, 'What should I do?' He knew Gibron, and I told Coach Stram that I was just starting with Haggar. He said, 'You stay right where you are.' I called Gibron back and told him that I was going to stay with Haggar."

Hunt got one more NFL offer to coach. This one came from Chuck Knox of the Los Angeles Rams, but again the former athlete said, "No thanks." He eventually retired from Haggar after 33 years with the clothing company. Now living in Charlotte, North Carolina, he works out five days a week, plays tennis, and does whatever he feels like. A season-ticket holder for Auburn games, he is a regular at Jordan-Hare Stadium in the fall.

"I really enjoyed my time at Auburn," Hunt says. "They say the best time of your life is in high school and college, and the older you are the more you realize it. Living in Graves Center on campus was really nice. There were a lot of crazy things going on, but nothing horrible. It was a lot of fun.

"The guys I got to play with and know I am still real good friends with. I had a good time in college. If I had to do it over again I would. Being able to play high school, college, and pros, that is about as good as I could ask for."

Chapter 11

CHUCK HURSTON

GROWING INTO A CHAMP

Despite a rather humble start, former Auburn standout and Super Bowl champion Chuck Hurston put together quite an impressive resume on the gridiron before moving to a successful career in business.

In fact, he was so slightly built when he started playing high school football that few could have pictured him as a future college player. However, by the time he was a senior at Jordan High in Columbus, Georgia, he had grown into a prospect whom Auburn, Georgia, and Georgia Tech battled to sign.

"It was probably about halfway through my senior year before I realized I was going to have a chance to play college football," Hurston says. "I was a slow grower. As a freshman I was 5-foot-8 and weighed about 135 pounds.

"I went out for the freshman team and as a sophomore they kept me on the freshman team," he remembers. "I got to the varsity as a junior. The December before my junior year is when I grew about two or three inches, and I wasn't quite as awkward as I had been before. I really started developing as an athlete and things just started getting better. Then, my senior year, I had a real good year and grew more."

Growing up with two brothers and a sister, Hurston was the type of prospect coaches are always looking for in any era—a good student and talented athlete with the potential to get bigger and better. "When I was a senior, I remember my coaches saying, 'Hurston, you have a good chance to get a scholarship.' But they were quick to point out, 'They will take a chance on you because your grades are so good. They won't have to worry about you failing out.'"

One of the highlights during the recruiting process was a culinary one. "A coach came down to see me and a guy who I think was from LaGrange," he recalls. "They bought us a big steak down at the old Ralston Hotel in downtown Columbus. I had never eaten a steak and totally fell in love with it."

In the 1950s, Columbus relied heavily on the textile mills built on the banks of the Chattahoochee River that separated Georgia and Alabama. "I was born and grew up in what you would call a cotton mill village," Hurston says. "Most people in Auburn are certainly familiar with the history of textiles in West Point, Lanett, and all of those places. A lot of good athletes who came to Auburn and played sports came out of those places, like David Hill and Bobby Hunt. All of their fathers worked in textile mills over in that area.

"Originally you rented those houses from the mills. They pretty much took care of you. They had doctors and nurses you could go to, even the kids. They had real good sports programs. I grew up running around the gym at Columbus Mill, which is owned by WestPoint Pepperell, where my daddy worked for 50 years. We had a gym and a full baseball field.

"Growing up, I used to watch my daddy play for Columbus Mill in baseball and basketball. He was a pretty darn good athlete. In fact, he had a brief tryout with the St. Louis Cardinals. I was on one of the first Little League [Baseball] teams that started in Columbus. I didn't play any other sports until high school. I went out for football, basketball, and ran track at Jordan."

Hurston's primary position was end, but he also saw action at fullback and even played quarterback for two games while the starter was hurt. He narrowed his choices to three colleges. "Georgia said they wanted to fatten me up and make me a tackle," he says. "That put them third on the list because I really wanted to play end, and Tech and Auburn said they were going to give me a chance at end. I wanted to major in engineering, so only Auburn and Tech had a school of engineering. So that made it between those two schools."

Originally, Hurston decided he would play for Tech. "There wasn't as much pressure then, but it was a lot of pressure on a 17-year-old kid whose family had not experienced anything like this," he says.

Chuck Hurston had a successful college and pro career.
Draughon Library Archives

"I was going to be the first child to go to college. After I said I wanted to sign with Auburn, they said I could sign at midnight." However, Tech didn't give up. The recruiting battle continued until the night before the Jordan High standout signed his scholarship.

Hurston remembers a Georgia Tech coach in his parents' living room saying, "I don't believe you are going to [sign with Auburn]."

"After that," says Hurston, "my father pushed everybody out. When I got up the next morning, I heard somebody in the kitchen talking to my mother. It was the Auburn coach, sitting there drinking coffee. He said, 'Are you ready to sign now?' I said, 'Yes, sir.' Erk Russell is the coach who recruited me, but it was Shot Senn who they sent over there to make sure I got signed."

Hurston started a trend, as his two brothers and his sister also attended college. John, who is also an AU graduate, played football for two seasons at Auburn. James played basketball at Columbus College before accepting an appointment to the Naval Academy and becoming an aviator.

TOUGH WAY TO PAY FOR COLLEGE

Hurston arrived at Auburn in the summer of 1960 and found out quickly he was just one of many talented freshmen. "It was probably a year or more before I really felt like I belonged on the field with those guys because there were so many good athletes," he says.

"In high school sports, especially if you don't come from a huge school, you have got one, two, or three good athletes. At Auburn, all of them were great athletes. They signed about 80 people back then and immediately began running them off. It was real tough—a lot of competition.

"College football is the hardest sport I have ever played. I played a lot of pro football, too, and nothing is harder than college football, especially the practices.

"I got a lot of encouragement from Coach Russell," Hurston notes. "They let me stay at end for a while and then they ran out of tackles, so they moved me there because I was a better blocker than most of the ends. We only played three freshman games and freshmen couldn't play on the varsity. It was a thrill to play in those games, but after that, all you could do was practice and you were just fodder for the varsity."

Being an honor student in high school, the adjustment to college academics went smoothly. "I had a good first couple of academic quarters," he says. "Then I fell into that malaise that you can get into in college. It took me about another year to scramble back up and decide, 'If you are going to stay in the school of engineering, you better get with the program.' I got a degree in industrial management from the School of Engineering."

Hurston's success as a freshman was a confidence-builder. "My sophomore season I began to think I could play a little bit, but I was redshirted," he says. "The coach took me on every road game, so I was part of the team—I just never played.

"I got a lot of valuable experience, especially watching guys like David Hill and how they played, how they handled themselves, and just what it took. Practicing with him every day, David Hill virtually took me under his wing and helped me an awful lot. That carried on when we played for Kansas City. Nobody wants to redshirt, because all you do is practice, but it was a very good idea for me because it helped me to develop physically and mentally."

Hurston saw his first varsity action in 1962. "It was a good year," he says. "I was on the first team at the start of the season. I played a decent amount, but most of it was when they needed a quicker guy in there to pass rush. I was about 215, so I was a little quicker than some of them. I was sort of a pass rush specialist until the Georgia game. I made the first rotation when one of the tackles was hurt, so I played tackle on the second unit. Back then, with the two-platoon football, we had a first unit and a second unit who played just about as much as the first. I finished the year at that position."

In 1963, the Tigers had a very talented team. "It was the greatest year I ever had in football, because we were 9-1 and went to the Orange Bowl," Hurston says. "We had two athletes who really jumped out. Tucker Frederickson and Jimmy Sidle were both All-Americans.

"Tucker, to this day, might still be the best all-around back I have ever seen in college football. He had an amazing amount of ability. He was big; he had a high confidence level. He was just a good all-around person and he loved to play the game."

Hurston's senior year was not as memorable. "It was disappointing as far as football is concerned," he says. "We went into the nation picked No. 1 by *Sports Illustrated*. We won our first game rather handily, but Jimmy Sidle got hurt against Houston.

"I will never forget that the next week we went up to Birmingham to play Tennessee, and we tried to keep it a secret that Jimmy couldn't throw. He had a bad shoulder. Before the game in the warm-ups, all of the Tennessee coaches stood there in a line at midfield watching Jimmy try to throw. Of course, he couldn't, so the first play of the game when we came out on offense, Tennessee put 10 men on the line of scrimmage and put one man back.

"We won 3-0, so that tells you what kind of game it was. After that, Jimmy moved to flanker and Tom Bryan came in and played quarterback. We had a disappointing season and finished 6-4. And we lost to Alabama, which is really how you judge your season."

THE GAME OF MY LIFE
BY CHUCK HURSTON

I still look back and say that the couple of times we beat Georgia stand out, being from Columbus. When we beat Alabama in 1963, that stood out as the best game. The game against Alabama, we were both 8-1. When you beat a team like that, a Bear Bryant team, you felt like you could play with almost anybody.

It was a real defensive game. You always remember your mistakes. I remember I got suckered on a trap block and their running back went about 60 yards for a touchdown. I said, "Oh, my God, I just lost this ball game." Of course, a lot of other people missed him, too, but I was the first one because he went through my hole. I really got worried, but then I was able to make a couple of plays near the end of the game that prevented them from making first downs, so that made up for it a little bit.

We didn't realize going into the season we were going to be as good as we were. We were coming off a mediocre 1962 season and finished just getting annihilated by Alabama. We went up to Tennessee and beat them on their home field. After that we started gaining more confidence, having a playmaker like Jimmy Sidle out there with Tucker, who just stood out. You fed off those guys and gained confidence. We had some really good players on that team. I think we all developed pretty well.

PART OF FOOTBALL HISTORY

When Hurston graduated in 1965, he didn't expect to embark on a successful career in the AFL. "I never thought I would even consider pro football," he says. "I had a job interview set up with WestPoint and a big iron company up in Birmingham, but I was drafted by both the American Football League and the National Football League."

A $4,000 signing bonus offered by the Kansas City Chiefs got his attention and he chose that AFL team over the Green Bay Packers. "I said, 'Shoot, that was great money.' I started playing pro football and played six years with Kansas City and one with Buffalo.

"With Kansas City, I was fortunate enough to play in the first Super Bowl and the fourth Super Bowl. We lost to Green Bay in the first one and we beat Minnesota in the fourth one."

The original Super Bowl featured four Auburn graduates who started for coach Hank Stram's Chiefs, with offensive tackle Hill joining center Wayne Frazier and safety Bobby Hunt in the lineup. Hunt and Hill were on the team when Hurston tried to make the roster as a rookie.

Hurston was approximately 6-foot-5, 220 pounds as a rookie, and would grow one more inch while playing for the Chiefs. "My entire job that season was on specialty teams," he notes. "David was two years ahead of me, and Bobby was three years ahead of me. They told me, 'If you just go down there and try to kill yourself on special teams, they might notice you and keep you around.'"

That advice worked. When the first Super Bowl was played in January 1967, in his second season as a pro, Hurston was a starting end.

"I remember that we were probably a little intimidated by the National Football League and also by the Green Bay Packers," he says. "I remember warming up before the game and saying to somebody, 'Good God, there is Bart Starr.' We lost pretty good, 35-10, but we realized after the game we could have played better and we could play with those guys.

"That was the first game matching teams from both leagues. We didn't play the NFL again in the regular season until the official merger in 1970, but we did have two or three exhibition games every year with NFL teams.

"I remember our first one was with the Chicago Bears, who had some great players back then. We were ready to replay the Super Bowl and they came in for an exhibition game, and I think we beat them like 35-10 or 40-10. We were ready to prove something and that is one way we did it."

Hurston and the Chiefs evened their Super Bowl record at 1-1 with a win in 1970. The AFL's New York Jets had beaten the Baltimore Colts the previous year, so the Chiefs' victory tied the series at 2-2. "That 1969 victory by the Jets in Super Bowl III put aside any doubt we could play with those guys," Hurston says. "We came into Super Bowl IV very confident after having to beat some really good AFL teams, like the Jets and the Raiders twice, to get there. We had a lot of confidence and we thought Minnesota really was overrated. We beat them pretty handily.

"I was a reserve linebacker in that game. They moved me two years earlier to linebacker because I had trouble keeping weight on. I started the season okay [around 235], but I would get worn down as the season went along and I would finish in the 220 range, which was beginning to be way too light for a defensive lineman.

"I played with some really good linebackers on that team. We had Willie Lanier, who is in the Pro Football Hall of Fame. We had Bobby Bell, who is in the Pro Football Hall of Fame. The third linebacker was Jim Lynch, who is in the College Football Hall of Fame, and the old Auburn guy, Chuck, was the fourth linebacker."

Stram, who died in 2005, was a hall of fame coach and considered one of the great personalities of the AFL. "Coach Stram was real loyal to his players," Hurston points out. "He was a real dapper guy, a neat man. My wife and I were fortunate to be able to go up for the induction when he entered the Pro Football Hall of Fame. He was in pretty bad health then, but it was great to see him one more time."

Hurston played for the Chiefs for six seasons before retiring after one year with Buffalo, where Hunt was the defensive backs coach. Through their contacts with Stram, Hurston and Hunt moved on to new careers with Haggar Clothing. Hunt is retired, while Hurston is working as vice president for sales of the firm he has been with for 34 years.

Although it has been many years since he graduated, Hurston is a regular at home games, making the trip to Auburn to watch the Tigers with family and friends. "I enjoyed my time at Auburn," he says. "I think it gave me a very good work ethic, along with what I learned from my parents. Auburn gave me an education and the confidence that I could succeed in the world."

Chapter 12

ED KING

KING-SIZE RECRUITING PRIZE

Big, fast, strong, and tough are all good descriptions of Ed King when he arrived on the Auburn campus in the summer of 1988. The high school All-American from Phenix City literally had scholarship offers from coast to coast, but when it came down to crunch time, he decided to stay as close to home as he could while playing major college football.

A player who first earned All-State honors as a sophomore, he was one of those rare offensive line prospects who was talented enough to overpower college juniors and seniors as a true freshman.

King had so many scholarship offers it was difficult to keep track of them, but he narrowed his choices to five colleges he had checked out on official visits. "I went to see UCLA, Florida, Colorado, Alabama, and Auburn," he says. "I actually committed to Colorado, but my last visit was to Auburn, and when it boiled down to it, my parents didn't want me to go too far out there to Colorado.

"When I weighed my options, playing at Auburn was a win-win situation. Auburn is close to my hometown. Phenix City is 30 minutes away and I had the best opportunity at Auburn to come in and play as a true freshman."

King recalls he felt good about his decision. "What I love most about Auburn is that there is a real family atmosphere. I remember going on my recruiting visit, and we were walking into the basketball arena. I don't remember who the game was against, but I remember seeing a big sign in the student section that said, 'Welcome Ed King.' I said, 'Oh, my God.'

That was just electrifying. I was just a high school kid, and to me that was like being on ESPN or something."

The big lineman originally thought he would be playing football as a jumbo size running back. "I began playing backyard football in the fourth or fifth grade," he remembers. "I was always too big to play in the Pee Wee leagues, so I didn't start playing organized football until I was in the eighth grade at South Girard Junior High. Believe it or not, I was a tailback. I was probably about 6-foot-3, 225 or 230 pounds, and could probably run a 4.6 or 4.65 40.

"My ninth grade year I was a fullback. In spring ball when I was still in my ninth grade year, the high school coaches had me at tight end. I remember having a very, very good spring, but I ended up breaking my foot. I was out of commission for about three months, so I couldn't lift weights, run, and be active like I normally was.

"When I reported to preseason varsity camp, I had picked up like 20 or 30 pounds. After that my dreams of being a running back, fullback, or even a tight end were pretty much squashed. After that I was an offensive lineman."

King started at tackle and had no problems with Coach Wayne Trawick's decision to move him to a new position. "I was very blessed to have gone through a school system like Central High School," he says. "The way we were worked out, the way we practiced, and the way we went about playing the games was very similar to the way Coach Dye did it at Auburn.

"I think a lot of that was because my high school coach got a lot of his coaching skills from Bear Bryant and Coach Dye. When I walked onto Auburn's campus, the football part of it was like going to a bigger version of Central High School."

A FRESHMAN STARTER

Although the Tigers were the defending SEC champions, Dye was looking for help at guard King's first year in college, so recruiting talk over the possibility he would play and even start as a freshman was right on target. King remembers his first fall on campus as an exciting time.

"A lot of the freshmen weren't used to the way we were practicing, but Coach Trawick had prepared me for Auburn or any college," he says. "I

Big Ed King was an instant impact player as a freshman.
Auburn University Media Relations

remember going through the preseason practices and thinking, 'This is okay, because it is a lot like high school.'

"Then I started getting some playing time. I remember I was able to rotate in and out with a senior named Stacy Dunn. I remember in the LSU game, when they beat us down there 7-6, I graded pretty well. I remember the homecoming weekend coming up and Coach Dye making the announcement they were going to start me. I felt like I was on top of the world. After that I started every game the rest of my time on campus at Auburn."

The Tigers finished the season 10-2 and were once again SEC champs. King earned Freshman All-SEC honors and went on to win first team All-SEC status his sophomore and junior seasons. In 1989, he became only the third Auburn player to be named a consensus All-American as a sophomore as he helped the Tigers win a third straight SEC title.

THE GAME OF MY LIFE
BY ED KING

Obviously, it would be the first year Alabama came to Auburn. The game had been played in Legion Field in Birmingham, which was home territory for Tuscaloosa. I just remember leading up to the game there was an electrifying atmosphere. It was so exciting that, for the first time in the history of the game, it was being played at Auburn and I had a chance to be a part of it. I remember Alabama was ranked No. 2 in the nation and nobody really gave us a chance to come out victorious.

I remember from the time the game kicked off until the last play, we as players were so excited and so filled with adrenaline we could have probably run through a brick wall. That was my sophomore year. Alabama had a very good player at nose guard, and before the game *The Birmingham News* had my picture on one side of the page all blown up and his picture on the other side of the page all blown up. The story was about how our matchup was going to be key and could make a difference in the game. I remember taking it as a personal challenge that I was going to make sure that I came out victorious.

That had to be the loudest atmosphere we played in, including the LSU [Earthquake Game] from my freshman year. From the beginning until the end of the game, we played hard and never looked back.

I truly think that game meant a lot to Coach Dye. From what I understand, they always tried to get the series to rotate between Auburn and Legion Field. I think it was a big thing for Coach Dye to be the first coach in the series with the game to be played at Auburn, and to come out victorious was really important to him. After the game, Coach Dye was very emotional. I don't think I have ever seen him like that before.

You better believe winning that game meant a lot to the players on our team, the students, and our fans. I have never seen anything like the buildup going into that game. It was so awesome.

We had a bye the week before, but as soon as Monday came on game week, the excitement was so high it was like we were playing the game the next day. I remember seeing the stadium packed with people. There were no seats open and even the ramps were packed with people.

TIME TO STAY OR GO?

After winning 10 games again in 1989, the Tigers slipped to 8-3-1 in 1990, King's junior season.

"I remember having pretty good freshman and sophomore years," he says. "My junior year, all of the sudden, I was like one of the top linemen in the nation. I was getting so much preseason pub I couldn't believe it. Here I am, just a regular player who loves playing the game and trying to help my team win and trying to do my best. All of the sudden, I am supposed to be one of the best linemen playing college football. I was like, 'Wow.'

"I remember trying to sit down with my mom and dad after the Peach Bowl and telling them that there was talk around if I left school for the draft, I would go pretty high. I asked them to tell me what they thought about it. My parents have always supported me. They always told me, 'Do what your heart tells you to do, and you will never go wrong.'

"I remember contemplating what to do for a few weeks after the bowl game and I remember meeting with Coach Dye. I love Coach Dye. He was always like a father away from home. When I told him I wanted to talk to him about something, I was pretty sure he knew what I wanted to talk about.

"When I got to his office, one thing that Coach Dye knew about me is that I am a straight shooter. I told him I was contemplating going into the draft. I remember he said, 'Ed King, you were a man from day one when you came on this campus and you are a man now if you decide to leave to go to the NFL. You did great at Auburn and if you leave to go to the NFL, you will do just as good.' That just floored me to get so much support from him."

King says it wasn't an easy decision, but after weighing the options, it made sense to declare himself eligible for the draft. He was taken as the 29th overall selection, going to Cleveland in the second round.

"I remember how it seemed like it was a dream," he says of his rookie season in the NFL. "Real quickly I learned having good talent and being strong and athletic wasn't going to get it, because everybody was just as strong, as fast, and as athletic as you. I was able, much like from my days at Auburn, to dig down and play hard every game to help our team to win. Every game in the NFL was like a bowl game."

He played three seasons with the Browns before moving to Green Bay; however, he spent the entire season on the injured reserve list. King went to New Orleans for the final three years of his career before retiring from the Saints after the 1997 season.

"It had gotten to the point where my knees couldn't take any more," he says. "I never had surgery on them, but they started to get bad. I knew it was time for me to hang up my shoes and move on to the next arena in my life. I have always been competitive, and once the injuries slowed me down and I couldn't compete at full capacity, I knew it was time to give it up."

College football is a good memory for the big lineman. "To tell you the truth, my collegiate career was very, very special to me," King says. "I don't think my professional career was as good, but it was a blessing. I played seven years in the NFL, and I believe the only reason I was able to get seven years in is because of what Auburn University and Coach Dye instilled in me and prepared me for after college."

Although he left college early, the lineman didn't forget about his education. "I started back working on my degree when I was in Cleveland," he says. "I kept taking classes when I was in New Orleans and I ended up finishing my degree in 2003."

King now lives in Columbus, Georgia, across the river from his hometown. He is a loan officer, a licensed realtor, and a family man. "I am enjoying what I am doing and it has been a blessing," says King, who notes that he really enjoys his five children, Alexis, Gabrielle, Edward Jr., Joshua, and Renee.

The former All-American has strong feelings for his alma mater. "I am truly proud to be an Auburn Tiger," he says. "Academics and sports, what I learned on the campus, helped me to be as successful after football as I was in football."

Chapter 13

MIKE KOLEN

CAPTAIN KANGAROO
TO CAPTAIN CRUNCH

In the history of Auburn football, few players have earned a more appropriate nickname than 1960s star Mike Kolen. A linebacker for Coach Shug Jordan's teams at the end of that decade, Kolen was known as "Captain Crunch" for big hits that excited fans. His leadership on and off the field made him one of the most respected players of the 1960s.

Kolen played a great deal of football before arriving at Auburn and a great deal more after graduating. He had a very early start in Termite League as a first grader in Montgomery, Alabama. He played every year until his family moved, when he put the sport on the backburner.

"When I came to Birmingham, I was real conscientious about my studies in a new school situation when I was in seventh grade," Kolen remembers. "I went out for football for three days before I quit because I didn't have enough time to study."

Kolen decided to return to football as a ninth grader, but unfortunately he couldn't play that year due to an injury. As a sophomore at Berry High, a new school with no seniors, he had the opportunity to play right away, and by the time he was a junior attracted attention from SEC programs. Kolen also played baseball and wrestled, but football was his primary sport.

Kolen took recruiting visits to Alabama, Georgia, and Tennessee, but when it was time to pick a college, the choice was not difficult. "I decided on Auburn because my mom had roots there," he says. "She was from Beauregard, which is a small community close to Opelika. When it was time to make a decision, I knew I had to choose Auburn, and I wanted to choose Auburn for a lot of reasons."

In high school, Kolen played linebacker as well as center, a position he also played occasionally as a freshman at Auburn. "I sure am glad they allowed me to stick to linebacker because I didn't like that center business," says Kolen, who notes that he only weighed in the 190s when he arrived at AU.

Another freshman in 1966, Tom Banks, became the chosen one at center. "Tom Banks was chiseled for that role," Kolen notes. "He was a great center and he and I were both out of Birmingham the same year. He was a great player at Auburn and became an All-Pro center who played pro ball for 12 years."

MODEST EXPECTATIONS, MAJOR RESULTS

A serious student, Kolen had a relatively smooth adjustment to college life, but his freshman season was still a challenge. "I don't know if I had any serious difficulty," he says. "I was never the type of guy who assumed anything or took anything for granted. I never assumed I would have an opportunity to play. When I got to Auburn I had some type of back problem that prohibited me from playing the first month or so, but after a lot of treatment, it worked out and I was able to play on the freshman team as a linebacker."

He received a rude welcome to SEC football in a freshman game against Georgia. "I was wearing one of those two-bar facemasks and was snapping on punts," Kolen remembers. "This Georgia guy just reared back with his forearm on my nose. Instead of it heading north and south after that game it was heading east-west, so that was interesting. That was my introduction to college ball. I never really got my nose straightened out until five or 10 years after my pro career."

Kolen's nose was far from the biggest change in his life as a freshman. "We had an FCA [Fellowship of Christian Athletes] chapter when I got there," he says. "Myself and several others like John Riley, David Campbell, and others kicked it off. Sometimes we had 75 players at an FCA meeting. So we had a good chapter, which I think meant a lot to us.

"When I got to Auburn as a freshman, like most anybody else, I didn't have a clue and I was a little misdirected. The later part of my freshman

Mike Kolen left Auburn for a successful career in the NFL.
Draughon Library Archives

year was when I got to know Christ as my Savior, and that is when I got involved in the FCA rather enthusiastically my last three years at Auburn.

"I remember in the off-season we used to have two or three speaking engagements a week. I tried to fill as many as I could do. I was up and down the state of Alabama during the off-season my junior and senior seasons all of the time, but that was really a big part of the fun in college—being able to influence so many young people."

One of the reasons Kolen became a popular speaker was because of his intensity and excellence on the football field. His first varsity season was 1967. He helped the Tigers post a 6-4 record, but didn't start until the finale, a defensive battle in the rain and mud in Birmingham.

"Robert Margerson, who was a nickname specialist and the guy who nicknamed me 'Captain Crunch,' he was a couple of years older than me," Kolen says. "He hurt his leg or something and, bless his heart, he was out for the Alabama game. I was second team behind Gusty Yearout as the strong linebacker. We played two outside linebackers and two inside linebackers in kind of a 4-4 defense. They moved me to the center linebacker spot in Margerson's absence, so I started as a middle linebacker against Alabama my sophomore year. That was a thrilling opportunity."

Alabama was ranked eighth nationally and AU wasn't in the poll, but the Tigers came close to winning before they fell 7-3 on a long run by quarterback Kenny Stabler. To this day many fans are still upset that officials let Stabler's run stand because it was aided by what they believe was a flagrant hold on Yearout.

Auburn improved to 7-4 in Kolen's All-SEC 1968 season. The athlete was a full-time starter and a really impressive one. Even though he was only a junior, he received the honor of being named co-captain.

"I remember that was just a good year," Kolen says. "I was able to play in the middle again and it was a privilege to be co-captain with [quarterback] Loran Carter. I remember we went to our first bowl game during my time at Auburn. It was a real fun trip, and we played very well and won the game."

The Tigers defeated Arizona 34-10 at the Sun Bowl in El Paso, Texas. That set higher expectations for Kolen's senior season in 1969. His play as part of a potentially strong defense was one of the reasons for that optimism. On offense, the buzz circulated over a pair of talented young players, quarterback Pat Sullivan and receiver Terry Beasley, who had been stars on the 1968 freshman team.

The Tigers finished the regular season 8-2 before falling to the University of Houston at the Astro-Bluebonnet Bowl in Houston, Texas.

Kolen again earned All-SEC honors and once more served as captain. The Tigers posted shutouts versus Wake Forest and Clemson, and held Kentucky and Georgia to just three points. To Kolen, however, the most memorable game was the regular-season finale, a 49-26 victory over Alabama.

THE GAME OF MY LIFE
BY MIKE KOLEN

We had a great game against Alabama my senior season. In those days, Alabama would always come out to the middle of the field with all of their seniors before kickoff. I remember the season before, Carter and I went out there and stared at 20 or more guys. So I asked Coach Jordan before the game if he minded if all of the seniors went out there with us.

Our senior class probably had about five more guys than their class. Tom Banks was the captain with me, and we went out to midfield with all of our seniors behind us and we kind of stared them down. We got off to a pretty good start and whipped them pretty good that day.

It was a hard-fought game. I think for the most part we pretty much had control of it and put some icing on the cake when Connie Frederick faked the punt and ran it in for a touchdown. That was just an unbelievable moment in my career at Auburn, especially considering we had lost my sophomore and junior years. And to win so convincingly, that was a great feeling. I can't explain the satisfaction and feeling that we all experienced after that game. It was sensational.

Sullivan and Beasley had a great game. I remember Alabama had a pretty hard-nosed guy at fullback by the name of Pete Moore. We go to the same church here in Birmingham now and I know him. He was just a solid fullback. I hit him a couple of times, and I tell him to this day my neck is still sore from that. It was a hard-fought game.

We had a couple of blitzes up the middle that day. As a middle linebacker, I would kind of get in an all-four position like a defensive lineman and just blast through the seam. I think I got through and got to their quarterback, Scott Hunter, at least one time. We tried to mix it up on defense and keep pressure on Hunter that day.

We were still playing our 4-4 defense that season. Coach Paul Davis, our defensive coordinator and assistant head coach, was big on that 4-4 with just three defensive backs. I don't think that would work today, especially against the teams that run the West Coast offense and spread it out across the field.

NO NAME FAME

Though considered a bit undersized for an NFL linebacker by some, the Auburn star quickly proved he belonged at the next level.

"We were fortunate to get to Miami in coach Don Shula's first year for his first training camp," Kolen says. "It was a very intense camp—four-a-day practices for four or five weeks. There was a strike by veteran players, and the rookies were one deep in every position for two weeks. I reported to camp at about 220. After about two weeks, I probably weighed about 210.

"I got acclimated to Shula's system, and I was fortunate they were looking for some new blood," he says. "A free agent linebacker from Amherst of all places, Doug Swift, and I both started every preseason game and played every play all the way through the season. Nick Buoniconti was in the middle. We got thrown into it pretty quickly. It is still a game of football and the fundamentals are what produce success."

Kolen's timing couldn't have been better. The Dolphins, an expansion franchise started in 1966, got a shot in the arm when Shula took over in 1970. "Shula turned it around," Kolen says. "Our second season was our first Super Bowl, and then we won the next two and had a perfect season in 1972.

"I was a little concerned initially being drafted by the Dolphins, although I was thrilled to be drafted because I was selected in the 12th round. In those days they had 16 rounds. It worked out well, though. Shula, his staff, and the players turned things around because of his leadership, and we had one of the brightest guys who ever coached football as our defensive coordinator, Bill Arnsparger, who went on to be LSU's coach, Florida's athletic director, and New York Giants head coach. He coached at San Diego, and I believe he is still consulting with them."

Arnsparger's celebrated group became known as "The No Name Defense," because it relied on teamwork rather than individual performances by star players. The Dolphins finished 17-0 after winning Super Bowl VII 14-7 versus the Redskins. It was the NFL's first and only perfect season.

"We thought we were going to have a big year, because the season prior to that was our first Super Bowl," Kolen recalls. "We learned a lot from that experience. We lost just a couple of games that year and started clicking the next year with one victory after another. The media started following it and it just continued. The ball had to bounce our way several times. I don't believe in luck much, but we were probably a little lucky at times that season to have a perfect year."

Kolen enjoyed his time as a pro player. "Probably a few teams had better athletes, but I don't think there was anybody that played more as a team than we did through those championship years," he says. "That was quite rewarding. By the time I was 25, I had been in three Super Bowls and been a part of two world championships. A lot of guys, bless their hearts, play for 10 or 12 years and don't even get into the playoffs. We were quite blessed and fortunate."

Kolen played through one knee surgery as a pro and continued to perform at a high level. However, midway through the 1977 season, his eighth in the NFL, he injured his other knee. "I figured it was time to retire while I could still walk," he says. "We moved our family back to Montgomery and ran our real estate business."

As part of his business, Kolen opened the Montgomery Athletic Club, which he ran for a dozen years before selling the establishment and moving to Birmingham, partly to be closer to his married daughter and future grandchildren. His other child, John, was a three-year letterman for the Tigers at linebacker from 1993-1995. After serving two terms of duty with the Army in Iraq, he now works with his father.

Kolen says he enjoys having his son involved in the business. He also has good memories of his days in both college and the NFL. "We still have a reunion every five years with our perfect season team, which is a lot of fun. It was a fun career. I am not a guy who lives in the past, but there were a lot of good lessons to be learned being around that quality of people and being a part of that atmosphere. There were a lot of good lessons for anything in life you will encounter."

He says the experience in college was special, too. "There was a great spirit there at Auburn and a lot of great friendships and camaraderie," he notes. "We didn't have SEC Championship years, but we had some pretty good years, especially our senior year."

Chapter 14

BEN LEARD

FROM RED AND BLACK
TO ORANGE AND BLUE

Growing up in the small town of Hartwell, located in the northeast corner of Georgia, Ben Leard learned early how to compete. That attribute has served him well and is a major reason why he had the mental and physical toughness to overcome a series of challenges he faced during his college days at Auburn.

Leard survived and eventually prospered through a tumultuous coaching change and came back from a series of injuries that would have sidelined a lesser person. He played a key role in helping coach Tommy Tuberville rebuild the program and in the process won the respect of his teammates, coaches, and fans.

"I have always been competitive," says Leard, who grew up with three brothers. "We were always competitive amongst each other. My dad and his brothers, being from a small town, they had been involved in high school athletics as far as playing, and my uncle was a really good high school running back. My grandfather was a very talented athlete when he was growing up in Albany, Georgia, and Adel, Georgia.

"I guess I started playing football when I was in second grade, probably seven or eight years old. I started in Pee Wee League. I just enjoyed the competitiveness of it. I played basketball and everything else just to stay busy. From there it kind of snowballed. I think I started playing quarterback when I was in my second or third year of playing ball."

Although he was born in LaGrange, Georgia, when his father was working at Callaway Gardens resort, the family moved back to Hartwell, his parents' hometown, when Ben was just a toddler. "My grandfather was a dentist in the area and my other grandfather was a veterinarian in the area," he notes.

Not long after he started playing high school sports, it was clear that Leard might have the chance to become a very good football player. "The timing hit really good for me," he notes. "When I was a freshman, there was a senior quarterback. There was some competition, but the slate was clean for me as a sophomore because I wasn't competing against a returning starter."

Leard won the starting job that year and put together an impressive high school career. Long before his senior season, major colleges like Auburn and his favorite since childhood, the Georgia Bulldogs, were courting him. Auburn went into the recruiting battle as a long shot. "Pretty much in my family, if you have got a college degree, you got it in some shape, form, or fashion from the University of Georgia," Leard says. "Even my wife has gone to Georgia. My mother and father both went there."

As Leard kept tossing touchdowns, he dreamed of one day doing it for the red and black of Georgia. Few doubted that he would be the first in his family to play the sport at the SEC level.

Leard says that he admired Georgia quarterbacks Eric Zeier and Mike Bobo when he was growing up, but also notes that someone he respected suggested that he keep an open mind during the recruiting process. "When I was a freshman in high school, one of our coaches, William Devane, gave me the advice to really take a step back and not be a huge fan of anybody. He told me, 'You want to look at everything through an even keel,' which I did for the next three years."

Devane had played on Clemson's national championship team, and his comments made sense to the young quarterback. When college coaches started writing and calling, Leard decided to take a serious look at schools such as Tennessee and Florida in addition to Auburn and Georgia. He also liked the offenses FSU put on the field, and Miami drew his attention, too. "I wanted to stay in the southeast—as far south as Miami, as far north as Kentucky—but I was really ready to listen to everybody who thought I was talented enough to play in their scheme," Leard says.

Ben Leard overcame injuries to make his mark at Auburn.
Auburn University Media Relations

He made his first trip to Auburn as a sophomore with his parents and brothers. The quarterback remembers being underwhelmed. "I think my expectations were way too high. I came to this big, huge stadium, but it was a spring game and there might have been 30,000 people in it. Nobody was really on campus. It was a morning kind of thing; you just went to the game and came home. I was somewhat disappointed. I put Auburn at the back of the list. It was the only spring game I went to all year, so there was no comparison there.

"As time went by, coach Rodney Garner [a former Auburn assistant now at Georgia] was recruiting two teammates who were a year ahead of me. He kept a watchful eye on my development. Going into my senior year, Auburn began their courting, for a lack of a better term. I was always interested in listening because of the tradition at Auburn and the players they have had who have been so good. At that time, it was when Auburn had just had the undefeated season and was at the top of the spotlight."

Although Auburn was on his list, the school certainly wasn't at the top of it. He didn't visit the campus as a junior and almost didn't return his senior season. "I had everything pretty much lined up in regard to Saturday visits and where I was going to go to unofficial visits and games my senior year," Leard notes. "About midway through the season, Coach Garner calls and invites me to go to some game called the Iron Bowl between Auburn and Alabama. I didn't really think too much about it because I didn't know a lot about the rivalry. A rivalry to me was Georgia versus Georgia Tech and Georgia versus Clemson. He gave me the whole spiel about that being a big recruit weekend, but I told him I had already made a commitment to go somewhere else.

"I hung up the phone and my dad, who never really stuck his nose in the process if everything was done right, casually asked me who that was on the phone. I told him it was Coach Garner and he was inviting me to some game called the Iron Bowl. My dad's eyes kind of perked up and he said, 'I think you need to call Coach Garner back and tell him we are going to come to that game and call whoever we were supposed to go see and cancel those plans.' My dad and my wife, who was my girlfriend at the time, attended that 1995 Iron Bowl game with me that Auburn won 31-27 in Auburn. That really put Auburn at the top of the list for me, along with some experiences I had on my official visits.

"I went to Georgia and coach [Jim] Donnan and I didn't exactly see eye to eye on some situations with them offering me a scholarship and me not being immediately ready to jump at it. I was going to Auburn the next week on an official visit and wanted to wait on that. So he didn't necessarily take to that too well. I came to Auburn the next week and had a great time and got to really find out what Auburn was all about. That was it. History was written at that point.

"It was hard to say no to the history of Georgia football and what I had grown up seeing, but it wasn't hard to say no to the interaction I had with Coach Donnan. Nothing against him, but he came on a little bit too strong for a 17-year-old kid whose parents weren't there. I am very tied to my family and I feel very indebted to them for what they have done for me. I wasn't going to do anything without their consent and he was insistent that [a verbal commitment] be done, and I didn't appreciate it. A lot of people make the mistake of thinking that Georgia passed on me, but it was actually the other way around."

ADJUSTING TO COLLEGE FOOTBALL

As a senior at Hart County High, Leard passed for 2,530 yards and 25 touchdowns. He received the honor of seeing his jersey retired, but when he reported to Auburn in 1996, he was just another young player trying to impress a demanding set of college coaches.

Leard says his decision to come to campus early after he graduated from high school was a wise one. "I was able to establish some relationships with upperclassmen and get an understanding of what was expected of us as athletes and students. The homesick aspect never really kicked in that summer because I was able to go home during the weekends. After we reported for practice and started in with two-a-days, that was a grind. You practice without a break for a month, and when you do that, you jump right into games. I was fortunate that I developed relationships with my teammates, so I never got homesick or thought about being one of those guys who goes home in the middle of the night."

Like many freshmen, Leard redshirted. "The speed aspect and becoming accustomed to what college football was like was night and day compared to what high school football was," he says. "I had a lot of growing up to do in every shape of the word. I had come from a high school where I was one of the biggest guys in the huddle and went to Auburn, where I was looking up to everybody, including most of the receivers. Fortunately, I was able to adapt, take the punches, and hang in there."

The next fall he played briefly as an understudy to standout senior Dameyune Craig, who led the team to the SEC West title. However, the next season was a rough one for Leard and the Tigers. Terry Bowden began the year as head coach, but left during the season when he found out he was going to be fired.

Defensive coordinator Bill "Brother" Oliver was named the interim coach and made it clear that Leard wasn't his choice to lead the team, even though the sophomore had put up solid statistics in his five games as a starter. The starting QB wasn't putting up the big numbers Craig had the year before, so Leard was a convenient scapegoat for fans who could not figure out why the Tigers were struggling. With Oliver as coach, Leard didn't step onto the field the final five games in 1998. Throw in a bulging disk problem that required surgery after the season, and it wasn't the best of times for the quarterback.

However, his luck soon changed. Auburn convinced Tuberville to leave Ole Miss and take over as coach. That meant a fresh start Leard's junior season. Leard notes that all he asked for was a chance to prove himself. When Tuberville said all starting assignments were open, it was exactly what Leard wanted to hear. He was ready to show what he could do—and that turned out to be a great deal.

Although the team's talent level was well below what it currently is, Leard set a school record and tied the SEC record with a 70.7 completion percentage. He posted a very impressive 170.78 passing rating, and his 0.23 interception percentage was also an SEC record. He began the season as a backup to current Major League Baseball player Gabe Gross, but got the call in relief on opening day versus I-AA power Appalachian State. He hit 10-19 passes for 159 yards and threw a 33-yard TD pass to Ronney Daniels that proved to be the game winner and avoided a potentially embarrassing debut for the Tuberville era.

Unfortunately for Leard, the Tigers had virtually no running game that fall, and opponents were able to attack him without much risk, resulting in the QB being injured much of the season. He missed four games and probably should have sat out more, but there was no keeping him out of the 1999 Auburn at Georgia game—the only chance he would have to play between the hedges at Sanford Stadium. As a senior, Leard started all 12 games, led the Tigers to the SEC West title, and passed for 2,158 yards with a lot of strong performances, but none of those games were as memorable as his night in the spotlight in Athens, Georgia.

THE GAME OF MY LIFE
BY BEN LEARD

There are two big things I recall that happened to me that season before the Georgia game. I had missed the game before against Central Florida because I had suffered a concussion two weeks earlier at Arkansas. Several weeks before that, against Ole Miss, I had separated my shoulder. Although I had what some people deem a successful season, I really hadn't played all that much. I didn't start the first game. We ended up winning that one and I started the next game against Idaho. I started against LSU. I started versus Arkansas and only got to play a quarter of that game, so it was kind of up in the air if I was going to play at Georgia. I was insistent that I was playing because it meant so much to me. I had always dreamed about playing between the hedges in Sanford Stadium, whether I was a visitor or at home, it didn't matter. So that was kind of a big buildup.

The anxiety of it was enormous. The wheeling and dealing of everybody I had to get tickets for was unbelievable. We worked it out between some of the Florida guys, where we did trades on games their families wanted to come to, and it worked out for the better when it was all said and done. I can remember being in the warm-ups seeing people from my hometown walking around the stadium. I want to say there were about 75 at that game. Some of their seats were near the tunnel where we came out on the field, and I talked to them before the game. It was something that will always mean a lot to me. They are Georgia fans. They were there to cheer for Georgia, but were there supporting me, and that meant a lot. The fact that we won and played well, and with those folks supporting me, those are things that I will always remember.

I can recall that game from the coin toss on. Haven Fields, Reggie Worthy, and I were captains that night. On the other side it was Orantes Grant, Quincy Carter, Richard Seymour, and Michael Greer who were their captains. I was on the far left and Quincy was on the far right. The colors of that game stand out to me. The bright red of Georgia and the bright orange of Auburn make for kind of a magical scene.

Georgia won the toss, giving them the opportunity to make the choice. They deferred, giving us the choice. Instead of him saying, "We defer, give the choice to Auburn," Quincy says, "We want to give it to 14 and see what he will do with it." We were all taken aback. I know that put a little spark in me, so we kind of went back and forth. Before you knew it, Reggie and Haven were gone and Michael, Orantes, and Richard were gone, and Quincy and I were just standing there in the middle of the field going back and forth at each other. I will always remember his last words. He said, "If you can do it, go ahead." I told him the biggest mistake he made was giving us the ball first, because when he got it back he would be down seven points.

At that game there were probably 15,000 to 20,000 Auburn fans in the stadium. Turning around and running back to the sideline and hearing those Auburn fans cheer and the Georgia fans cheer their players is something that was unbelievable. We got the ball, and the first play we ran a reverse, and Tim Carter got about 15 to 20 yards. I think we had two fourth-down conversions to Travaris Robinson, who was a freshman in that game. He later ended up playing free safety for us. We drove down the field and I threw a touchdown pass to Clifton Robinson on what we call a pivot route. For a lack of a better term, it was "on" from there.

Our defense played phenomenal football that night. We got the ball back and I threw a touchdown pass to Ronney Daniels, just like that. Then I threw another one to Ronney and another one to Markeith Cooper on a wheel route. Then we came out in the second half. I threw a ball to Ronney that he went up and got, and he carried about three Georgia guys down to the two-yard line. We went in after a play or two and I scored on a quarterback sneak. That put us up 38-0 and [offensive coordinator Noel] Mazzone shut it down. It was one of those nights that we could see what they were doing before they did it, and they kept doing the same things we had killed them on previously.

Georgia was playing the corners up real tight and the safeties weren't in position to rebound if those guys got burned. Our receivers could do no wrong that night. It was not hard for me to throw the ball to them and make a big play. My eyes would light up and our receivers would see what they were doing, and all of them were just itching to see who would get the ball next. The last time I got ready to [audible to a hot passing route], I remember looking to the sideline and seeing Coach Mazzone waving at me not to check, just run the football. He said we already had enough points. We just needed to run the ball to keep the clock moving. That is what enabled Heath Evans to get his yardage running the ball.

I remember we drove the ball down to about their 13 or 14 just before the half. I threw a curl route to Reggie Worthy. He caught the ball on the goal line, but the ball never crossed the plane. With time running out with maybe a second left, Clifton Robinson turned around to the referee and called a timeout. That was a heads-up play. Everybody was running off the field for halftime, but they called everybody back and we were able to kick a field goal and get those three points we would have missed if Clifton hadn't called timeout. Our defense played great. They were causing turnovers and Quincy didn't know which end was up. Their running game was shut down and their defense continued to do things we had an answer for, and they wouldn't listen to reason when we told them to stop.

I think that was probably my best game numbers-wise and all around and for what it meant to me. I think it also meant a lot to us as a team, because we had hit a dry spell and lost several games that season. Earlier in the year we had gone down and beaten LSU really badly [41-7] and we should have beaten Ole Miss [a 24-17 loss in overtime]. We went to Knoxville and played Tennessee really tight. We were just waiting for something to show us we could compete. Georgia was ranked 12th in the country and we were 4-5 at the time. That turned the light on for us and showed us we could compete with anybody if we came to play.

PROUD TO BE AN AUBURN MAN

Even though Tuberville decided to run the clock and not run up the score, Leard's passing numbers in his big game versus Georgia were memorable. He set a school record with 416 passing yards while throwing for four touchdowns. Auburn left the crowd of 86,117 and a national TV audience stunned at halftime as the underdogs took a 31-0 lead into the locker room. The Tigers stretched the lead to 38-0 early in the third quarter before relaxing on the way to a 38-21 victory.

Leard completed 26-37 passes with no interceptions. He hit freshman Daniels nine times, and the former pro baseball player finished the night with 249 receiving yards. By halftime Daniels had six catches for 180 yards, including spectacular TD plays of 59 and 78 yards.

Leard, who today lives and works just a few minutes from the Auburn campus, says that the university had a profound effect on his life. "It's hard to put it all into words what Auburn did for me, but the old cliché I think is best. It made a man of me. It got me to where I am today. I am sure people who follow Auburn football are aware of all of the things that happened to me in my career, like being benched in 1998 and coming back and starting and the injuries. Whether you think I was a good quarterback or not, I could not care less. It developed me personally and made me into a mature person because I was able to rebound and rely on support from others and become stronger.

"At the time, the most important thing was to become a better football player. Now that that is gone, Auburn means so much to me because of what it stands for, how much we put into it, and the impact that we were able to see we had on people's lives—whether it be a child or a grown man or woman. I will say it for years and years to come, regardless of what I went through, I wouldn't change it for the world because it made me into a person I am extremely proud of."

Leard earned a degree in mass communication in August 2000 and played his redshirt senior season that fall. He led the Tigers to nine wins, a berth in the Capital One Bowl, and earned All-SEC honors. He had a brief stint with the NFL's New England Patriots before moving to Decatur in north Alabama to begin a career as a pharmaceutical sales rep. He did that for three years and then began training others to do the job. He decided to move back to the Auburn area in 2005, where he opened an insurance agency in Opelika.

He says he thoroughly enjoys living in the area and having the chance to see current AU athletes, as well as ones from other eras. "A common thread of all of the Auburn players is that there is a work ethic that you find with them," he says. "There is kind of a lunch-pail mentality that comes along with being an Auburn player, and that is something I grew up with. It was the mentality that my mom and dad had and that my brothers have. Auburn is a place where I always felt like I fit in. The Auburn-Opelika area is a place that I plan to call home the rest of my life."

Chapter 15

TOMMY LORINO

BORN TO RUN

Growing up during the 1940s in the steel mill town of Bessemer on the outskirts of Birmingham, Alabama, Tommy Lorino was a natural athlete. A key player for Shug Jordan's teams in one of the most successful eras of Auburn football, he was a blue-chip recruit who certainly lived up to his billing as a two-way standout for the Tigers.

Lorino learned at a young age the advantages of being fast and elusive. "I got into football real early," he remembers. "As a small kid, when I was eight or nine, I played with older kids from around the block—guys who were in high school. I could run and play, so they would let me play with them. We would play touch football in the streets, and when the game was over, they would always chase me home because I was the smallest one. Many a day I had to run all the way home to get into my dad's old mom-and-pop grocery store."

He would use those skills learned from playing with the big boys when he joined his first organized football team. He got to participate in a charity fundraiser event called the Toy Bowl in Birmingham that drew what he notes was a rather amazing crowd of 35,000 fans to Legion Field to watch the kids play. "It was a great thrill to be part of that," says Lorino, who would be involved in numerous big games at that stadium.

"Many times I think about my history at Legion Field," Lorino says. "I played there as an eight year old. I played high school football there. I played in the Crippled Children's Clinic Game, which was a famous [high school] game in the 1940s and 1950s. I played there in college and I refereed SEC games there."

When he was 12 years old, the Lorino family moved to the Woodlawn area of Birmingham and stayed there for four years. He was good enough to play for Woodlawn High as a ninth and 10th grader, which was considered unusual. Woodlawn was one of Birmingham's "Big Five" powers of that era, and the level of competition was so high mostly juniors and seniors got to play.

Lorino, who had one sister, was the only athlete in his family, but was encouraged to compete in sports. "My dad wasn't an athlete," he notes. "He was born in Italy and came over here as a young kid, at two or three years old, and he worked all of his life. He ran a grocery store and was never into sports himself. He was thrilled to death with me playing sports. He emphasized it, he supported it, he did everything that he could to see that I got all of the opportunities to play.

"I grew up in an era when there weren't organized sports. We didn't have Little League Baseball. We didn't have football except for the Toy Bowl. He was the dad who would get the kids together, put them in a car, and take them to another section of town and play a little team over there. We didn't have uniforms; we didn't have enough gloves to go around. Everybody would use each other's gloves. We had two bats and two balls. He would umpire or another parent would umpire and we would just play on a sandlot field."

Prior to Lorino's junior year, his family moved back to Bessemer, where he became a star for Alabama High School Hall of Fame coach Snitz Snider's team. As a senior he led Bessemer to the state title and became a prospect sought by colleges around the country.

"I was highly recruited to a lot of schools," Lorino remembers. "I really wanted to go to Georgia Tech. Bessemer had been kind of a feeding ground for Tech back in the '50s. Jimmy Thompson, Duck Stephenson, Maxie Baughn, Frank Christy, and three or four other guys had gone from Bessemer to Tech and I wanted to go over there, too. They had those pretty tearaway jerseys, they played wide-open football, and coach Bobby Dodd was kind of the thing in the early 1950s and the mid-1950s, but my dad didn't want me to go to Tech. In those days kids did what their parents told them to do. He just wasn't going to let me go to Tech—it wasn't going to happen."

His father wanted Tommy to attend college in the state. "Alabama was down—that was the [Ears] Whitworth Era," Lorino points out. "I had a

Tommy Lorino was a popular 1950s standout for the Tigers.
Draughon Library Archives

chance to go to Notre Dame, but I really didn't want to go that far off. I had a chance to go to all of the schools in the SEC, but decided, and he decided, I was going to Auburn. And I did. Of course, it turned out real well. I had a pretty good career and we won our school's only football national championship. I was privileged and honored to be a part of that. I surely hope that the day will come when there will be another one of those. A lot of times I speak to people at different quarterback clubs and meetings and they always introduce me as 'Tommy Lorino, who played on Auburn's national championship team.' I always open and say, 'One day I would like to be introduced as Tommy Lorino, who played on Auburn's first national championship team.' I think we are getting close. Coach [Tommy] Tuberville is getting closer and closer. Hopefully soon that will come to fruition."

Tuberville has brought many talented players into the program in recent years. Coach Shug Jordan did the same thing in the 1950s. "Buck Bradberry was my primary recruiter for Auburn," Lorino remembers. "Back in those days it was legal for alumni to help with recruiting, and everybody did. They had alumni assigned to areas. Auburn had a guy named Trez Feaster—bless his heart, he is passed away now—who recruited me. He is the guy who worked with Coach Bradberry, my dad, and my family. They worked real close together. I never will forget that they tried to hide me out right before signing day. They got me together with a hunting trip down in Eufaula. I didn't know anything about hunting. I was kind of a city boy and I didn't know anything about guns. They got Fob James [an Auburn running back who later became governor of Alabama], myself, [Auburn lineman] Frank Reeves, and maybe some others. We went off to Mr. Trammell's plantation that was known for hunting birds and those types of things. I went down there for three days before signing. The whole deal was to get me out of sight so nobody could make contact or get to me.

"We used to sign in December," Lorino points out. "We would all meet at a hotel, the old Thomas Jefferson in Birmingham, about 10 at night and then we would sign at 12:01 a.m. I was there along with Jerry Wilson, Frank LaRussa, Nicky Prosh, and a couple of other people. They took us over to see a movie at the old Ritz Theater in downtown with all of those alumni around us so nobody could get to us. They kept us at the movie until about 11:30 and took us back to the hotel, and then we signed there. It was like espionage, keeping us out of sight and hidden."

After he signed, Lorino notes that he was excited about the opportunity and knew how important it was to take advantage of it. "If I hadn't played football, I would have never gone to college. No one in my family had ever been to college. We were just working people. Back in those days I would have probably ended up at U.S. Steel or at the pipe shop working in one of the industries around Bessemer."

Unlike many freshmen, Lorino's transition to college was smooth. "I didn't have a problem with that," he notes. "Like everybody who came with me in my freshman class in 1955, we knew this was our opportunity to have a better life. We all had working parents. Nobody had money. Nobody had cars when they got here. We were pretty average, common people. We were serious about school.

"[Auburn graduate and novelist] Paul Hemphill told me years later that there is a composite picture of the 1957 national championship team with the sophomores, juniors, and seniors. There are maybe 65 or 70 people in that picture. He said that 92 percent of them earned their degrees. That is unusual and we had an unusual group of people. We had people who became lawyers, doctors, and had other impressive careers. It was a group of players who had a chance and took advantage of that opportunity. It was a good group of guys."

Playing college football is always a physical and mental challenge at the SEC level, no matter what the era. In the 1950s, it was particularly tough. "My freshman year we didn't play on the varsity," Lorino says. "We had a freshman team and would play around three or four games. I remember we played Alabama and Georgia and maybe Florida. The game was Neanderthal in those days. We just hit, hit, and scrimmaged. That is all we ever did. There were no practice days in shorts. You put the pads on every day. The linemen would be hitting even before we did calisthenics. Practices were three or four hours a day with no breaks. No water breaks. That is just the way it was. When some of us talk about it now, it is a miracle that some of us didn't die in the heat. That was the era when they didn't believe in giving you water. The only way you got out of practice was if you had something broken. And you better have been hurt or you would get a reputation that you were slacking.

"The team practiced where Haley Center is now," Lorino remembers. "That was the varsity practice field. Down below, where the coliseum is now, is where we used to practice as freshmen. They called it 'coming up the hill' when we went up to scrimmage against the varsity. We were just fodder. They put us in there and they would beat us to death, and the fittest or lucky ones survived. They had 55 scholarships they could give [each year], so they were trying to weed them out. They had so many players. Of the 55 who came in with me, maybe 30 would be left going into the sophomore year and then you lost some more during the sophomore year.

"I remember the toughest, hardest, meanest football game I ever played in was as a freshman over at Georgia. The Auburn and Georgia coaches had a good relationship. Georgia had guys over at Auburn and Auburn had guys on the staff over at Georgia. They basically told the referees to stay out of the way and let them go. We didn't really play 15-minute quarters. We just played until they said stop. A lot of us remember that game."

Lorino says intimidating as that day was, he never considered quitting. "We had no alternative. There was no, 'I don't like this, I am going home.' That wasn't an option. Going home meant going into the mines or going into the steel mills. We adjusted quickly and stayed there. My daddy brought me down to Auburn in August, gave me a $20 bill, and I didn't see him again until Thanksgiving. I think we got $15 a month [laundry money] and that was it. You lived off of that. Of course, gas was 25 cents a gallon and you could go to the movies for 15 or 20 cents, so $15 would go a long way."

The coaches wasted no time taking advantage of Lorino's skills when he joined the varsity as a sophomore and earned All-SEC honors. He started at halfback on offense and in the secondary. It was an era in which players were required to go both ways. "I played safety on defense," Lorino says. "I ran back punts, I was a kickoff return man, and I held for extra points and punted. Once you were in the game, you were in the game and you had to do everything. The only way you got out was when you were hurt or ran up a big score. We didn't get out a lot because we normally didn't run up big scores. We would win games like 6-0 and 6-5. I remember we beat [Georgia] Tech 3-0."

Lorino was a key player on teams that lost just three games during his three-year varsity career, despite a lack of offensive firepower. "Our offense was so pure vanilla and it had no imagination at all," he says. "Even though we had me and Bobby Hoppe in the backfield in 1957, and we were both on the cover of *Life* magazine as the two top backs in the country coming out that year, we would play games where Bobby would run the ball three times and I would run four, or he would run five times and I would run it three. We didn't even touch the ball. We ran the fullback up the middle and would throw five or six passes. We had no offense. We would run option a little bit to try to get wide, but we didn't do much of that, either. I think that Coach Jordan figured that we just needed to play defense and win. That was back in the days where we were still quick-kicking and punting it out of bounds."

GAME OF MY LIFE
BY TOMMY LORINO

The most memorable to me was beating Alabama 40-0 in 1957. I had a particularly good game that day. I ran for over 100 yards. I intercepted three passes that day. I punted for an average of 40-something yards and I ran one interception back for a touchdown 79 yards. Being from the Birmingham area and being able to go home and do that was just outstanding.

That was a special football team and a special game. It was a combination of things that made the 1957 team so good. When you are in the middle of it you don't think about it that much, but looking back on it, that team had some great athletes. We had [Jackie] Burkett, [Zeke] Smith, [Red] Phillips, [Jerry] Wilson. Those are fine players and tremendous athletes.

It also goes back to having that 92 percent graduation rate. We had the kinds of kids who were determined. We had good citizens on that team. Like everybody, we had a few fights and a few guys getting drunk, but back in those days that type of thing didn't get into the newspaper. The campus police would go to Coach Jordan with anything we did and they would handle that inside and nothing got out. In that era, drugs were what you got at the drug store. That wasn't going on. We didn't know anything about that. There was a little beer drinking, but you had to drive to Opelika to get a bottle of alcohol and none of us had cars, so that kind of curtailed that.

There was just a tremendous amount of talent on that team combined with a lot of good people. On top of that, we had a coaching staff that had been in place. Coach Jordan had that same staff with maybe one or two changes for the past five years. He believed in the KISS system—keep it simple, stupid. We didn't do anything other than run the ball off-guard and off-tackle and throw the football five or six times a game. The theory was if you threw the ball there was a chance to make a mistake, so we didn't throw it much.

Our team had just an unbelievable defense. That was what made us so good. It wasn't our offense. I don't know if Auburn has ever had a better defense than the 1957 team. I remember we were leading Alabama 34-0 at the half and Coach Jordan put the first team in to start the second half. We scored right away to make it 40-0 and then he took us out. We didn't go back in until Alabama got inside the 20-yard line to keep them from scoring, and we did that. I remember people were hollering, "Go for 57 points" because we got beat 55-0 by them in 1948 [the renewal year of the rivalry], but Coach Jordan wouldn't do it. He sat us down again after we stopped the scoring threat and didn't play us the rest of the game. I believe Coach Jordan did that because he and Coach Whitworth were assistant coaches at Georgia before Coach Jordan came to Auburn and Whitworth went to Alabama. It had to be his respect for Whitworth.

ALL-AROUND ATHLETE

Lorino's skills learned on the sandlot included baseball, and he was also a standout on the AU team. "I call the time I was at Auburn our golden era," he says. "We won our first SEC baseball championship. Jackie [Burkett] and I were part of that team, along with [quarterback] Lloyd Nix. We won the SEC championship in basketball. Of course, we always won in track in those days because coach [Wilbur] Hutsell had a great team. Our wrestling team was winning championships, too."

Off the field, Lorino excelled in the classroom. He earned Academic All-SEC and Academic All-America honors while completing a degree in business administration he would use to start a successful career. However, before that began, he made time for more football. "I went to Edmonton and played Canadian football for one year," Lorino says. "I got drafted by San Francisco of the NFL. Back in those days the NFL didn't pay any money. They wanted me to pay my own way to come try out. If you made the team, the contract was like $3,500 or $4,000 per year.

"The Edmonton people came down and said they wanted me to play for them. I told them I was too small, but they said they really wanted me. I could just come up there and punt and they would pay me a $1,500 bonus. They said, 'If you make the team we will pay you $3,000.' Well, that was a lot of money then—enough to buy a brand new car for $1,500 and a house for $3,000. I said, 'Shoot yeah, I will go up there and just punt for that kind of money.' Well, they lied.

"In Canadian football you could have 15 Americans on your team," he notes. "They played 12 men on the field and they needed to play their Americans all of the time to have a chance to win. It was obvious after I got up there I was going to do more than just punt, so at 160 pounds I played offense, defense, and punted. It didn't turn out the way I expected, but I stayed up there for one season and didn't go back after that."

After returning home, Lorino joined the Air National Guard. His unit, which included teammates and other friends from college, was activated and spent a year in Europe during the Cold War. When he returned to the U.S., Lorino got married in 1961 to "Pete" Thomasina, the sister of former

AU teammate Junior Thomasina, and began selling insurance. He later went to work for Xerox and retired after more than 20 years with the company. But during that time, football was still a part of his life.

"I was an SEC official for 24 years," Lorino says. "I got into it doing high school games. I had a cousin, a guy named Fagan Canzoneri, who played football at Auburn in the '40s who was in a Birmingham school system administrative position. I was a young guy who was working and needed money. Back then a B-team game would pay $7.50. I think it was $20 for a varsity game. I was trying to raise a family [two sons] and it was a little supplemental money. I started in 1965, so that was pretty good money then. I was happy doing that and didn't ever think about doing college football. They scout like everybody else and they were looking for guys they might bring into the SEC.

"It was a very political thing, becoming an official in the Southeastern Conference. You have coaches on the selection committee and a couple of officials. The way it always works, Bear [Bryant, former Alabama coach] might say, 'I have got this boy who used to play for me. I want him in.' Then Shug would say, 'I have got this guy; I want him in. If you vote for him I will vote for your guy.' Of course, there were other coaches on the committee, like [Ole Miss'] Johnny Vaught and several others. I had gotten about five years of experience and was coming along. They called me and asked if I was interested, which was very unusual because they don't usually do that. Usually you have to apply, and sometimes you have to do it for two or three years before they finally check your application to start the process.

"Hootie Ingram, the ex-Alabama AD, was working for the SEC. He called me and said, 'Have you ever thought about getting into the conference?' I said I hadn't really, and he said, 'Why don't you think about it then?' I knew then something was up, so I sent in an application and got in the first year."

Lorino quickly became a respected SEC official and was the first Auburn graduate to officiate Alabama games, something previously not done because of the rivalry. He also called every major bowl and was present for five bowls that decided national championships. One of the most memorable was the January 1, 1984, Orange Bowl. "It was the one when Nebraska went for the two-point conversion at the end of the game," Lorino remembers. "You have to give [Nebraska coach] Tom Osborne credit. He could have gone for the extra point, tied the game, and probably could have won or at least shared the national championship. That was the game that started the Miami dynasty. Before that, they had been nothing in football. That same night Auburn beat Michigan 9-6 in the Sugar Bowl.

I still believe Auburn would have won the national championship if the team would have scored a touchdown versus Michigan." Miami jumped the Tigers in the final polls while AU stayed third.

After retiring from Xerox, Lorino started another career with IKON Corporation. He did that for a dozen years before retiring to Auburn, where he enjoys the college town atmosphere and football Saturdays. Like many from his generation, Lorino has redefined the word "retirement" with still another career. This one is in the restaurant business, helping his son David manage The Golden Rule Bar-B-Que and Grill, located not far from the campus where the small, do-it-all player made a big impact on Auburn football.

Chapter 16

BUDDY
McCLINTON

A GROWING EXPERIENCE

Going back to his earliest memories, Buddy McClinton was passionate about sports. Although he was a good athlete, he was smaller than the kids he competed against and few would have predicted the young boy from Northwest Alabama would grow up to be a future star on SEC football fields.

"Like most kids in Jasper, I started out playing Toy Bowl football, which is just Pee Wee football," he says. "I just loved it, but none of the uniforms fit. Everything was too big for me. I probably looked like a clown out there, but I really, really loved the game and the contact.

"Somebody asked me if football was always my love, but I grew up with baseball as my first love," he notes. "I was really a good baseball player from the time I was a young boy because it doesn't matter how big you are.

"Growing up, I had a September birthday, so I was always a year behind everybody and candidly, that is one of the reasons [Auburn head coach "Shug"] Jordan took a chance on me—because he knew I was a year younger than everybody in high school. Age-wise, I was like a junior, even though I had graduated high school. When I played my first game at Auburn, I was still 17 years old."

When the athlete's mother remarried, the family relocated to Montgomery, a hotbed of football in that era. McClinton, who was 10, kept competing in both of his favorite sports, but had it not been for the intervention of his coach at Goodwin Junior High, Auburn fans would have been deprived of seeing one of the best safeties in school history.

"Football was always so hard for me because I was so small," McClinton says. "By the time I got to junior high school, I was getting beaten up so badly in football. I think in the ninth grade I weighed 115 pounds. I was just getting killed every day in practice. I tried to quit, although I had never quit anything in my life. But I got all beaten up one day and I didn't go back. I was thinking, 'This is not any fun, it's too hard.'

"I was playing for a guy, Jackie Spencer, who had actually played for Auburn returning punts back in the 1950s. He was a little guy growing up, too. After practice the next day he sent a bunch of my teammates to get me. I was down at the YMCA shooting a basketball. They told me he wanted to see me. I said, 'I don't want to see Coach, he is going to be mad at me.' I was expecting him to just blast me, but he didn't. He said, 'You remind me so much of myself at your age. I was always little and I was always getting beaten up, but I made a decision I was never going to let my size keep me from playing ball.'

"He said he was able to go and play at Robert E. Lee, which was the pinnacle of high school football then, along with [city rival] Lanier. They were competing for state championships every year in the '50s, '60s, and early '70s. He said, 'Then I went on to play at Auburn even though nobody ever thought I would be able to play college ball because when I signed I was only 150 pounds.'"

McClinton rejoined his junior high team and became an undersized star for coach Tom Jones at Robert E. Lee. At just 5-foot-8, McClinton was not exactly a prized recruit. However, Jones knew how much potential McClinton had. After McClinton's senior season at Lee, Jones was moving up to the college ranks, accepting the post as head coach at Troy State, about an hour's drive southeast of Montgomery.

"Coach Jones is the only reason I got to Auburn," McClinton says. "Auburn hired him away from Troy to become the head coach of the freshman team. He had talked me and Keith Green, a defensive tackle on the Robert E. Lee team, into going down to Troy with him. He said, 'It is so late that all of the scholarships are gone, but I will get you one if you come down to Troy with me and help me get a program started.'

"We were going to Troy with Coach Jones, but he switched to Auburn after getting the opportunity to go there. Rather than forget about us, he came to us and said, 'Guys, I want you to come to Auburn and walk on.' We said, 'Gosh, Coach, we aren't going to be able to play up there.' He

Buddy McClinton was a superb safety in the 1960s.
Auburn University Media Relations

said, 'I have had you for three years, and I wouldn't tell you to come do this unless I thought it was the right thing for you.' So Keith and I were vacillating about what to do. We had already signed up, got our paperwork done, and were accepted at Troy and were planning to go there.

"Literally, two or three days before we were to report, Coach Jones called me and said, 'Buddy, I need you all to meet me at Keith's house at five o'clock. And bring your mother.' So we go over to Keith's house and his mother and dad were there. We had no idea what was going on. Coach Jones had talked Coach Jordan into giving us scholarships and we got the last two Auburn had, so we went to Auburn."

SMALL EXPECTATIONS, BIG RESULTS

Jones obviously knew what he was doing by convincing McClinton to play for the Tigers. The Auburn staff put the defensive back on a weight training program as he played on the freshman team and the coaches prepared him for varsity competition as a sophomore for the 1967 season.

Secondary coach Bill "Brother" Oliver liked what he saw in McClinton. "Brother Oliver never held being small against me," McClinton notes. "He stuck me out there that first spring my freshman year and I was able to hold on to that spot the rest of my career."

Even though McClinton worked hard to get bigger, it took a while for the training to pay dividends. "The size thing got to be such an important issue in college, because you got beaten up so badly," he says. "We hit the weights big-time in college and I responded just like kids who had never hit the weights before responded. I gained a lot of weight, a lot of muscle mass.

"We also had a lot of exercises to make sure you didn't lose your speed as you got bigger, and I actually got faster. It was a blessing because my sophomore year they had me listed at 170 pounds in the program. I probably weighed 158. I hit those running backs and it was just brutal—I was taking all of the punishment, but I hit them for all I was worth. My senior year, when I was 5-foot-10, 195 pounds, it was fun to be able to come up and hit them and know you were delivering the lick to them, not them delivering the lick to you.

"Back then, nobody lifted weights in high school," McClinton points out. "I went to Auburn in 1966 with no expectations other than just thanking the good Lord that Coach Jordan was giving me a chance and Coach Jones had recommended me. The rest is history. I was very blessed to be at the right place at the right time with great coaches and having an opportunity to play where people believed in me."

That belief was well founded. McClinton broke into the starting lineup as a sophomore and stayed there all three varsity seasons, helping Auburn bounce back from a 4-6 campaign in 1966 to post winning records (6-4, 7-4, and 8-3) his sophomore through senior seasons. A two-time All-SEC player, McClinton earned All-America and Academic All-America honors and set school records that are still standing today for interceptions in a single season (nine) and career (18).

THE GAME OF MY LIFE
BY BUDDY McCLINTON

My senior year, Florida had a phenomenal team, but we used to own Florida. Auburn beat Florida almost every year. They were good, but we just had their number. They had a quarterback by the name of John Reaves and a receiver by the name of Carlos Alvarez. We had a great passing combination, too, with Pat Sullivan and Terry Beasley.

The Florida guys were getting all of the press and they were leading the nation in completions and yardage and were scoring 40-something points per game. They came into Auburn the seventh game of the season and were undefeated and ranked seventh in the nation. They were just blowing everybody away.

Bill Oliver came up with a defensive scheme that was just absolutely phenomenal. We played the old Notre Dame 40 defense to take advantage of the great linebacking we had—Mike Kolen, Sonny Ferguson, Bobby Strickland, and people like that. We had four linebackers and we only had three in the secondary. We played a three-deep secondary. It isn't like it is today. I wasn't a free safety. I was the safety, so I had a lot of responsibility. I didn't get to roam. A lot of people said, "You got to go where you wanted to," but that wasn't the case. We had a lot of territory to cover up.

Coach Oliver came up with a scheme where ostensibly I would become a free safety and Sonny Ferguson, who is a judge in Birmingham, basically became a strong side safety instead of a rover linebacker. What he did instead of playing his typical role, he started going not always to the strong side where the tight end was, but sometimes he would go to the weak side because they loved to run a back out of the backfield when everybody was trying to double-up Alvarez on the other side. They were making huge yardage with these plays out of the backfield. It was a very innovative offense.

Sonny moved around and they never knew what was going on. Sonny would be where he always was, four or five yards off the line of scrimmage, and I always played 12 to 15 yards deep as the deep safety. Now, I was lining up four or five yards off the line of scrimmage on the other side, and they didn't have any idea of what in the world I was doing. What it amounted to, one time when I was up there it was purely decoy because as soon as I anticipated the snap count I was leaving the tight end, although it appeared I was playing him man to man. The linebacker would immediately pick up the tight end and I would take away the quick slant or the quick out to Alvarez when it looked like I was guarding the tight end.

The next time I was standing in there, Larry Willingham at cornerback walked up on the line of scrimmage with the old bump and run technique, but nobody played Alvarez like that because he was as fast as Larry was, and Larry was a great athlete who also ran on the track team. Nobody could play Alvarez like that because he was so gifted, and Reaves would immediately check off for a deep pattern because he knew that Alvarez could get away from anybody.

What I was doing the moment the ball was snapped, I was headed to the deep outside on a dead sprint, because we knew they loved to throw that fade pattern. I really believe they may have been one of the earliest teams in college that threw their passes to a point. They didn't throw it to the receiver. They had a point on the field. Alvarez would go down and cut here, here, and here and when he was doing that, Reaves would throw the ball and then the ball would be there. That is why they were so successful.

Brother Oliver realized that, and it is why we baited them to throw to areas. One time I would sprint back there and I would have him deep, and another time Larry would cover him deep and I would cover any inside slant. They never knew what we were doing. We intercepted nine passes, which set an NCAA record for one game. We beat the stew out of them and they never knew what hit them.

After the season I ended up in New York or Chicago at an All-American program. It might have been *The Bob Hope Show.* Carlos Alvarez was on the team and he said, "I couldn't wait to meet you. You have got to tell me what in the world you were doing. We could never figure it out. When I thought I was man to man, you were doubling me. When I thought I was facing zone, you had me man to man." I kind of sat down over a beer and talked to him about it. They said even after looking at it on film, they couldn't figure it out. It just blew them away.

It was just a wonderful, wonderful game. It was so memorable because it was so intriguing to do something we had never done before, which was basically allowing me to be a free safety.

INTERCEPTIONS GALORE
AND A BIG FINISH

When the final whistle blew to end the 1969 Florida game, the Tigers had set a record with their nine interceptions. When the final whistle blew to end the season, the Tigers had 34 interceptions in 11 games, which stood as an NCAA record for a quarter of a century.

The only setback for McClinton came at the end of the season. Auburn beat its oldest rival, Georgia, by a score of 16-3, but the safety was injured. Throughout a two-week break before wrapping up the regular season with a showdown against in-state rival Alabama, the Tigers looked like they might have to play without their All-American. His last chance to beat the Tide, McClinton desperately wanted to play despite being on crutches.

"The final game of my career was special when we beat coach [Bear] Bryant and Alabama 49-26," he says. "What a great victory that was. Alabama pretty much owned us back then. They were beating us every year. We scored more touchdowns—seven, the most any team had ever scored against Coach Bryant. We had a truly great game."

Fittingly, McClinton intercepted a pass that day, even though he was far from full speed. "I was hurting," he remembers. "I had gone through all of the cortisone shots and the treatment 24/7. When I walked out to Legion Field for the walk-through, it was the first time I had been off crutches for two weeks, but I told Coach Oliver, 'Whatever it takes, I am going to play.' He said, 'Let me tell you something, whatever it takes, you are going to play.' It was one of those deals where, thank goodness, we were able to take control of it and score a lot of points."

SAYING NO TO THE PROS

McClinton notes that he arrived at college with no expectations a pro career would follow, but the opportunity was there after he graduated with honors in 1970.

Signed by the Atlanta Falcons, who were coached by Norm Van Brocklin, McClinton was one of the top rookies on the team along with No. 1 draft choice John Small, a linebacker from The Citadel.

"John Small and I were the only rookies to play in every preseason game," he remembers. "Back then, I think we played eight preseason games, and I really had a great preseason. The last game we played was up at Buffalo against O.J. Simpson. When I came back to Atlanta on Saturday, my secondary coach, Fred Brunne, called me and said, 'Buddy, you made the team.' The final cut was Monday and I said, 'Coach, do you think I could go home? My girlfriend, who I have been dating for years, is getting ready to go off to college and she is leaving Sunday. Do you think I can run over to Montgomery and see her?' He said, 'Absolutely. Why don't you stop over in Auburn and see your coaches and let them know you made the team.' He liked all of those guys over at Auburn and I was on cloud nine. I saw Brother Oliver, Coach Jordan, and everybody and told them the good news, and I went on to see my girlfriend.

"I got back to Atlanta on Sunday and Coach Brunne called me in and said, 'I have got some tough news for you, but I don't want you to overreact to this. One of the offensive linemen got hurt in the Buffalo game, so we are going to need to carry an extra offensive lineman instead of a defensive back for at least the first two or three weeks until we can get him back. Van Brocklin wants to put you on the taxi squad.'

"I had already told my family and my coaches that I was on the team, and being on the taxi squad you made half your salary, which wasn't much then, and you didn't get to dress out for the games. You were just meat. You were nothing but a practice squad guy. Back then the salaries weren't much. I am not sure you could pay rent on an apartment. So I was really devastated. I said, 'Coach, I am not going to do that. I feel like I have done everything you have asked me to do and even more.'

"Of course he tried to talk me out of it. He asked me to go see Coach Van Brocklin. I said, 'I don't want to see Coach Van Brocklin. You are my coach. You told me I made the team; now you are telling me I have to be on the taxi squad. I am going home.' I got in my car and went home."

The Falcons, hoping McClinton would return, kept him on their roster until late in the season when they released him. Pittsburgh owner Art Rooney then called the safety to convince him to sign with the Steelers, who had watched McClinton play at Auburn.

"By this time, the season was almost over and he wanted me to come up for the next year, but I had a good job, my girlfriend was out of college, and we were getting engaged," McClinton remembers. "I said, 'You know, I think I am just going to stay in commercial real estate.' I have been in it for 36 years. It was the best thing I ever did. It was a wonderful decision. The Lord knows what his plan is for us.

"I thought it was catastrophic when they put me on the taxi squad," McClinton notes. "I thought it was the worst day of my life. Actually, it was the best day of my life. I went home, married my sweetheart, and have had a fabulous career in real estate. I have four children and three grandchildren. Who knows how any of that would have worked out if I had stayed in Atlanta or gone to Pittsburgh the next year?"

Now a developer, McClinton and his firm in Montgomery, McClinton and Associates, builds shopping centers, Wal-Marts, movie theater complexes, and a variety of other major projects across the Southeast.

The All-American notes that he has strong feelings for his alma mater, teammates, coaches, and professors. "I loved Coach Jordan," he says. "He was truly one of the finest gentlemen who ever graced the sideline. His door was always open. In all my years at Auburn, I never went by his office one time when his door wasn't open. He wanted to let you know you were always invited to come in and sit down with him. It didn't matter what you wanted to talk about and it didn't matter if you were first-string or fifth-string. I truly enjoyed getting to play under such a gentleman."

McClinton says that he was also fortunate to play for a smart defensive coordinator, Paul Davis, as well as his position coach, Oliver, who the safety calls a "defensive genius."

"Brother Oliver understood offense better than most offensive coaches did," McClinton says. "He was way ahead of his time. He had us breaking down film of opponents, studying tendencies for down and distance. He taught us how to think like a quarterback. Larry Willingham, who was a world-class athlete, played in the secondary along with Don Webb, my roommate, and Merrill Shirley. Larry is really the only one of us who had great athletic ability, but Coach Oliver took us and molded us into one of the finest secondaries in the nation." Willingham went on to an NFL career with the St. Louis Cardinals and finished Auburn as an All-American, too.

"Being a part of something like that, it was what being a team was all about," McClinton adds. "We weren't great individually, but being able to play like a well-oiled machine, some of us got to get some accolades we would never have been able to get. I always thought Auburn got the best out of me. They always made me better than I was capable of being, and that was true on the field and in the classroom."

McClinton says he closely follows the fortunes of the Tigers and says he is pleased with current AU coach Tommy Tuberville's emphasis on signing players with a love of the game and a willingness to work hard both on and off the football field. "It's a system that is working very well right now at Auburn," says McClinton, who knows better than anybody how far an athlete can go on brains, athletic ability, and a big heart.

Chapter 17

PATRICK NIX

TOTALLY A TIGER

As the son of a high school football coach, Patrick Nix lived a nomadic lifestyle as a youngster. However, throughout his travels several constants remained, such as the future Auburn quarterback's love of sports and his dream of one day playing for the Tigers.

Nix laughs when contemplating the moment he first became interested in sports. "With my dad being a coach, it was probably when I was in the womb," he jokes. "I don't remember a day in my life not being around sports at a gym, at a basketball game, at the baseball park, or at the football field. When you are a high school coach's son you are a gym rat, and that is all you do."

The son of Auburn graduates, Nix began playing organized baseball and basketball when he was very young, but had to wait longer to put on pads and a helmet. "My dad wouldn't let me play football until I was in middle school, but I was always around it," he says.

Conrad Nix was coaching at Ocilla High in Georgia when Patrick was born. Soon after, the family moved to Warner Robins, Georgia, with stops in Hayleyville, Alabama, Fayetteville, Georgia, and Albertville, Alabama, before moving to Rainbow City, Alabama, where Nix became an All-State quarterback for his dad's Etowah High team. He played varsity football in mop-up roles as a freshman and started the next three seasons.

"It was probably the fall of my junior year when I realized I was going to have some opportunities to play college football," Nix says. A trip to Auburn in December made that clear when he had a conversation with Coach Pat Dye, whose team had just defeated its rival in the historic first

Auburn vs. Alabama game ever played in Auburn to close the 1989 regular season.

"After the game we were standing in the lounge area outside the museum, and Coach Dye came up to me and told me they wanted me at Auburn," Nix says. "I will never forget it. They told me they didn't know if they were going to sign a quarterback with this class that was coming in before mine. They told me they wanted me the next year. I was kind of taken aback. Either my dad or I asked if he was serious and Coach Dye said, 'I am serious as a heart attack.' When I heard that it was like a dream come true, because playing for Auburn is something that I had always wanted to do.

"I think I was in shock when Coach Dye asked me if I wanted to play at Auburn. Of course, I agreed I wanted to do that, but I didn't really push it. Recruiting was different then. You didn't commit early. Deep down they knew I was coming and deep down I knew I was coming. Yes, I did take some visits and yes, although I am ashamed to say it, I went over to Alabama for a visit and I watched them play a game. I think it was against Florida in the fall of 1990. I think Florida won and I was kind of happy about that. Auburn played Ole Miss that day. I spent more time listening to the Auburn game on the radio than I did watching the Alabama game."

CLIMBING THE TOTEM POLE

Nix joined the Auburn team in the summer of 1991. He says the move to college was challenging. "I had my good and bad days, that is for sure. I came from a smaller environment where you kind of knew everybody and knew what was going on. I was the low man on the totem pole just trying to survive. It wasn't easy at all.

"It wasn't as hard as what it felt then, but at the time, for an 18- or 19-year-old kid, it seemed pretty tough leaving home, leaving the family, the girlfriend, and all of that kind of stuff.

"The great thing though about coming in as a football player is that you start playing right away after you get to college. Once the season got going, I was having so much fun being on the sideline at games the other things didn't matter."

Nix figured he would redshirt while learning the system from quarterback coach Pat Sullivan. That is what happened, although injuries almost changed those plans.

Patrick Nix lived his dream of playing quarterback for the Tigers.
Auburn University Media Relations

"Corey Lewis, who was the backup quarterback, got hurt and our starter, Stan White, got hurt before the Florida game, and I practiced with the first team all week," Nix recalls. "Coach Sullivan calls me into the office on Wednesday night and actually calls my parents and talks to my dad and tells him, 'I don't know if we are going to be able to redshirt Patrick. We may have to play him this week.'

"I was thinking I was going to start against Florida my true freshman year, but Stan was able to come back and practice some on Thursday and then some more on Friday and then play in the game. I wanted to play, but I am glad it turned out the way that it did. It was an interesting year, a fun year. I learned a lot about myself."

Nix, who has a good sense of humor, remembers the thrill of running onto the field opening night in his Auburn uniform, but notes he had a humbling experience on the way to the stadium. Like the other redshirts who weren't scheduled to play, he didn't participate in the Tiger Walk pregame ceremony. Instead, he and the others put on their uniforms at the football complex and walked past the coliseum to get to the stadium.

"I remember a little kid running up for my autograph, and his father says, 'No son, you don't want his autograph. He doesn't play.' I can remember that like it was yesterday." Little did that father know that Nix's name would be plastered throughout the Auburn record book before he graduated.

The Tigers struggled as Nix redshirted, finishing 5-6. The next season, 1992, was just as disappointing. "We felt like we should have been better," he says. "We missed an opportunity to go to a bowl. Then Coach Dye resigned at the end of the year, which was very frustrating, because all of the guys loved Coach Dye. He recruited us and we had a ton of respect for him. It hurt us and shocked us.

"Back in those days you didn't have the Internet and we didn't know what was going on. We didn't know the NCAA was investigating and all of that stuff. There was a lot of turmoil and confusion. When Terry Bowden got hired, all of the players were home for Christmas break and we were all calling each other and finding out who our next coach was going to be."

The following spring, Nix was trying to impress Bowden and his third college QB coach, Jimbo Fisher. "For me, the transition went okay," Nix says. "I saw it as a new life, a chance to compete. I thought I had a better spring than I really did. Looking back at it, Stan beat me out. He was really playing well. I just wanted to believe that I should be playing and was frustrated that I wasn't.

"It was tough for all of us," Nix adds. "When Coach Bowden came in, there wasn't a lot of loyalty. He didn't recruit any of us. He just had to get guys doing what they were supposed to do to give him the best chance to succeed. It was one of those times when you knew you better do what you were supposed to do and work extremely hard."

Nix missed Dye's staff, but was impressed with Fisher. "I have a ton of respect for Jimbo. He is a great football coach. He really related to us well, being closer to our age and being very competitive. All of us were very competitive.

"I was very fortunate. I had Coach Sullivan my first year and I respected him a ton. Then Randy Campbell came in as my quarterback coach and I really got a great perspective from him, being a former player and quarterback, about what is expected at Auburn. Then Jimbo comes in and he has no ties to Auburn. It was just straight football. We really got after it about becoming a better quarterback."

The Tigers weren't expected to be one of the SEC's top teams in 1993, but opened the season on a winning streak and finished 11-0. The only negative part of the season was in the team's probation, which meant no bowl game or national title.

"It was obviously one of the best seasons in Auburn history," says Nix, who played a key role in a much-anticipated showdown with the in-state rival to close the year. "Obviously, the Alabama game was big," he says. "I think that was the single moment that has probably changed my life as much as anything in my career in football."

Nix's first play of the game is one of the most remembered in Auburn football history. When White went out with an injury against the Tide, the sophomore threw a long touchdown pass to Frank Sanders that sparked the Tigers to a 22-14 victory. "I only threw three passes in the 1993 Alabama game, but people think I must have thrown 30 and been 30 of 30 that day, the way the stories were told.

"That game sort of catapulted me into the starting role. If that hadn't happened, I am not certain I would have gotten the chance to be the starter the next spring because Dameyune [Craig] was sort of the [new coaching staff's] guy and obviously a great player. I had to fight him off the whole time."

Nix was the full-time starter as a junior in 1994 as Auburn's winning streak reached 20 before the season ended with a tie versus Georgia and a loss to Alabama. "We had a lot of our players back and we had a really good team," Nix notes. "The LSU game that year was incredible, with all of the interceptions and the defensive touchdowns. How frustrating it was for me that we didn't move the ball and I got benched during the game. It was sort of a trying time for me.

"I went from that to going to Gainesville and upsetting Florida when they were No. 1. We were 17-point underdogs and beat them in the last seconds. I remember Georgia at the end of the year getting lucky and tying us because of our mistakes when we didn't get the job done at the end of the game. I remember the frustration of losing to Alabama 21-14. It was never fun to lose to those guys."

Nix spent long hours studying football. That didn't change his senior year, even though he got married over the summer. "It changed my life just a little bit," he says. "It gave me a whole new perspective and it actually made things a lot better for me. I am very thankful some of those two-a-day mornings at 4:45 a.m. when I didn't want to get up, [Krista] kicked me out of bed in the morning because I might have just slept through them and been in a lot of trouble."

With Nix calling the signals, Auburn put up impressive offensive numbers. However, the defense wasn't as good in 1995 as it had been, and the Tigers finished 8-4. "My senior year we were extremely young and we played a lot of true freshmen," Nix says.

"We battled and lost a heartbreaker at Arkansas and one at LSU. It was very frustrating that we didn't get those wins. We got beat by Florida at our place. They were a very good team that year, and ended up winning the national championship the next season. Then we ended up beating Alabama at home. Just knowing that we beat Alabama in that final game in itself was probably as satisfying as anything out there in my career."

Nix wrapped up his playing days in a muddy monsoon, as Auburn lost its bowl game in Tampa versus Penn State. But all things considered, he says he had a great experience at Auburn. "It was a rollercoaster ride. It was a crazy five years and I basically got to experience about everything you could experience over a five-year period."

THE GAME OF MY LIFE
BY PATRICK NIX

No doubt it was the 1995 Alabama game because that was my last chance to play them. I know a lot of people would think my choice would have to be the 1993 Alabama game or the 1994 Florida game, but the 1995 game was the most memorable one for me. I circled that date when I committed to Auburn because I knew I was probably going to be redshirted because we had the quarterbacks ahead of me. I figured that was going to be my last football game I ever played in Jordan-Hare Stadium and my last chance to beat Alabama as a player. Beating Alabama was my life. It was as good as anything you could ever do, and to beat them at home just put the icing on the cake.

It just seemed like we had control of the game and we were playing really well. I remember coach [Terry] Bowden, [offensive coordinator] Tommy Bowden, and Jimbo talking during the week, and we noted we hadn't done anything against them offensively since Terry had been there. In 1993 we didn't really move the ball great on them, and in 1994 we didn't move it until the second half when we really spread them out and started throwing.

They decided we were going to spread them out and start throwing the ball a little more in the first half than we had in the past. We did that and had a good first half. I think we went up 24-14 and we were really feeling good.

I remember them coming back in the second half and actually taking the lead 27-24. I remember sitting on the sideline thinking, "There is no way I can lose to these guys." And sure enough, we found a way there at the end to make a few plays and Fred Beasley scored to put us ahead 31-27 and we won. Then at the very end, we had to hold our breath for four plays while they threw it into the end zone. Fortunately, they didn't score.

The best memory of all is being able to take a knee—which is something I had dreamed of—which is basically making them submit, knowing the game is over. For me, it was a great night and a great way to finish. It was not a great career, but it was great for me to be able to play at Auburn and experience everything I did. I remember the end of the game thinking about all that I had been through, everything that I had done and seen.

LIKE FATHER, LIKE SON

Nix graduated in the fall of 1995 with a degree in education and quickly moved into the coaching ranks as an assistant at Jacksonville State University. He first coached running backs and also spent two years directing the quarterbacks. He did a good job and was named head coach at Division II Henderson State in Arkansas. He spent two years there before moving back to Alabama, where he coached receivers at Samford.

Before the year was finished, however, Samford's head coach was fired and the offensive coordinator was promoted. Nix moved up to offensive coordinator. Prior to the team's next season, he took a job at Georgia Tech, where he spent his first year coaching running backs and four more directing QBs. In 2007, he moved to the University of Miami to become offensive coordinator.

Those who knew him in college are not surprised that, like his dad, who is having a successful second run at Warner Robins High in Georgia, Nix now coaches for a living. The quarterback was a smart player who enjoyed the strategy of football.

"I never really thought about coaching for the first few years in college. Then, as I went into my junior and senior years, I realized I had better start thinking about what I was going to do," he says. "The only logical thing for me to do was to go into coaching. Other than going into some type of ministry, coaching is the only other thing that I absolutely loved. I just knew that I wanted to be around young people and football.

"I was very fortunate," adds Nix, who is raising two young boys, Bo and Caleb, and a daughter, Emma, with his wife, who he met at Auburn. "It was a storybook type of career I had in college for a kid who honestly didn't have a whole lot of ability. But the good Lord blessed him and gave him an opportunity.

"I was just very fortunate to be around a lot of guys who were really good players. I was very, very average. I still have my high school highlight tape, and sometimes I will go back and watch it and think, 'I wouldn't even recruit myself now.'"

Despite Nix's comments, he did more than just prove he could play SEC football. He produced two of the top 10 passing seasons in Auburn history and threw for 4,957 yards, which should keep him in the record book for many years to come.

Chapter 18

AL PARKS

NO MORE TOOTHLESS TIGERS

You would be hard pressed to find an Auburn fan who lamented the end of the Earl Brown era after a winless 1950 season. Nobody understands better than Al Parks why replacing the former Notre Dame player with former Auburn standout Ralph "Shug" Jordan was a really good idea.

Parks was the starting quarterback for Brown in 1950 and for Jordan in 1951 as the Tigers rebounded to finish 5-5 overall and 3-4 in the SEC. In Brown's three seasons as head coach, the Tigers won just three times, lost 22, and tied four.

"My senior year I played quarterback again and cornerback, too, but I didn't play as much defense," says Parks, who competed in an era in which most players went both ways.

"With Coach Jordan taking over my senior year, it was like a night and day difference," Parks recalls. "He came in here knowing what he was going to do and what he was going to run, who was the backfield coach, and who was the line coach. We didn't try this today and try that tomorrow. It was very positive. The enthusiasm and the confidence of the players were like night and day. We turned it all around."

Jordan would go on to coach for a quarter of a century at Auburn. His name was added to the stadium, partly because he recruited bigger and more high-profile athletes than Parks, who Brown was fortunate to get as a walk-on. Parks contends that he was the lucky one, getting a chance to play at a place he grew to love.

"There wasn't much demand for 150-pound blocking backs," he says with a laugh. "I came to Auburn because an alumnus flew two of my buddies to Auburn for a tryout and they brought me along. I tried out and [assistant coach] Shot Senn, bless his heart, told me I could walk on and work in the chow hall. That was the greatest thing."

In 1948, Parks graduated from Central High in Jackson, Mississippi, where he was a three-sport athlete who played basketball and ran track. "I am really from a lot of places," he says. "Jackson is where I went to high school. My father was a superintendent of a deaf school in Mississippi."

As his dad took various jobs, Parks grew up in Arkansas, California, and Georgia, as well as Missouri, where he was born. Parks notes that he had a passion for sports for as long as he can remember. In seventh grade, he played as a member of the varsity in Cave Springs, Georgia. By the time he graduated in 1948, he had participated in seven seasons of high school football.

Parks remembers his transition to college went smoothly on and off the field because he really liked the campus and the people there. "I didn't really work too hard as a freshman because I was a walk-on," he says. "Coach Brown was our coach and he just kind of put you where he thought you might play. I started out at cornerback and I played some quarterback, but just in practice."

Parks played on the '48 freshman team and watched the varsity struggle to a 1-8-1 record in Brown's inaugural season, which ended with an embarrassing 55-0 loss to Alabama in the renewal of an in-state rivalry that hadn't been played since 1907. The 1949 season was a little better for the Tigers as Parks moved up to the varsity. Auburn finished 2-4-3. "That was the season we beat Alabama 14-13, and I got to play in that game," he says. "I played a whole lot against Wofford the first game in Montgomery, but I played sparingly until the Alabama game."

As a junior, Parks' role with the team became a major one. "It was real funny," he says. "We were at practice one day and Coach Brown came up to me and said, 'I have been noticing that you can throw the ball pretty good.' This is when we were warming up.

"He said, 'Why don't you try out for quarterback?' I said okay and started playing there. In those days, Coach Brown didn't really know what offense he wanted to run or what defense he wanted to run. It would change from week to week."

Altering offensive and defensive systems every game was a recipe for disaster. Parks did his best to help the team win, rarely leaving the field on either offense or defense, but the 1950 Tigers finished 0-10. "I also played

Al Parks started for Shug Jordan's first Auburn team.
Draughon Library Archives

cornerback that year," he notes. "I averaged 52 minutes per game on the field."

After the Tigers lost every game and looked really bad doing it, Parks says the players, students, and alumni were thrilled when Jordan was brought home. He notes that it didn't take long to figure out that Jordan and his assistants were going to make good things happen. When Parks lined up at quarterback as a senior, he did it with a chance of success.

Opening day of the 1951 season, Parks and the Tigers upset a Vanderbilt team led by future NFL star QB Bill Wade. Tiger fans were ecstatic. Although short on talent and depth, AU managed to break even at 5-5, Auburn's first non-losing record since 1945. Parks notes that everybody realized that better days were on the horizon.

THE GAME OF MY LIFE
BY AL PARKS

Football, in Coach Jordan's day, he didn't call plays and he didn't have a staff up in the press box. He would just say, "Al, I think maybe the belly series will work," or he would say, "Al, maybe the dive play will work," or he would say, "Try this or try that." Now, he did call a play that won the game against Florida in 1951.

Jackie Creel, from Dothan, Alabama, who played at about 130 pounds, blocked a punt on the 30-yard line. We had about a minute and 30 seconds to go. Coach Jordan called timeout and called a play. He said, "Al, fake the dive, fake the handoff, and hide the ball on your right hip. Lee [Hayley], go down there and stand in the left side end zone corner. Al, throw it to him as hard as you can throw it." We had never run that play in practice, but Lee caught it for a touchdown and we won the game 14-13.

I remember going into the game against Florida that Coach Jordan told me we wanted to run the option, which meant I got to run the ball a lot that day. I ran about 25 yards to score the first touchdown. Then they scored. I was also playing defense too, and somewhere in the game I intercepted a pass. Then, late in the game we threw the pass to Lee to win the game. I remember that was a very hard-fought game.

A FASCINATING CAREER

Parks graduated with a degree in education in 1952. He moved on to a rather exotic series of jobs, but other than one year as a coach, he wasn't really a teacher.

"I went into ROTC to stay out of Korea and I went into the Air Force because I was in the ROTC," says Parks, whose deceased first wife, Mary

Jo, had been a student with him at Auburn. "Everybody goes to Lackland Air Force Base [in San Antonio, Texas] for their basic training, but I didn't. I was selected to go to Carswell Air Force Base [in Fort Worth, Texas] to play football for the Carswell Bombers.

"In those days, service football was big. Bud McFadin, the all-time All-American from Texas, was there. We had Lloyd Lowe, the little All-American from North Texas State. We had a coach from West Point who played with Doc Blanchard. We had some good players. We averaged 42 points per game against service teams, so I played football there. I wouldn't go to work there until 2:30 p.m. I was planning to just stay four years in the Air Force and then play Canadian football, which was real big in those days."

However, a flight he took with a captain got him excited about flying, so he changed the game plan to become a pilot.

"I ended up staying in the Air Force for 27 years," Parks says. "I had 490 combat missions over North Vietnam. I flew the 101, which is a reconnaissance plane. In 1964, the only airplanes in Vietnam were reconnaissance. I was actually stationed in Okinawa, but our squadron would send 30 guys down for 30 days. We lived in a three-story, 15-bedroom house right across from the palace. Alex P. Butterfield, the man who would later release the tapes of President Richard Nixon, was our squad commander.

"I got 100 missions in 101s and I went back to Okinawa. I was going to be there for two more years, so I went to the wing commander and said, 'Look, I need to check out in the 105.' That is the fighter. Nobody checks out in the 105 in the field, but this wing commander pulled a lot of strings and let me do it.

"After flying 100 missions in that, I went to Nellis Air Force Base in Las Vegas and flew the F-111, which was a swing-wing plane—a horrible aircraft. The wing commander said, 'Why don't you be the test pilot of tactical air command?' When they build a new airplane they make a book on what it will do and what it won't do. It was my job at Nellis to make that book. Then one of my good buddies said, 'How would you like to go to Laos?' That is where the CIA ran the war."

Parks accepted the assignment with the spy agency. Much of what he did in that time frame is still classified as a government secret, but there is no doubt he was involved in high-risk, life-or-death situations as both a pilot and a major decision-maker. He was granted multiple Purple Heart awards for his service.

After the assignment with the CIA was completed, he returned to Las Vegas and worked for a short time at a desk job before retiring from the Air Force. He took a job in sales with the MGM Grand Hotel in Las Vegas and also worked in other parts of the country, like Snowmass, Colorado, before returning to Auburn to become the athletic department's pilot, a job he handled for a decade. One of his primary assignments was flying head football coach and athletic director Pat Dye to and from numerous meetings and recruiting trips. Dye only wanted to fly with Parks as the pilot.

"I really enjoyed doing it, but my schedule was tied to Coach Dye's schedule and I was ready for break," Parks says. "I went in to see him one day and said, 'Coach, I need to do something else besides fly.' He said, 'Why, Al? I am happy with your service.' I said, 'Every time you take a vacation I can take a vacation, but if you don't, I can't. I am tied to you.'"

Dye then made Parks a surprising offer. "He said, 'I am going to fire that women's tennis team coach.' He knew I used to play tennis with [basketball coach] Sonny Smith, [baseball coach] Hal Baird, and [P.E. department head] Dennis Wilson every day at noon. He said, 'Why don't you coach the tennis team?' I decided to do it and I enjoyed that. It was a lot of fun. My son was a manager on the football team and he was my manager, too."

In his one season as head coach in 1987, Parks' team finished with a 20-7 record, still one of the best marks in school history, and his players had a lot of fun playing for a coach who brought a dynamic and upbeat personality to the job.

Living in Auburn with his wife, Floyd, Parks notes that he is enjoying his retirement. In addition to liking life in the college town, the location is ideal because it is not too far from his three children and their families. One son, Lee, is an attorney in Atlanta, his daughter, Jody, is a computer specialist in Huntsville, and his other son, Mike, is a banker in Birmingham.

The quarterback says he thoroughly enjoyed his time at Auburn as a student, an athlete, and later a pilot and coach. He says that having the opportunity to play on Jordan's first team is a special memory.

"Coach Jordan was the first great coach of our era," he says. "He came in and knew what he wanted to do. There was great excitement from everybody when he came. He was such a gentleman. He could run you to death up and down the field and you would still love him. I am glad I got to play football for him."

Chapter 19

KEN RICE

THE RELUCTANT RECRUIT

It would be hard to find a former Auburn athlete—or any graduate—who has a stronger love for his alma mater than Ken Rice. The All-America tackle is one of the best players to ever suit up for the Tigers, but had it not been for others' major persuasion, Rice would have never played a down of football at Auburn.

Recruiting Rice to Auburn was work, and once he arrived on campus as a freshman, the job wasn't finished.

"It was very tough for me adjusting to college," says Rice, who grew up in a tiny town with scarcely more people than he found in some of his freshman classes.

"I had never been away from home," Rice notes. "It was very tough on a country boy to come over to the big city and be around all of these folks. The first year was really an adjustment period. In fact, twice I quit and went home.

"The first time, before I got there, coach [Dick] McGowen was already at my home waiting for me. The next time he just called ahead to my dad and told him that I was on my way and to send me back. It was a tough adjustment for me."

Auburn's coaches wouldn't have bothered retrieving some freshmen. However, they knew Rice, with a rare combination of size, speed, and athleticism, was special. The staff's judgment was obviously good, as Rice became a major contributor the first year he could play varsity football as a sophomore in 1958.

"I was born in a little town in South Georgia that most people have never heard of called Attapulgus," Rice says. "It is right on the Florida line, right there in the southwest corner of Georgia. I got interested in sports, and football in particular, in 1950. I had an older brother who was going into the ninth grade. He wanted to play football. Attapulgus didn't have a team, so we moved to Bainbridge where they did have a team. He was on the varsity and I began to play junior varsity. That was my introduction to organized football."

It didn't take long for Rice to show what he could do. He became a four-year high school standout in football, basketball, and baseball, as well as track and field. He was a three-time state champ in the shot put and won the discus title once. It's not every day you see a 260-pounder running sprints, but Rice competed in the 100, 220, 440, and 4x110 relay, along with the high jump and long jump.

"In high school, I started playing football in August," Rice recalls. "Coaches would give me a week off when football was over before I started practicing and playing basketball. As soon as basketball was over I went right into track and baseball. Even after school was over we were still playing some baseball. Sports took every waking hour in my high school career."

When Rice, the team's fastest and largest player, was moved to fullback as a junior, his coaches told him that he was on track to play at the next level. "The thought of going to college never crossed my mind," he says. "No one in my family had ever gone to college."

McGowen, head coach of Auburn's freshman team, got a tip about Rice from a Bainbridge coach. "Coach McGowen never saw me play a single football game, and in those days they didn't have any film of high school games," Rice notes. "He came to watch me play basketball and he said the reason he offered me a scholarship was that he saw me stand under the basket and dunk a basketball. He knew then I was a football player."

However, it took more than a scholarship offering to convince Rice to attend Auburn, also known as API in that era.

"When I was a junior in high school, we used to play Thomaston in football," he says. "They had a super crackerjack quarterback over there, a kid named Bryant Harvard. Bryant was a year ahead of me, and for some reason, his senior year he chose to go to this little school, API. I said to myself, 'Why in the world is a guy like that, who could go to Georgia or

Ken Rice was an All-American for coach Shug Jordan (right).
Draughon Library Archives

Georgia Tech or Florida or Tennessee, going to API?' It was the first time I had ever heard of Auburn.

"I anticipated Georgia was where I would probably end up. Florida State wanted me to go down there, but it wasn't too far removed from being a girls' school at that time. It was about 20 miles from home and I didn't think I wanted to go there. Tennessee and Georgia Tech offered me scholarships."

In that era, alumni were allowed to help with recruiting, and McGowen enlisted the aid of Dr. Herman Jones, a 1926 Auburn graduate. "He was head of the state crime lab in Atlanta," Rice says. "I think on four different occasions that man got up early on Saturday mornings and drove from Atlanta to Bainbridge, 220 miles, to take me to games. In those days there were no expressways. They were two-lane roads."

Rice's first road trip with the Auburn recruiter was to Gainesville to see the Tigers play Florida, and the last was to Birmingham, where the Tigers closed the season with a 34-7 win over Alabama.

"The weekend we played Alabama, he drove from Atlanta to Bainbridge to Birmingham and then retraced his steps," Rice recalls. "It seemed to me that if this man loved Auburn this much to do these things for me, there had to be something good about it. Between Dr. Jones and Coach McGowen, they were the ones that convinced me that Auburn was where I truly needed to be."

YEAR AND CAREER TO REMEMBER

Despite trying to go home during his freshman season, 1957 turned out to be a memorable year for Rice. Auburn won its first national championship that fall and the freshman began building relationships that are still strong a half-century later.

"Auburn has been my life," he says. "I came in August of '57. [1960 All-American] Ed Dyas, [future associate athletic director] Buddy Davidson, and I all showed up the same day and have remained good friends through all of these years.

"I also moved in with a couple of pretty good roommates. My upperclassman roommates were [star running back] Tommy Lorino and [starting quarterback] Lloyd Nix. To this day, we are still good friends. Within two years at Auburn I met my wife, Billie Ann, and we were married 48 years ago. My whole life, my whole beginning, really showed up down there as a 17-year-old kid, and Auburn took care of it from there."

Rice played on a talented freshman team that was good enough to provide a test for a varsity that finished undefeated that fall. "I always kid those guys that I made them what they were because we got to play against them every day," Rice says.

In the fall of 1958, Rice got his chance to play tackle for the varsity and became an immediate contributor. "We didn't lose a game that year, but we got tied by Georgia Tech," he says. "My two roommates were still there and my best friend at Auburn, Cleve Wester, was there, so it was a good, good year.

"We had what coach [Shot] Senn called the tackle shuffle. There were six of us. In those days, you had to play practically the whole ball game, so the way it worked out my sophomore year, each of us got to play about five minutes in each quarter. We were always fresh and we were always able to beat the other guys down simply because of it. It gave me a chance to ease into college football rather than being thrown in with the wolves, so to speak."

Going into Rice's junior year, the Tigers hadn't lost a game since the one he watched as a recruit at Florida in 1956. The 1959 team was good enough to extend the streak, but it didn't happen. "We went up to Knoxville for the first game. It must have been 110 degrees in the shade that day and we lost 3-0 to Tennessee," Rice says. "Cotton Letner kicked a field goal for them. It was real hard to take. Coach [Shug] Jordan didn't let us forget that. Any time you lost you would have the Toilet Bowl, and he didn't care who you were, you were out there scrimmaging on Monday. Coach Senn would tell you, 'We'll quit when I see blood.'"

The Tigers finished 7-3 and were ranked as high as seventh nationally. Rice was named an All-American and was thrilled when he received the news. "It was probably the greatest day in my life other than the one I got married," he says.

"We were going up to Birmingham to play Alabama, and in those days we would take the train up the day of the game. The week before, I found out I was an All-American. The game was on Saturday and I was going to be on the *Perry Como Show* on Sunday in New York City. Somehow I had to get from Birmingham that Saturday afternoon to New York that night so I could be on television. For a country boy from South Georgia, that was a long stretch. Billie Ann and I drove from Birmingham to Atlanta. I took the plane that night and I was on the show the next day. Staying up there in the big city and being on national television, that was really a thrill."

Auburn finished 8-2 Rice's senior season. The Tigers were ranked as high as eighth. Rice was named an All-American again and was a player who excited pro scouts.

Pat Dye, an All-American at Georgia who later became head coach at Auburn, says Rice was a special player who belongs in the College Football Hall of Fame. "I played against Ken for four years, and there is not a more deserving player who ever played in the SEC to be in the Hall of Fame," Dye says. "He was big and fast—just a great player on both sides of the football. On top of that, he is an even better person than he was a player."

THE GAME OF MY LIFE
BY KEN RICE

In those days Georgia Tech would not play us unless we came to Atlanta and played them at Grant Field, so we would take the train up to Atlanta the day of the game. Tech had scored early in that 1958 game but had missed the extra point, and they were up 6-0.

We had a young quarterback that year by the name of Bobby Hunt. We were driving about 30 or 40 yards and finally got to around the 10-yard line and came up with fourth down. A field goal was not going to win the game, so we had to score a touchdown. In those days, there was a penalty called "coaching from the sidelines," which was a five-yard penalty, so the coach was not allowed to tell the quarterback what play to call or anything else.

Bobby was a sophomore. He sort of puckered up and he looked over at me. I was right tackle and Joe Leichtnam was right end, G.W. Clapp was left guard and Wayne Frazier was the center. He looked at me and I told him, "Bobby, run the dive. We can get him in there." Bobby called the play, faked a handoff, kept it at the end, and scored the touchdown. Bobby, later on, had to open his mouth and tell Furman Bisher about it, and it wound up in the newspaper. I became offensive lineman of the week for *Sports Illustrated* because of that story. It wasn't Ken Rice. It was Joe Leichtnam, it was G.W., it was Wayne, it was Bobby, it was Auburn. But I guess that is the game that made me feel like I maybe had a future. That was my coming-out party. I will always remember that, being a Georgia boy. I never lost to a Tech team, and that was important to me, although we tied them once. We lost just once to Georgia.

The Tech game was a big rivalry then because [coach] Bobby Dodd wouldn't leave Atlanta to play us, and he flat out told Coach Jordan, "If you want to play us, you have to come up here." Our game at Georgia Tech became an institution. The train would stop in Auburn around 6:30 a.m. or seven o'clock the day of the game. We would get on the train and all of the students who were going would get on, and then every stop between Auburn and Atlanta our fans would get on the train.

By the time we got to Atlanta we had it loaded with fans, and we would literally take over North Avenue with our people. Coach Dodd always said he loved to see Auburn come to Atlanta because win, lose, or draw, they were the best fans and best crowd he ever had.

PLAYING FOR DOLLARS AND BILLS

Rice graduated from college in 1963, a little later than scheduled, but had a good reason. He was the No. 1 player chosen in the AFL's draft, so he was only able to take classes part-time while becoming established as a pro. He was also selected by the St. Louis Cardinals in the first round of the NFL's draft as the No. 8 overall pick.

"After being the first player drafted in 1961, I got the real big money," Rice says with a laugh. "I got a signing bonus of $2,500 and the salary was $12,500, so I got $15,000 for a year of playing football."

However, he notes it was an exciting offer. "For a kid from South Georgia, that was big bucks, but in this day and time that is nothing. They throw more away than that on a weeknight. With the two leagues, I had a choice. With the American League being the new league, I thought I would have an opportunity to play quicker with Buffalo. And I did. They made me the starting left tackle."

Playing time, even as a rookie, was no problem for Rice. "In those days we only had 32 players on the team, which was a league rule," he says. "We only had one extra offensive lineman and one extra defensive lineman. During the season one offensive lineman got hurt, so there was no coming out. Then two defensive guys got hurt and they came to me and said, 'Can you play defensive end?' I said, 'I played both ways in college, so I can do it.'

"The last four games, I was the starting left offensive tackle and I was the starting right defensive end. I was also on the punting team, the kickoff team, and the field goal team. When they blew the whistle, I played; when they stopped blowing the whistle, I was still there.

"I went into that season at 255 pounds and I came home at 228. I was in the best shape I had ever been in during my life. That was my indoctrination into the pros. It was a real eye-opener, but it was fun."

Rice played in the AFL's first all-star game his rookie year. He moved west to play for the Oakland Raiders in 1964 and '65, and notes he really enjoyed being part of Al Davis' team before ending his career after two seasons with the Miami Dolphins.

"Like everybody after they finish playing, I thought I would be a coach," Rice says. He talked to Jordan and other coaches who offered jobs, but they also told him that he would have to be willing to be mobile to advance in the business. "I had been moving around for seven years in pro football and I was tired of it," he says. "I was ready to settle down and wasn't ready to make that commitment."

Rice then checked into being a high school teacher and coach, but decided the salary was too low to support a family. "I knew Tom Cousins, the developer up in Atlanta, because his wife Ann was the daughter of Ralph Draughon, the Auburn president," he says. The former Tiger asked Cousins if he had any openings, and was in luck when the developer offered him on-the-job construction training at a housing project. Rice learned a lot about the business there and took another assignment managing construction of an apartment complex.

After that he worked for a new mortgage company Cousins started, but too much travel convinced Rice to change his career. "I left after a year and I started my own construction company, building homes and light commercial," he notes. "That is basically what I have been doing until eight years ago, when I started doing development work selling off residential lots."

Rice and his wife developed a love for Lake Martin near Auburn when they were students. They have a house there, as well as a home at Big Canoe in north Georgia. A regular at games, Rice says seeing the Tigers in person and spending time with former teammates and others is special. "Auburn is my life," he says. "It gave me my friends, it gave me my family, and it gave me my occupation. I went over there as a 17-year-old and it has been my love ever since."

Chapter 20

QUENTIN RIGGINS

A QUICK LEARNER

Although he got a bit of a late start in athletics, by the time Quentin Riggins arrived in college he looked like he had been playing linebacker since he was in diapers. An immediate impact player as a true freshman in 1986, Riggins, who always seemed to be at the right place at the right time, was a major contributor to three SEC championships and a key member of the 1988 team, which featured one of the most talented defensive units in Auburn history.

"I never thought about playing football when I was young," he remembers. "One day I went and watched my brother play at Georgia Washington Junior High School in seventh grade and it just struck me. I said, 'I need to do that.' I hadn't been playing any type of organized sports before that."

Quentin's brother, Marlon, who is a year older, was a defensive back, safety, and halfback—and a good one. "It was kind of a big brother syndrome with me," Riggins explains. "His interest became little brother's interest and took off from there."

It didn't take long for the younger brother to develop a passion for the game. "I just jumped right in," he says. "There was no big learning curve. It was real interesting. It was contagious—not so much the sports part of it, but being on the team, in the locker room, in the huddle, and being around guys from different backgrounds and interests. That is what I really liked."

After getting a taste of competition in football, the future Tiger decided to compete in basketball and track. "As I got older, I quickly realized I wasn't a track guy and I wasn't a basketball guy," he says. "When I got to Lee High School, what stuck was football."

As a 10th grader, Riggins played tailback and was an old-fashioned, straight-on placekicker. The Generals, who had previously been one of the powers in Alabama high school football, were struggling when Riggins joined the team. "I think we went 1-9, 2-8, or something like that," he recalls. "We were just a very bad team.

"Spence McCracken came in to coach us when I was in the 11th grade. He just walked into the weight room and watched film on everybody. He said to me, 'Hey, you are not a tailback. You are a linebacker—a middle linebacker—and I am moving you today at practice. Good luck.' After that, I played linebacker. I stayed as a kicker. I kicked field goals and kicked off."

McCracken, one of the most successful coaches in the state, knew what he was talking about when it came to Riggins, who developed into a prospect at his new position. In addition to Auburn, Riggins was recruited by North Carolina State, Memphis, Georgia Tech, Texas A&M, Southern Miss, and others, along with UT-Chattanooga, where his brother was playing football.

"It was like night and day when Spence took over the team at Lee," Riggins says. "What he instilled in us is that we were winners, and if we worked hard enough and competed it would pay off in the end. Everything about him was work ethic. Spence always believed we could win on the field and we started seeing that."

Lee won the area championship when Riggins was a junior and senior. "After I left, they won the state championship," he notes.

Auburn had several advantages in recruiting Riggins. In addition to being close to Montgomery, former Lee assistant coach James Daniel was assigned to convince Riggins to play for Pat Dye's team. "We just hit it off," the linebacker remembers. "I didn't go to any camps or anything like that. I didn't know anything about camps. After practice and after school I always went to work at McDonald's. I only went to one game at the major college level. It was Bo Jackson's first game against Southwestern Louisiana. I went to Auburn for an official visit and I went to Memphis for an official visit, and that was it."

Riggins notes his parents were supportive of the boys playing sports, but kept a close watch on their activities. "My dad had a neat trick," he says. "My parents worked out of town and he always wanted to know where we were going to be at all times, so when we hit 16 we went to work. I went to work for McDonald's and worked there until I went to Auburn.

Quentin Riggins (41) was a four-year contributor for the Tigers.
Auburn University Media Relations

"When I got home from work on a night shift on the weekdays at 10:00 or 10:30, my dad would be there waiting on me to go through my homework and would say, 'Let's finish it before you go to bed.' It was just a natural routine."

A GOOD FIRST IMPRESSION

Riggins was excited about signing with a program that was winning a lot of games. He arrived on campus as a 5-foot-11, 200-pounder who didn't take long to impress linebacker coach Reggie Herring and defensive coordinator Wayne Hall.

Riggins says he thought he was in good shape when he reported to campus, but he wasn't prepared for the intensity he found. He adjusted quickly, although he lost 10 pounds in the process during preseason. But that didn't matter as much to the coaches as what Riggins did between the white lines.

"With Coach Herring you always knew where you stood," Riggins says. "He would get so pumped up when you made a play. You just always played that next play hoping you would hit that button that would get him excited about you, and I did.

"I remember the very first short-yardage scrimmage. It was the second-team defense against the first-team offense. For some reason that had to do with attrition, I was running with the second team on the goal line that day. I just slipped through a little crack and popped [tailback] Tim Jessie in the backfield on fourth and one on the goal line. Before I hit the ground, Wayne Hall and Reggie Herring were congratulating me. That is when I figured out I had arrived."

A strong preseason got Riggins on the field opening day as Auburn defeated Chattanooga 42-14. He can recall that game for several reasons. "I played on all of the special teams that day. The very first tackle I made was on the punt team going into our student section in the south end zone. My brother was actually on the field for Chattanooga and he clipped me into the ball carrier. He got a penalty for that and they marked it off after the tackle."

Later in the game, Riggins saw action at linebacker. He developed into a key backup on the team, which finished 10-2.

Although he didn't start as a sophomore, Riggins played a major role for a team that finished 9-1-2 on its way to winning the SEC. "I probably played as much as a starter that year," he says. "I backed up Eddie Phillips at mike linebacker and played sam linebacker as well, where I backed up Kurt Crain. After the third defensive series, I rotated in and I stayed in until the fourth quarter unless we had a pretty good handle on it. Out of 60 snaps, I would easily get 30 to 40 snaps in the rotation."

The linebacker's most memorable game in 1987 was AU's 27-11 win at Georgia. "Wayne Hall had looked at film and saw that Ole Miss had run a 5-3 defense against Georgia's running attack. He wanted to slip it in. We had never run it before, so he took out a strong safety and put me in the game. They had never seen me on the field at the same time with Kurt and Eddie. Our plan was to blitz them on the weak side. I blitzed for just about four quarters and I think I had three tackles for losses against the quarterback, Jackson."

As a junior, Riggins earned All-SEC honors with 120 tackles on a defense loaded with standouts. AU finished 10-2 and won another SEC title.

"That was the best defense I played on," he says. "It was so easy standing in there behind Tracy Rocker, Benji Roland, and Ron Stallworth.

I will never forget the 7-6 loss to LSU when we just played lights out. We could just see everything coming to us. We were just a play away from winning.

"I remember the Florida game down at Gainesville that year. I think we could still be playing and they still wouldn't have scored yet. We were just so prepared. We could see what they were doing. Emmitt Smith was out that day and Willie McClendon was the tailback. We just ate him up."

Riggins' senior season was another memorable one as he earned All-SEC honors with 165 tackles, a total no AU player has matched since. Although the defense wasn't as dominating, the Tigers finished 10-2 again and won a third straight SEC title. The linebacker finished his AU career with victories over rivals Georgia and Alabama, followed by a 31-14 bowl game whipping of Ohio State in Tampa.

That Alabama game, first ever in the Iron Bowl series to be played at Auburn's home field, is still considered the most intense atmosphere for any football game in Auburn history.

THE GAME OF MY LIFE
BY QUENTIN RIGGINS

Anybody who was on our 1989 team who walked down Tiger Walk that day from Sewell Hall to the stadium will tell you that, by far, that was the best thing about the whole season. The 1989 Alabama game was one we were playing for other players—the Zeke Smiths of the world, who didn't get a chance to play this game at home against Alabama, guys like Tucker Frederickson and Freddie Smith, all of those outstanding guys.

In 1989, Homer Smith was Alabama's offensive coordinator and Alabama had an outstanding offensive game plan, an outstanding scheme, in which the tight end and the fullback were the leading receivers. Everything looked the same. We couldn't cheat. We couldn't line up and expect a run out of this formation or a pass out of that formation. We had to beat them straight up. We ran a lot of 52 with cover three behind it and just lined up. We didn't blitz. We just tried to beat them man to man.

I remember the student section and how we fed off of that energy. I remember Alexander Wright making the big early catch on third down and Reggie Slack just putting the football downfield perfectly. I remember the poise that Slack had. He would always come to the sideline and say, "Defense, just give us a three and out and we will get it right." It was just a confidence that he brought to the team.

I remember watching Shayne Wasden catching a little seam route from Slack. If it wasn't for Keith McCants running him down from the backside he would have scored, but we just started feeling the momentum from that point. [Alabama running back] Siran Stacy couldn't get going. He was frustrated, yelling at his offensive linemen. We just got after them.

It was the most intense atmosphere I have ever played in. We could see things in Alabama's first score. We saw it coming, but we were just out of position. We should have made the play. Once we stopped them, we felt like they couldn't move the ball on us. We were just absolutely confident that they couldn't move.

When we got in the locker room at halftime, we made some little adjustments. The coaches said, "When you see this formation, they are going to run the little pick plays. Just pass it to the next guy." And that is what we did.

After the game in the locker room, it was really interesting hearing the fans yelling, "It's great to be an Auburn Tiger!" My only regret is that we didn't go back out on the field to thank the fans, but you could just hear them. It was just a tremendous feeling.

A LESS SATISFYING EXPERIENCE

Riggins won the respect of Dye, and the feeling was mutual. "What was remarkable about Coach Dye is that he remembered details about you and would share different stories on Thursday night and Friday night with the team and you would think, 'I didn't know that about Reggie Slack,' or 'I didn't know that about Craig Ogletree.' He wanted you to know that you were playing with a person, not just a jersey. He never wanted you to forget that there was a special person in that jersey."

Riggins was considered too small to play in the NFL, but wasn't ready to put away the pads after college. "For some odd reason, I decided to play Canadian and World League Football," he says with a laugh. "It was a huge drop off from playing on our level. People play for different reasons. They weren't playing because they loved the game. They were playing for money and they could not care less about their teammates. Some of them did, but others did not. I quickly decided that I wanted to leave liking the sport. We won the Grey Cup [league championship] when I was in Canada in 1990."

Riggins says that, after his great experience with football at Auburn, Winnipeg was disappointing. "It was cold and the general manager was just a bad guy—genuinely a bad guy. He didn't play the best players. To me, he didn't have the team's best interest at heart. It was about the organization.

"It gave me a real good dose of what the business side of the sport is about. I just went and told the general manager, 'This is not what I want to do. You are not being fair to people and I don't want to be a part of any organization that is not fair to people.'"

After playing one season for the Raleigh-Durham Skyhawks in a new summer league that quickly folded, the linebacker decided two unsatisfying years of pro football was enough. He returned to Auburn, finished his degree, and took a job with the Alabama Department of Revenue.

He later returned to the university, where he took a position with the Office of Student Affairs. "I did that for about three years before I got pulled into politics," he notes. "I am senior vice president for governmental affairs for the Business Council of Alabama. I enjoy doing it. You still have some people to deal with, like the Winnipeg Blue Bombers, people who are embarrassing, but you can't just leave it to them. Maybe I packed it in too early in Winnipeg and should have stayed around and been an example of what was right. Now I want to hang around and do what is right in politics if I can."

In order to stay close to political action, Riggins lives in Montgomery with his wife, Kimi, and their eight-year-old daughter, Madison, who also knows daddy as her softball team's coach.

During football season, the linebacker is a well-respected radio sideline reporter for The Auburn Network. However, it took some convincing to get him to try it. Mike Hubbard, once general manager of the network, talked Riggins into working a game in 1990 after the CFL season was done. A year later, he became a regular on the broadcast crew.

Riggins says he enjoys being around a new generation of players, particularly guys who put their heart and soul into playing their best down after down. A defensive player at heart, Riggins notes that he really enjoys interacting with AU defensive coordinator Will Muschamp and other members of Tommy Tuberville's staff.

"I love them," he says. "Will Muschamp reminds me so much of Reggie Herring. He has so much excitement and energy and is such a perfectionist. He is scary bright. I love Eddie Gran. I just admire how he has dealt with the challenges in his life, handled them, and excelled. I like how Coach Tuberville is straight up and honest. He doesn't pretend. What you see is what you get."

Riggins says he still gets excited when returning to campus. "Auburn is the place where I got a chance to go from being the guy who sat at the back of the classroom and knew the answer but was too shy to share it or raise his hand to a guy who is not afraid to walk into the governor's office and sit down and talk policy matters with him. Auburn is where I learned to be a productive person. I loved the fact that I got to meet my best friend Craig

Ogletree there and a guy like [wide receiver] Pedro Cherry. It was a special time for me, and every time I go back I don't forget that."

Chapter 21

GERALD ROBINSON

BIG FISH IN SMALL POND

Little Notasulga, a tiny town in Macon County less than a half hour drive west of the Auburn campus, has a long history of producing talented athletes. The most successful of the bunch was Gerald Robinson, who became an All-SEC player for Pat Dye's Tigers and later a defensive end in the NFL.

Robinson played sports year-round, looking to follow in the footsteps of his older brother Willie, a star football and basketball player for the Notasulga High Blue Devils. Gerald accomplished that assignment and more. He dominated on the football field and was a standout in both basketball and track and field.

Robinson became the focus of a recruiting battle between two College Hall of Fame coaches, up-and-coming Dye and Bear Bryant, who was nearing the end of his career at Alabama.

"When I was in 10th grade, I started getting recruited by colleges like Auburn and Alabama," Robinson recalls. "That is when I figured out I had a chance at being a pretty good athlete. My friends all played football, so to hang out with my friends I played every sport. We were such a small school that we needed everybody to play everything. We had 34 people in our senior class, which may still be the largest in school history, so you can see our school was very small."

Robinson notes that, as a youngster, he wanted to be like his big brother. "Willie was a great athlete and a big influence on me. I think he might have been good enough to play pro football if he wanted to do that.

"He had offers to accept scholarships to attend college, but he turned them down to go into the service to fight in the Vietnam War. He chose that over college. He is 6-foot-4, about 250 pounds, and rock solid. My brother is hardcore and a tough guy."

Little brother, who could toy with most of the small school athletes he faced, was an impressive physical specimen himself. Making the adjustment to college football easier was the fact that Robinson arrived with a strong work ethic, essential for success in Dye's program. Physical and emotional maturity helped him to become an immediate contributor as a freshman in 1982.

"My parents were an especially big influence on me, teaching me how to be an adult," Robinson says. "They were good teachers. They taught me how to make a living in life. They taught me to never quit. They always told me to 'shoot for the stars, and even if you don't reach them, you can still be successful.'"

When it came time to choose a college, Robinson decided to make the short trip to Auburn for a variety of reasons. "It really was an easy decision because Auburn was so close to home and it is a great university," he says. "I knew I wanted my mom to watch me play every Saturday, and I knew she could be there without having to fly and drive all over the place. After I talked to Coach Dye, I knew there was no doubt about where I was going to school.

"I think it was a perfect time to come to Auburn," he adds. "It was Coach Dye's second year and I came in as part of what I think was the best recruiting class to ever come to Auburn, with guys like Bo Jackson, Steve Wallace, myself, and many others. We had a lot of guys in our class get drafted into the NFL. I think that 1982 class got Auburn jumpstarted back into national prominence."

TURNAROUND TIME FOR TIGERS

Dye and his assistants had no doubt when they signed Robinson that he could be special. A 6-foot-4, 215-pounder who ran very well, was physical, and wanted to be good, Robinson's report for preseason drills was eagerly anticipated by AU's coaches.

"Coming to Auburn as a freshman was probably one of the most exciting times of my life, but it was also one of the most nerve-racking times of my life," Robinson recalls. "Going from playing in front of 200 or

---

Gerald Robinson was a big-play defender for the Tigers in the 1980s.
Auburn University Media Relations

300 people on Friday nights at Notasulga High to playing in front of 80,000 people at Jordan-Hare Stadium, I can't explain the feeling I had." However, it didn't take him long to make the adjustment.

Robinson impressed his coaches enough to play immediately as he contributed to Auburn's 28-10 opening-day victory over Wake Forest. "I remember coach [Joe Whitt] calling my name about 50 times to go into the game, and I was thinking, 'Who, me? Who, me?' But once I stepped on the field, it was a done deal. I never questioned my ability to play football at the college level even though I had come from a small school.

"I did question my ability to achieve academically. I wasn't sure I was prepared for Auburn coming from a little Class A school. I was concerned they hadn't taught me enough to be successful at Auburn. It was a slow start for me academically, but I hung in there and I eventually got my degree."

On the field, Robinson and his talented freshman teammates made a huge difference. The year before they arrived, Dye's first Auburn team finished 5-6 overall and 2-4 in SEC. In 1982, the Tigers improved to 4-2 in the SEC and 9-3 overall, with a victory at the Tangerine Bowl in Orlando over Boston College, led by future Heisman Trophy winner Doug Flutie.

Playing outside linebacker in a 4-3 defense, Robinson quickly established himself as a big-play guy. An athlete who would later move to end as he grew, Robinson played in numerous memorable games. One of his favorites was during his freshman year, when the Tigers defeated Alabama 23-22 to end a losing streak that had begun against the Tide in 1973.

"Beating Alabama is something that really stands out from my first season," he says. "That is probably the most exciting game I played in my whole life, counting both college and pros.

"I will never forget when I went to visit Alabama on a recruiting trip and I sat in Bear Bryant's office and I talked to him. "He said, 'Don't go to that cow school. They will never beat us,' and blah, blah, blah. And then Coach Dye came to my house a little while later and told me, 'We are going to change things at Auburn. Do you want to be a part of it?'

"I liked Coach Dye's motivational approach and to me, Bear was a little arrogant. When we beat them my freshman year, it was the most exciting time of my life."

Robinson and his teammates kept on winning. In 1983, the Tigers finished 11-1 as SEC Champions. Their only loss was a 20-7 setback to Texas in game two, and many people believe by the end of the year the Tigers were the nation's best team. Auburn finished 9-4 Robinson's junior season and 8-4 in 1985, as he established himself as one of the top defensive players in the Southeastern Conference his senior year.

THE GAME OF MY LIFE
BY GERALD ROBINSON

One that sticks out was the Florida State game my junior year. We won 42-41 in 1984. I had back-to-back sacks at the end of the game to clinch the win and a blocked field goal in that game. I just had an all-around productive game. It was at Florida State and it was a wild game, a wild atmosphere that night. I will never forget that one.

It really got started when the Seminole mascot came riding out to midfield on horseback and then came over in front of our bench and threw his spear down into the ground. The crowd went crazy, but I don't know why they did that. It fired me up even more to get ready for that game. Once I saw that, it was wartime. That was an exciting night.

There were a lot of big plays in that game and some unusual ones. One of the best ones was a bloop kickoff by Florida State that we fumbled. Eddie Graham picked it up on a big bounce. He grabbed it on the run and ran it back all the way for a touchdown.

I also remember celebrating the win with all of the players who came in with me in our freshman class—great guys like Jeff Lott, Rob Shuler, Tommie Agee, Tim Jessie, Randy Stokes, and a lot of others. We had a great time together. That game was so much fun to play in.

ONTO THE NFL

Robinson had steadily added size and muscle during his four years in college. As a senior he was a very impressive looking 6-foot-4, 254 pounds, and the pro scouts gave him their seal of approval. He was chosen by the Minnesota Vikings as the 14th player selected in the first round of the 1986 NFL Draft.

The Auburn star played 10 years of pro football, including three seasons with the Vikings, two with the Chargers, and five years with the Rams. Robinson says he enjoyed the pro game, but admits it was frustrating at times, even though he quickly proved he could play at that level. He was named NFL Player of the Week as a rookie after making three sacks in one game.

"The thing about my pro career that was disappointing to me was that I was hurt a lot," Robinson points out. "My first year, I broke my leg. The second year, I tore my ACL. The third season, I missed the whole year completely because of my ACL. My fourth year, I missed half a season because I had a cartilage injury.

"My first four years in the NFL were filled with injuries. I think most people would have been out of the league after all of that happened to them, but I thank God I was able to play six more years without injuries. My NFL career didn't turn out the way I wanted it to be, because I wish I had been healthier, but that is one of those things you can't do much about as a player.

"I weighed around 250 as a senior in college, but the pros wanted me to be bigger to play defensive end in the NFL," says Robinson, who notes his average weight throughout the NFL was around 265 pounds. "I think that was part of my problem in the pros. They wanted me to get a lot bigger and I gained too much weight too fast and my body wasn't used to it."

After putting in a decade in the NFL, Robinson returned to Auburn and finished his degree. He then took a position with the Boys and Girls Clubs in the Atlanta area. "I have been doing that, taking care of my family, raising kids, and coaching my son in baseball and football and enjoying life," he notes. "Right now I am taking some time off and taking it easy, spending more time with my family."

Only a couple of hours away from Auburn, he returns to his alma mater to watch several games each fall. "I try to support the team," says Robinson, who notes that he really enjoyed his time at AU.

"It's truly a humbling feeling, playing for Auburn. I don't know of any university that has the great camaraderie that Auburn has. When you meet Auburn people all over the world, it is just a different feeling. There is a lot of love in the air when Auburn people say, 'War Eagle.' It means something to them."

Chapter 22

BENJI ROLAND

UGA'S LOSS IS AUBURN'S GAIN

Growing up "country strong" in the central Georgia town of Eastman, Benji Roland became one of the standout defensive players in the decade of the 1980s, a period that featured some of the best defensive teams in Auburn history. Roland was a major part of that success as a four-year contributor for Pat Dye's teams, which won SEC Championships his junior and senior seasons.

An athletic lineman who stood out even in an era when the Tigers had lots of players who fit that description, Roland got an early start in sports. "Growing up in a small, southern town, there was a lot of community involvement and we played sports throughout the year," he notes. "Whatever was in season, I was playing it. I started playing football in a league for five- and six-year-olds. I really enjoyed it, and then I started getting a little size on me and I became pretty good at it."

Roland, whose father worked for Stuckey's Candies, moved to Albuquerque, New Mexico, and later to Swainsboro in Georgia when his dad was transferred, but spent most of his youth in Eastman. "I grew up in Eastman and my family is from that area," he says. "My dad was a twin, the youngest in a family of 10. My grandfather was a farmer. On my mother's side of the family they owned the first dairy there. My grandmother would wrap my mom up in a blanket when she was a baby and early in the morning they would deliver milk to families around Eastman.

"Eastman is the county seat and the town is the kind of place where you know everybody," he says. "There are probably 8,000 to 10,000 in the town and we probably had 150 in our graduating class at Dodge County High. If you got a speeding ticket on Friday night they knew it at the coffee shop on Saturday morning. It was a good place to grow up. I am from a small town and I liked the small-town atmosphere of Auburn."

A Reynolds Aluminum plant is located in the area, but Roland says the main industry is farming, something he learned about at an early age. "My best friend, his uncle, and his cousin ran a big farm and we loaded watermelons for $20 a day," Roland remembers. "We would load two or three transfer trailers a day that would come down from the north." He also did other jobs, like setting up irrigation systems and harrowing land. They helped him grow up strong and attract college coaches to Dodge County.

"I was recruited by a lot of teams, like Auburn, Alabama, Tennessee, Georgia, and Notre Dame, but basically being from a small town in the middle of Georgia, which was Bulldog country, I grew up as a Georgia fan," he notes. "I used to go up there on Saturdays for games with my parents, who were Bulldog people. There were not many Auburn fans there in the area.

"Coach Ray Goff recruited me for Georgia," Roland says. "He supposedly started looking at me in eighth grade because there were some alumni there who were friends with him and Dicky Clark, but it really didn't start to dawn on me that I was going to be a college prospect until about 11th grade because that is when you start getting the letters. A lot of them were just form letters, but when I started getting phone calls from Pat Dye, Vince Dooley, Ray Perkins, Bobby Bowden, and people like that, I started realizing I had the chance to move on in my career."

Roland remembers that when the word got out that he and his family were Georgia fans and that Dooley's Dawgs were offering a scholarship, the recruiting attention waned. "I guess everybody thought or assumed I would go the University of Georgia with me being a fan," Roland notes. However, Auburn was not one of the colleges to back off.

"I remember Coach Dye came down to see me, and Frank Orgel is the coach who started recruiting me for Auburn," Roland says. "Coach Orgel took a shot in the dark, I think. He thought he might have a chance and he hung in there through the recruiting process. He was real honest with

---

Benji Roland was a force for the Tigers on the defensive front.
Auburn University Media Relations

me. I came over to Auburn and visited with Coach Dye. I thought they had a program on the rise. I liked what he said. My parents really liked the atmosphere in Auburn. That is why I decided on Auburn."

Roland points out that his decision to spurn the Bulldogs wasn't a popular one. "There was a sign on our street that read, 'This neighborhood has gone to the Dawgs.' It was put up on behalf of [longtime SEC football official] Jimmy Harper, who had actually gone to school at the University of Georgia. One time after I went home after we beat Georgia, we painted it to say, 'But now it belongs to the Tigers.' When Georgia beat us, it was returned to me. A couple of times after we lost to them, people put a couple of hundred pounds of dog food on our driveway.

"I did catch some flak about not going to Georgia, but what people didn't understand was that I was making a decision on where I wanted to go to college for four or five years. I wanted to make the best decision I could, and that was to go to Auburn. If I could do it over again I would do the same thing. It was the best decision of my life to come to Auburn."

OFF TO COLLEGE

After arriving on campus in the summer of 1985, the lineman found the adjustments challenging on and off the field. "When you come to college you feel like you have all of this freedom, but I remember I was real focused on school when I first got there," he says. "Then you get to thinking that in the off-season you don't have a curfew. You really have to be a disciplined person to be successful. There are opportunities, and you see it every year where kids who are great athletes let the academics catch up to them. I struggled academically for a while because I didn't have my priorities right."

A meeting on that subject with the head coach got the freshman's attention. "When Pat Dye gets on you about your academics, it is time to put your priorities back in line," Roland says.

On the field he had to prove himself to a demanding position coach, Wayne Hall, who was also the defensive coordinator. "I was very fortunate. I played for a great guy, Wayne Hall. We didn't always see eye to eye, but I knew he was always looking out for my best interests.

"When we came in as a freshman, we had three or four days prior to the upperclassmen reporting to work with the coaching staff. I was the only defensive lineman Auburn had signed that year, so I could get a pretty good crash course in playing my position. I wasn't as strong as I needed to be, but I was fortunate to be able to play second team as a freshman and not get redshirted. I had a lot of guys up in front of me who really helped me with the mental aspects of the game and the speed of the game. What people don't understand is that in high school, you have one or two guys who are really good athletes who are better than everybody, but when you line up in the SEC, the guy in front of you was a high school All-America-caliber player, too, especially at levels of programs like Auburn, Tennessee, and Alabama.

"It took a while for me to realize the importance of gaining strength," Roland notes. "I had never been a gym rat—a guy who is going to go in there and lift a lot of weights. God gave me a lot of ability and I would just say that I was country strong. At one time, I was the fourth strongest guy on the team. That is not saying that I am hugely strong, but I just had a God-given ability that He gave me. I have some strength there and I don't have to lift a lot of weights.

"It took a while to develop those priorities—making sure I was in the weight room, making sure I was working on my weight, keeping it down, turning fat into muscle, and then transitioning into the speed of the game, the quickness of the game, the strength of your opponents and film study, because you can always pick up something by watching other people on film.

"I was very fortunate to be able to play behind Harold Hallman, who taught me a lot of technique. He helped mentor me along, as did Gerald Williams and Gerald Robinson. Those guys had a lot of games under their belts. They helped the underclassmen develop because that was the future of the program. We did that, too, as we developed as players."

Even though Roland was lanky for a nose guard as a 6-foot-4, 260 lb. freshman, he was able to play immediately because of his natural strength and athletic ability. "Now you have linebackers who weigh that much," he says. "I added some weight and played at 270."

Roland notes he gained more weight before he left college—sometimes too much. "If you caught me around bowl time, I would weigh around 300. I wasn't the most disciplined player, but Coach Hall would get it off me."

The defensive lineman notes that playing for Hall was seldom dull. "Wayne Hall was a moody guy. If he had a bad day, he was going to take it out on the defensive front. We were doing a pass rush drill with Wayne and our offensive line coach, [current UAB head coach] Neil Callaway. Our manager [Anthony Freeman], who we called Boss Hogg, would stand seven yards deep and we would make a move to try to get to him. A lot of times that is how we would get in our conditioning at the end of practices. If we had a good pass rush drill we wouldn't have to run as many sprints.

We would have to touch Boss and run back to the line. It was one thing to get blocked, but don't stay blocked—you had to get off the ground immediately.

"Well, I get by [future NFL player] John Hudson, who is about 280, and he pulls me down from behind. I am trying to get up and sprint back. Wayne has been on my ass all day for something, and as I start back, he starts toward me and we sort of collide. Wayne was a guy who would put his hands on his players. He was a feisty linebacker for Bear Bryant and all of that. Coach Dye always told him, 'If you put your hands on the players, you are on your own.' So actually, Wayne and I got into a fight. We are fighting and cussing. Callaway grabs me and [offensive lineman and future Georgia coach] Stacy Searels gets in between us. Wayne actually reaches over him and rips my helmet off from behind and says, 'Get back in.' I had been starting for years and I said, 'Screw you, I quit.' And I am not a quitter by any means. He started yelling, 'You don't quit on me!' And I said, 'No, I quit.'

"After practice he talked to me and said, 'Look, I just want you to be the best player you can be.' I said, 'Coach, I understand that, but I am a man and if you back me into a corner I am going to fight, so don't put your hands on me.' He did it to Tracy Rocker and Harold Hallman, too. It didn't matter who it was, he would grab you and throw you around. [Team trainer Hub] Waldrop talked to me and I decided to stay. I am not a quitter. I didn't go back in that day, but the funny thing is that we were walking out to practice the next day—me and Coach Hall and Coach Dye were side by side—and Coach Dye says, 'I was pulling for you yesterday, Benji.'

"I said, 'Sir, what do you mean?' Coach Dye said, 'Well, if I have players who can't whip their coach's ass, they aren't going to play for me.'"

Roland, who earned All-SEC and All-America honors, played on teams that lost just nine games in his four seasons. The Tigers played in the Sugar Bowl twice, the Cotton Bowl once, and the Citrus Bowl on the other trip.

THE GAME OF MY LIFE
BY BENJI ROLAND

There are so many games that come to mind. Being from Georgia, you especially want to beat the Bulldogs. I realize Georgia versus Auburn is a super rivalry, but you don't realize what the impact of the Auburn-Alabama game is until you participate in it. I guess the first year I actually got to participate in the Iron Bowl (in 1985), (Alabama kicker) Van Tiffin made the 52-yard field goal to win the game. That sticks in my mind. After you lose a game like that and have to live with it for 365 days, you realize that it means a lot to both universities, the fan base, and the media.

If you look at that game, and (former Tide coach) Mike Shula mentions it a lot, they ran a reverse late in the game. I was in at nose guard as a true freshman. We ran what we call an X-stunt, where the tackle comes inside and I loop outside and have containment. I am sitting there thinking, "It is third or fourth down and if I make this play, we win the game." I sort of got blindsided by Shula, and he still rags me that I got decked by a quarterback. I tell him that it was a clip. It meant a lot to win the following year, but the game that really sticks out is the one that we shut out Alabama 10-0 in 1987. We led the NCAA two years in a row in total defense and rushing defense. To go into Legion Field and shut them out means a lot to me. It was a hostile environment. They used to say it was split 50-50, but that wasn't true. It was a lot more crimson than it was orange and blue.

It also meant a lot to do it playing with great teammates like Tracy Rocker, Aundray Bruce, Nate Hill, Kurt Crain, Eddie Phillips, and the other guys. You bleed and sweat with those guys and it feels great to win what I consider to be the best college rivalry in the country.

There were several keys to the game when we shut them out. One of the biggest plays was when they were fourth and goal with inches to go and we knocked them back. It was a back-and-forth, back-and-forth game. We knew if our offense could get three points we were going to win the game, because we didn't believe they could score on us. I think we had a little arrogance about us. I don't know if it was arrogance or confidence. We knew we were going to play well and whip somebody in front of us. It was just a question of how bad it was going to be. That is something Coach Dye instilled in us.

I think there were different times in the game when Alabama could have gained the momentum, but we were able to stop them. Winning the conference championship that year was special. We won it again the next year, too, when I was a senior.

Our defense was really good in 1987. People don't realize what experience can bring to a football team. If you look at guys like Tracy Rocker, Nate Hill, Ron Stallworth, myself, Aundray Bruce, Kurt Crain, Carlo Cheattom, Tommy Powell—all of those guys—you have got players who have 20 or 30 games under their belt. With the leadership and experience we had on that defense, it was really special. The best way that defense has ever been described—and it was that way in 1988, too—was that we played like we were all chained at the ankle, because when one of us got to the ball, the other 10 were right there behind him.

GOING OUT AS A CHAMPION

Roland finished his playing days at Auburn in 1988 on a team that he believes was the strongest during his time in college. "I really believe we were the best team in the country that year," he says. A maddening last-minute 7-6 loss to LSU in Baton Rouge, known as "The Earthquake Game" because the celebration at Tiger Stadium registered on the Richter scale, kept a national championship from happening.

"If we had won that game like we should have, I believe we would have won them all and beat Notre Dame in the Sugar Bowl and been national champions," he says. "I thought we had a special group of guys. It was just heartbreaking to lose a game like that. LSU couldn't do anything against us for four quarters."

Roland became so fond of Auburn that he still lives there today. "I married a local girl, so I can say that coming to Auburn was a blessing for me, although she might not say that," he says with a smile. "We have three kids.

"After college I was drafted by the Minnesota Vikings in the seventh round. I don't know why they drafted me, because they had the No. 1 defense in the NFL at the time. They released me and they wanted to sign me back to the practice squad to move me to the offensive line because they had just done it the year before with a guy named Brian Habib. Atlanta picked me up off waivers and signed me to the practice squad. Being from Georgia, I would rather be in Atlanta than Minnesota because they know what grits and sweet tea are."

After spending a year in Atlanta, Roland played one season with Tampa Bay before returning to Auburn to finish his degree. He worked as a student assistant coach and later took a job with the city of Auburn. "After I graduated, we didn't have any kids and I decided I wanted to stay in Auburn," he says. "The city was building a new softball complex. I played softball growing up and interviewed for that job and got it, so I ran the softball complex for a couple of years."

Roland then got back into coaching as a graduate assistant on Terry Bowden's Auburn staff for two seasons. "I have always had coaching in my blood and I would do it tomorrow, but I don't want to leave Auburn and it is hard to do that," he says. "I had opportunities to leave and coach, but they were going to pay me $15,000, $16,000, or $17,000 a year. Not that I am saying that I didn't know that I had to break into it somewhere to climb the ladder, but with my wife being pregnant and her family living in

Auburn, I made the decision to get out of coaching and go to work for Price Oil."

Roland switched careers again and for the past 13 years has been in pharmaceutical sales. He is with Bristol-Myers Squibb and his specialty is cardiovascular medicines. He notes he has turned down opportunities to take other positions around the country because he thinks the quality of life in the college town where he played football is so high.

"I still enjoy coaching, but I do it by staying involved in my kids' lives, coaching their teams," he says. "There is a lot more job security in T-ball, coach pitch, and softball than there is coaching at Auburn University. This is a phenomenal place to live and raise my kids and I am glad to be here."

Roland also notes that he enjoys watching the bigger kids arrive on campus every year and grow up as college players. No matter how big they get, few are likely to have more success playing the game than the four-year contributor who lined up in the heart of some of the best defensive teams in Auburn history.

Chapter 23

GEORGE
ROSE

A PEACH OF A PROSPECT

Playing during a period in which the Tigers had a large number of talented two-way players, George Rose was one of the most impressive. Rose, who moved on to a successful career in pro football, had the talent to be a standout in any era of Auburn football.

A heavily recruited high school All-American, Rose attended Glynn Academy in Brunswick, Georgia. Signing the athlete was a recruiting coup for Shug Jordan and his staff. A player who rushed for more than 1,000 yards as a junior and senior, Rose chose Auburn from a group of around 50 colleges who offered scholarships.

"I liked Georgia because I was a Georgia boy, but when Auburn invited me over for a visit, I was really impressed with Coach Jordan and all of the staff," Rose remembers. "I loved Auburn. It was a smaller town. There wasn't a whole lot of hoopla back then. I figured I could go over there and get an education and play some football. Plus, Auburn was No. 1 in 1957. They started recruiting me in 1958 and 1959. I went to their game against Florida when they beat them 6-5 down there, and I was just impressed with them and decided that was where I wanted to go."

Rose developed an interest in sports at a very early age. "I grew up in Brunswick," he says. "I played Little League Baseball and Midget League Football. We had a real good recreation program. I loved football more than I loved the rest of them and I went on from there to high school, to Auburn, and then on to the pros."

Rose is the middle brother of three boys who competed in sports, but he was the only one who played at the collegiate level. He figured out early in high school that he could have a chance to play in college.

"I was always pretty good when I was smaller in Little League Football," he notes. "When I got into high school as a ninth grader, you couldn't play varsity ball. You had to play freshman football. That year they pulled me off the freshman team to run against the varsity in practice, so I figured I must be pretty good.

"I started the next three years at Glynn Academy, which is the high school in Brunswick. I played fullback and defensive halfback. Most players had to play both ways back then. They usually kept the same 11 players out there then until you got tired or got hurt.

"We were undefeated my junior year and lost 12-6 in the state playoffs to LaGrange," he recalls. "They had a running back named Jimmy Burson, who also played at Auburn. They went on and won the state and we were ranked second right behind them."

Rose also started in basketball and was a sprint star in track, but stuck to football in college. Auburn's track coach, Wilbur Hutsell, did give him pointers on how to run faster. "I was just fast naturally and I got faster at Auburn," Rose says. "Coach Hutsell taught me quite a bit about running, about getting everything going in the right direction."

Rose, who had rushed for close to 3,000 yards at Glynn Academy, remembers arriving in Auburn in 1960 surprised at the level of competition, even on the freshman team. "That first year was pretty shocking to a young boy. I think they signed 50 players that year. They didn't have a limit, I think.

"The players were from everywhere and they were all good. You were just one man in the apple pie over there. It makes you find out right quick if you fit in."

The coaches quickly figured out Rose was going to fit in both on the field and in the classroom. "Coach Jordan always required his freshman players to go to study hall, and I think that really helped me," he says. "In high school, you don't always have good study habits. Once I got over to Auburn I was lost like every freshman is, I guess, but we went to study hall every night and, because of that, I didn't have a big problem."

George Rose was a standout for the Tigers in the early 1960s.
Draughon Library Archives

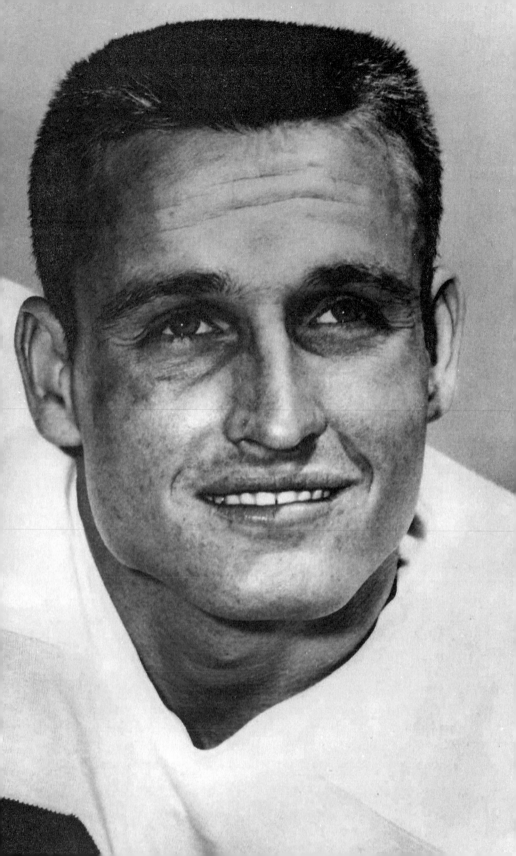

The next fall, Rose moved up to the varsity and saw action on offense and defense. "I played behind Don Machen, who was captain on the 1961 team," Rose says. "I played enough to letter. I ran back the kickoffs and played a little bit of offense and a little bit of defense. I think I did good for my sophomore year, but I didn't excel or play a lot until my junior year.

"My junior year I started getting letters from pro scouts after my third or fourth game. The scouts at Dallas ranked me in the top four or five defensive backs in the country. I had the speed and the ability to cover people man on man and we played mostly man-on-man coverages back then. I was just blessed with the ability to do that.

"I ran back kickoffs and punts that year. Jimmy Burson and I did that. I played left halfback on defense and right halfback on offense. We played a three-deep backfield then. I don't think we ever had a four-deep coverage unless it was a prevent defense."

Rose says he was fortunate to be coached by assistants Billy Kinard and Hal Herring. "Both were very good. Hal went on to the Atlanta Falcons and was coaching there when I was playing with the Vikings. He was a really good defensive coordinator."

Rose put together another big season as a senior, the kind of year that attracted scouts from the NFL and the upstart AFL.

"My senior season was probably our best year," Rose says. "We were 9-1 and were ranked fourth or fifth in the country. We lost to Nebraska in the Orange Bowl 13-7 in a game we could have very easily won. I played with a bunch of great athletes on that team. We had a team that gelled together and worked together really well.

"In the backfield we had Larry Rawson, Tucker Frederickson, myself, and Jimmy Sidle. That was probably one of the best backfields in the nation at that time as far as all-around ability. We moved the ball on everybody and we had a great defensive team. We lost one game to Mississippi State [13-10] by a field goal. We could have very easily won that one. We could have been national champions that year. I believe Texas ended up No. 1 and I think they were 9-1. We ended up No. 5."

THE GAME OF MY LIFE
BY GEORGE ROSE

The Alabama game my senior year when we beat them 10-8 is one that stands out. They had beaten us four years in a row. [Alabama coach] Bear Bryant came out in *The Birmingham News* before the game saying that Auburn would never beat them while he was there. He had to eat those words, because we beat him that year. They had a great team. They were ranked in the top 10, too. They had Joe Namath and a lot of good players.

We had been playing good football all year long going into the game. I remember that team more than any of our other teams, because most of us were real good friends off the football field, too. Jimmy Sidle had a great year, but he got hurt that game and Mailon Kent came in at quarterback and did a real good job. Mailon had started the year before. They had X and Y teams in 1962 to give players a rest, because you played both ways and Mailon had started on one of those. That was his fifth year. He had already graduated, I think. Thank goodness he came back in 1963.

Both teams were good defensively and offensively. It was a real hard-fought game all the way through. I remember Alabama had a good receiver for their quarterback Namath to throw to that year. He was catching some balls on us early, but after the first quarter I just covered him man to man the rest of the game and shut him down.

It was time we beat them and it sure did mean a lot to Coach Jordan. At that time he wasn't getting the respect he deserved. He was one great coach and I am glad I played for him.

NFL SUCCESS, TOO

Those coverage skills were Rose's ticket to a successful pro career. "They had two leagues, the American Football League and the National Football League, and both of them drafted me that year," he says. "I was the 30th player drafted that year by the NFL. There were 14 teams that year, so I was the second player drafted in the third round.

"I was also drafted in the third round by Buffalo in the American Football League. I signed with Minnesota because the AFL had just been formed in 1960 and I wasn't sure they were going to make it. They weren't making a lot of money, but the next year they got that big contract with ABC. That helped them make it and things got better for the AFL.

"I don't have any regrets going to Minnesota," says Rose, who made the NFL's All-Rookie team in 1964. "I went up there and I started my first year and I led the team in interceptions, kickoff returns, and punt returns. I played all 14 games and had a good start.

"I ended up playing six years, but not all at Minnesota. I played three years at Minnesota and started all three years. Then I started at New Orleans in 1967. Then I was a backup in San Francisco in 1968 and 1969."

The defensive back says he has good memories of his days as a pro. "The NFL was the best league at the time and, being a fan all of my life, I remember the first game I played in we went against Johnny Unitas, who

I had been watching on TV all of my life," Rose says. "It was very exciting to be able to get out there and compete against people like him."

Before joining the Vikings, Rose got a test run versus the pros. "I played in the College All-Star Game, which was really my first pro game. We played against the Chicago Bears at Soldier Field. They picked 40 players out of the college ranks and you played against the NFL champions. I played with some great players in that game. I think six or seven are in the hall of fame. Mel Renfro was on that team, Charlie Taylor, Carl Eller. I started at left cornerback. We could have beaten the Bears if we could have driven down and kicked a field goal."

Rose finished his physical education degree in 1966 and put it to use as a coach. "My first year out I coached at Glynn Academy, my old school, and then I went to East Carolina," he says. "Sonny Randle was the head coach there and he had played with me at San Francisco, and he hired me as the head freshman coach. They played freshman football back then. I was there one year and Coach Jordan called me and hired me. I was at Auburn until he retired in 1975. When he retired, they hired Doug Barfield and I was not held over on his staff.

"After that I went into business for myself. I bought a Western Sizzlin' Steakhouse franchise in Bloomington, Indiana. I went up there and opened the steakhouse and stayed there for six or seven years. Then I went home and opened a sporting goods store in Brunswick. I left there and went with Georgia Crown Distributors out of Columbus, Georgia, and I worked in the Auburn and Montgomery areas."

Rose retired in 1995 and lives off the Georgia coast not far from Brunswick on St. Simons Island. He still closely follows the fortunes of the Tigers. "I go back to Auburn and see some of the players I coached, and they turned into great people," he says. "Like all Auburn people, they are great to be around. Just about every game I go back to, I see some of the old guys there."

Rose notes that he really enjoyed his days as a student. "I would say my time in college was four of the best years of my life, being an Auburn Tiger and playing there. I have friends to this day that you don't ever forget. I have a place in Auburn and I love to go back. It is like going home. Most of the players I played with, we stay in touch and we are friends to this day. And we will be until we are gone."

Chapter 24

KENDALL SIMMONS

HE WAS BIG WHEN HE WAS LITTLE

If Kendall Simmons had been a guest on the old TV program *What's My Line?*, the game show's panel could probably figure out what he does for a living without asking many questions.

When Simmons arrived on the Auburn campus as a thickly built, muscular 321-pounder, he already looked like he could be playing football in the NFL. In fact, several of his fellow freshmen assumed he was one of the coaches before they found out he was their teammate.

After a collegiate career as an All-SEC performer and winner of the Jacobs Trophy as the league's best blocker, the offensive lineman makes a living playing professionally.

Growing up in an athletic family in Ripley, Mississippi, Simmons was always a guy his teammates could look up to in more ways than one. A standout in a variety of sports, Kendall wasn't a small guy even when he was young.

"I weighed 140 pounds in the third grade," he notes. "When I say that, you may think I was big and fat, but that wasn't the case. I was just as tall as most of the teachers. I was just a tall, big kid. From first grade all of the way up to the second and third grade, I had to have desks from the fourth and fifth grade rooms because I couldn't fit in the ones in our classrooms."

By the time Simmons was in high school, he was a standout in three sports. "Everybody in my family is athletic to a certain degree," he says. "My mom was a pretty good basketball player in high school, my dad had a chance to play a little semi-pro baseball, and my sisters ran track and played basketball. My brother, who is 13 months younger than me, he played every sport, too.

"I threw the shot put in track, in baseball I played catcher, first base, and right field, and in basketball I did all of the dirty work. Football was always my best sport."

Simmons began youth basketball and baseball as an eight-year-old. His first chance to play organized football was as a fifth grader and he was a natural. By the time he was in the eighth grade, coaches on the high school team needed a big lineman to replace a star player who had quit. Simmons was their pick.

Playing on the offensive and defensive lines, Simmons was discovered as a prospect his sophomore season. "We played Amory, the undefeated state champions, who hadn't been beaten in three years," he says. "They had at least eight guys on each side of the ball who were going to get Division I scholarships. Amory had Joe Gunn, Rufus French, Darius Burns, Chris Rainey, and others. They came to Ripley and played us, and a Tennessee scout was there and several others to see them play.

"My coach told me if I wanted to make a mark for myself with the college coaches, this was the game to do it. He said, 'They are definitely not here to look at anybody on our team.'

"We got beat 65-0, but I had 14 tackles, three sacks, two forced fumbles, and played both sides of the ball. That got me recognized. It was kind of like the turning point for my whole football career."

Simmons, who was also a good student, became a coveted recruit, and Tennessee was his early favorite. "It was Tennessee at first, because that was who was at my school first and that was the school that sent me the first letter I ever got from a college. Also, I loved Reggie White, and when I found out he went to Tennessee, that got my interest. I wore his number in high school.

"This is going to sound bad, but at one point I seriously considered going to Alabama," he says. "My athletic trainer, who was at my high school, was a graduate of Alabama. I kind of looked up to him and I went to some games with him. I had never been anywhere outside of Mississippi, really, so I liked Alabama at first.

"Then coach [Rick] Trickett and coach [Pete] Jenkins from Auburn came into the picture. I just loved Coach Jenkins and I just knew I was going to come to Auburn and be on the defensive line. Coach Trickett kept

---

Kendall Simmons was one of AU's top performers in the 1990s.
Auburn University Media Relations

coming by and kept calling and I was thinking, 'This guy is pretty persistent.' I liked his whole mentality and everything."

The big lineman notes that once he visited Auburn and got to meet the players, he knew that was where he wanted to be.

ALMOST A BIG MISTAKE

Simmons arrived on campus in the summer of 1997 to play for coach Terry Bowden's Tigers. He had been All-State as a junior and senior and, unlike most freshmen, he was physically ready to compete in the SEC.

However, the mental part of college football was tougher. "Man, that was the roughest time I have ever had in my entire life," he remembers. "My first semester I was very, very close to going home. I was having such a hard time. I got thrown right into the fire once I got to Auburn. I didn't start the first game, but after that I was starting for the rest of the season."

The staff decided to play Simmons on offense, and that meant he had to please Trickett, a coach with the personality of a Marine drill instructor. "I was already trying to deal with Coach Trickett, and then having 17 hours of classes was tough," Simmons says.

"My schedule was to spend two hours in study hall after class, and then I would go home and sleep and get up at five or six in the morning to work out. It was just wearing me out. I was just at my breaking point one night and I actually packed my bags to go home.

"I decided to call my momma to tell her I was on the way home and tell her I couldn't deal with this any more because I was too tired to study with Coach Trickett just wearing me out.

"My momma said, 'Remember what you told me about all of the guys growing up around you who could have made something out of themselves and the people in your hometown who said, "Yes you are a good athlete, but you can't play at a Division I school"?'

"That motivated me to stay. I was really close to hitting I-85. It would have taken about four and a half hours to get home. If I had done that, I don't think the coaches would have been able to get me to come back. It would have been the worst mistake I ever made, but that first semester was rough."

On the field, Simmons quickly demonstrated he could be a star. "Football went well," he says. "It was second-nature-type of stuff. Jeno James and Colin Sears helped me get through it. Colin can tell you that Coach Trickett had me talking in my sleep at night, he had me so messed up. He just chewed on my butt so much. I had never been through that. My high school coach only screamed at me a few times.

"One thing I learned about Coach Trickett, if you show him he can't break you, then he loves you to death. If you show even an ounce of weakness, he will keep chewing on you until you are tough enough or gone.

"I put a lot on him getting me ready and making me a better player at Auburn and in the NFL. I felt like if I could deal with what he put me through, nobody else could crack me or even bother me at all. I respect him for that and I still talk to him."

After a stressful start, Simmons' academic situation improved, too. Arriving on campus with art skills, the athlete decided to study the subject. "That is something that my mom and dad did," he says. "We can all draw pretty well. I think my brother and I came out on the long end of it.

"Letting us draw is something my mom did when we were younger in kindergarten and first grade to keep us from tearing up the house. It was kind of hard for her to get things done having two little boys around when she was trying to work. She would bring home school supplies, put us on the floor, and let us draw.

"I also had friends who would draw and we kind of had our own little group to see who could draw the best. Whenever the schools had contests, we would draw things and see who would win. You could get things posted on the wall next to the principal's office and get a little recognition. I didn't have a clue what I wanted to study when I came to Auburn. The only thing I knew that I could be good at was drawing, so I headed on over to the art building and that is what I fell into."

Simmons was part of a strong team his freshman season and assumed that would be the case again in 1998 as a sophomore. However, that didn't happen.

"It was a kind of crazy year at Auburn," he says. "The year before we went to the SEC Championship and we lost to Tennessee by one point. I was thinking, 'This is how college football is supposed to be.' It was exciting and I was playing with all of these big-name guys, like Takeo Spikes. The next year, we still had what should be a pretty good team, but we went 3-8 and Coach Bowden left during the season." The big lineman remembers the news "threw me for a loop.

"We were so messed up as a team that year," he adds. "The offense and the defense weren't getting together and we were pointing fingers. That is something I hadn't been through."

Defensive coordinator Bill Oliver took over as interim coach but was replaced by Tommy Tuberville after the season. Hugh Nall arrived with Tuberville from Ole Miss to become the offensive line coach.

"I had ankle surgery at the end of the year and I was fine, and then we got Coach Tubs and his staff," Simmons says. "It was kind of weird, because when they were at Ole Miss they recruited me hard. I didn't want to go to Ole Miss and I never wanted to go to Ole Miss. I would have gone to Mississippi State before I would have gone to there. I decided I would go out of state if I could go to somewhere bigger and better, but I ended up with Coach Tubs anyway.

"That was a bit of an adjustment for both sides. It took a while for me and Coach Nall to get cruising and now I love him to death."

Simmons started at guard the first three games in 1999 as a junior, but ankle problems cut his season short. He received a medical redshirt and was back in 2000. He moved outside to tackle and was a terrific blocker. "That was a great year," he says. "That is when Rudi [Johnson] came in at tailback and started dominating. We got to the SEC Championship Game again and Rudi was player of the year in the SEC. That was a lot of fun."

In his final season, 2001, the Tigers tied for the SEC West title, but didn't go to the championship game. "My senior year Rudi and Heath [Evans] both left for the pros. We had Carnell [Williams] and Ronnie [Brown], but we just didn't have as much firepower on the team as we did the year before. We got beat by Alabama and that is something that is hard to deal with your senior year when you are playing your last game at home."

Simmons says he made huge strides as a player at Auburn. "I really had a chance to leave for the pros after my redshirt junior year and I seriously considered it," he says. "You have to be careful not to fall into a trap when people are telling you how good you are. I had my progress report sent in to the NFL and it came back telling me that at best I would be a third- to fourth-round pick. Physically, I didn't think I was ready for the NFL coming back from my foot surgeries, but I wanted to see what they said about me. Mentally, I think I could have handled it.

"I think it helped me out to play left tackle my last two years at Auburn, because it showed the [NFL] a little more versatility than just playing guard. I went out there and played against guys like Julius Peppers, Dwight Freeney, and Alex Brown, who are all pro-bowlers, and other guys who are in the league now. That would have been a mistake if I left for the pros after my junior year."

THE GAME OF MY LIFE
BY KENDALL SIMMONS

My junior year when we played Florida and they were the No. 1 team in the country is my favorite. It was raining like hell and Damon Duval kicked (a field goal) 10 yards outside the goal posts and it curved back in to win the game. That was the most fun I had. Alex Brown and I battled it out the entire game. Our defense did a great job of shutting down their quarterback, Rex Grossman. He was just on fire that year, but we beat him and the Gators 23-20.

I still have the end zone marker from that game. I kind of tease Max Starks with it. Max kind of laughs at me that I led our team in rushing that game, because I had about two yards off a fumble I picked up and I got killed, too, when I did that. That game was so much fun. I will never forget it.

The Alabama game my freshman year when we came back and beat them at the end was really memorable, too. That and the Florida game are the ones that really stand out to me, but the Florida game is the one that really stands out because I had developed a lot more as a player. I think the game with Florida had a little more meaning to me because of my rivalry with Alex Brown and the fact that they were ranked No. 1 in the country. I felt like I had a really big role in that game.

The weather was real bad. I remember the wind was blowing so hard the rain was coming down sideways. It was a game in which both defenses were doing very well. We were doing just enough on offense to stay in the game and kick some field goals. I remember how much effort we put into it and how tired I was after the game. I don't think I have ever been as exhausted after a game as I was after that one.

The fans were so excited that they stayed into the game even in the rain. When we got a chance to tote the goal posts around the field, the students passed the goal posts up the stands and were going to throw them over the edge of the stadium. They had to come on the PA system and say, "Please don't do that because there are people walking around down there." I have never seen a stadium so excited.

FIRST ROUND DRAFT PICK

Pro scouts had been watching Simmons closely. His decision to return as a fifth-year senior proved to be a wise one when the Pittsburgh Steelers made him their first-round pick in the NFL Draft.

After earning his degree in graphic design in 2001, he made a successful transition to pro football. But just as when he arrived in college, it wasn't easy. "I don't think I have ever been so exhausted my whole life because of how many games we had to play," notes Simmons.

"You tell young guys who are coming into the NFL, 'You better condition yourself now.' You want to enjoy your first year in the NFL, go out, go to the parties, and all of that stuff, but if you are playing you better be smart about it, because you have four exhibition games, 16 regular-season games, and as many as three or four more in the playoffs. That is eight to nine more games than you play in college.

"What you don't realize is that the eighth or ninth game you hit the wall, and it was so bad for me my rookie year I couldn't get in my stance it hurt so much," he says. "My coach was laughing at me and calling me an old man. He said, 'You need to find some kind of fountain of youth because we still have eight games to go.'"

Simmons handled the challenge. A starter at guard, he was named the Steelers' top rookie and made *Pro Football Weekly* All-Rookie team. With the exception of missing the 2004 season with an ACL injury, he has been a regular in Pittsburgh's starting lineup and was a standout in his team's Super Bowl victory.

"It's great that I was able to make it to the Super Bowl in my fourth year," he says. "There are a lot of great players, guys who are Hall of Famers and legends in the game, who never had a chance to play in the Super Bowl or never won it if they did."

Simmons is so fond of Auburn that he lives there in the off-season with his wife, Celesta, and two young daughters. "I always feel good when I come back to Auburn," he says. "I don't know if any of the other guys on my team in Pittsburgh feel the same way about their schools. Since day one when I got there, I have worn my Auburn stuff and still do. When I work out, under my shoulder pads I have my old Auburn 4XL cutoff sleeve T-shirt.

"My O-line coach with the Steelers said to me one time, 'You aren't at Auburn anymore. Take that T-shirt off.' I said, 'I am not taking this off unless somebody rips it off me because this is where I came from and this is what got me here.' Even now, when those shirts get holes in them I come back to Auburn, talk to the equipment manager, and I get a couple of more shirts with the sleeves off of them.

"I am proud of where I went to school," Simmons adds. "To the other guys on the team, I want to make it clear where I went to school. I can honestly say I enjoyed every bit of my time at Auburn."

Chapter 25

FREDDIE SMITH

AN IMPRESSIVE START

In the history of Auburn football, few freshmen have made anything close to the impact on their teams as Freddie Smith did. A heavily recruited high school star, Smith exceeded even the most optimistic expectations through his contributions in the fall of 1976, the year Doug Barfield took over as head coach.

A two-time All-State running back who scored 37 touchdowns his senior season, Smith was also a standout at linebacker. His athletic ability generated countless discussions as to where his talents could best be used on a team that needed help on both sides of the ball. With the greater need on defense, Smith was tried at linebacker and he didn't disappoint.

"It didn't matter to me whether I played defense or offense as long as I could help the team win," he says. "I think I could have excelled at either position. If they had wanted me to play both ways, I would have. When I got over there at linebacker, I liked it. I said it was better to give than receive."

It didn't take long for Smith to launch his campaign of giving. He opened the season as a backup as the Tigers lost 31-19 to Arizona in Tucson. When they returned home to face the Baylor Bears, he was a first stringer.

"Everything went pretty well for me on the field my freshman year," Smith notes. "I remember [defensive coordinator] P.W. Underwood telling me they were going to get me ready to start for the second game and everything went pretty well."

"Well" might be an understatement. Although the Tigers lost again, Smith put on a show for the home folks versus Baylor. Paul Ellen, who was the stadium public address announcer that day, notes that time after time he kept saying, "Tackle by Freddie Smith." It happened so often that Ellen says he questioned his spotter to make sure he was certain that it was really one player making so many stops.

Smith's 22 tackles set a school record. However, it took the linebacker, who earned the nickname "Fast Freddie," just one week to break his record as he finished with 24 tackles as the Tigers won their SEC opener, defeating Tennessee 38-28 in Birmingham.

Tennessee was one of a large number of colleges that had recruited Smith. He considered in-state offers from Alabama and Alabama A&M and offers from a variety of SEC teams like Ole Miss, Mississippi State, and Florida, and even from colleges as far away as Penn State. However, he decided to stay in state and play for the Tigers, who had just come off a disappointing year in Shug Jordan's 25th and final season as head coach of the Tigers.

"I remember Auburn invited me to come to campus, and the people there seemed more down to earth," Smith says. "They really welcomed me in like they had known me all of their lives. The people who were there were real friendly. They made me feel real comfortable, and that is why I chose Auburn."

As he joined the Auburn Family, he left a rather large one back in Athens. "I am one of 14 children," he says. "I had six other brothers. That is what got me started in sports in general. I grew up watching them compete. We would play backyard football and basketball and we competed against each other and the kids who were in the neighborhood. It really helped me in sports."

The linebacker notes that he enjoyed having so many brothers and sisters. "There was always something going on all of the time. We had a lot of fun with each other growing up. We made each other better."

Smith says having 14 kids kept his parents busy. "My dad was a construction worker and my mom stayed at home and made sure we all we got fed. My dad did a lot of work."

Smith began playing organized football as a seventh grader and was a natural. He also excelled in basketball and track, but football was his ticket to college. He rushed for more than 1,000 yards each year as an All-State junior and senior. "I guess it kind of hit me that I was a college prospect just before my senior year," he remembers. "That is when different colleges came through and started talking to me."

Freddie Smith (31) goes airborne to attack a Georgia runner.
Auburn University Media Relations

The recruiters who stopped by Athens High knew what they were doing. By the end of the 1976 season, Smith led the Tigers in total tackles with 125, including 76 individual stops. However, the freshman almost didn't stick around to put up those big numbers.

"College was a new experience," Smith says. "I got homesick and I told Coach Barfield I was ready to go back home. He called my mom and talked to her and she called me and told me it was best for me to stay there.

"It was my first time away from home. It was a major adjustment, trying to juggle my time and understand my purpose there. Once I got that on track, everything went fine. My freshman year turned out to be a lot of fun. It might have been my favorite season."

Smith's impressive play continued as a sophomore. His 1977 tackle total of 193 is the school record, a mark that has never been seriously threatened. A high-energy performer, Smith totaled 114 solo stops that fall, making tackles all over the field.

"My sophomore season started like my freshman year," he remembers. "I kept doing the things I had been doing. I worked hard to be successful and I didn't let anything stand in my way. I was determined to become the best player I could be."

The only season he didn't lead the team in tackles was his junior year. "I had a knee surgery during that summer," Smith notes. "I made it back by the Tennessee game, which was the third game of the season. When I got back out there, I felt like I picked up where I left off."

As a senior he had another monster year with 162 tackles, the third highest total in Auburn history. "I felt like I picked up where I left off and played to the expectations of myself and what the other players had for me," Smith says.

"I tried to give them everything I could," he adds. "I feel like that was my best year as a player. I was more mature and more equipped to do the things I needed to do. We went 8-3 that year and that was the best team I was on in college."

THE GAME OF MY LIFE
BY FREDDIE SMITH

My very first start is the one that stands out. It was against Baylor. I was scared stiff when I found out I was going to start. After I got out there and I got hit for the first time, I said to myself, "I am never going to be the last one around the pile." That really got me started. I was determined to be the first person there for every tackle that was made on the field.

I didn't realize I had made that many tackles (22) that game until Coach Underwood came to me and said, "Did you know you had that many tackles?" He also told me that I had made SEC Player of the Week, so I was just ecstatic about that. That was probably my most memorable year.

Toward the end of the game, they pulled me out and the people in the stands were yelling, "Freddie, Freddie, Freddie!" I was thinking, "What is that?" It just went on from there.

We were in a 5-2 defense and I was the weak side linebacker and Mike McQuaig was the strong side linebacker my freshman year. They set it up so I could roam because of the speed that I had. Out on the field I was thinking like a running back, getting to the hole where the running back is supposed to be.

After getting hooked up at linebacker, I really enjoyed that position. I always had plenty of confidence in myself and I felt that, given the opportunity, I was going to make the best of it. Once I got the opportunity I never looked over my left shoulder or my right shoulder. I kept my focus forward and stayed on my track. I wasn't going to let anybody turn me around.

"FREDDIE, FREDDIE, FREDDIE"

Smith finished his Auburn playing days with his name throughout the record book. He was certainly a favorite of the fans, who loved to chant his name. "I don't know for sure why they did that," he says. "I assume it was because I was always playing from sideline to sideline and my name was called a lot on the loudspeaker during games. That is what sparked it."

The linebacker says he enjoyed his college days. "I would say what stands out most are the people I met and the players I played with, like Joe Cribbs, James Brooks, and William Andrews. Those guys had a lot to do with keeping me positive. I would talk to them and they would give me words of encouragement.

"I truly enjoyed being coached by Doug Barfield," Smith adds. "He was a heck of a good coach. He turned the program around from [4-7] my freshman year to 8-3 my senior year, and he was a real gentleman."

Smith wasn't finished with football after the 1979 season. "After college I tried out for the Minnesota Vikings," he says. "I went to their camp and got released on the last cut. Then I went to Canada and played there for one year. I played in Winnipeg, Manitoba, for the Blue Bombers in the CFL. The game there was well suited for me with the wider field and 12 guys. It was different, but I enjoyed it.

"Then I came back to the States and played in the USFL with the Birmingham Stallions in 1983 and 1984. After that, I knew it was time for me to get out of it. I was tired of it.

"After I finished pro football, I went to work," he says. "I decided it was time to find a job. I guess from 1985 to 1987 I was in car sales with Toyota. In 1987 and 1988, I opened a video store and then sold that. I went to work for a company called Brasfield & Gorrie, and I have been with them for 18 years."

Smith and his wife, Gwendolyn, have two children. Freda is 29 and Timothy, 17, is a three-sport athlete just like his dad. He plays for Midfield High, where he has shown the potential to be a college athlete.

The former linebacker notes that he enjoys keeping up with Auburn and has a good relationship with the coaches. "I came back to school in 1998 and 1999 and finished my degree," Smith says. "It was part of Operation Follow Through. It is an excellent program for guys who want to come back and finish their degrees. I think many more players will do that as long as the program is there.

"I am really pleased with how the team has been playing and how the whole program is being run. We have a really quality head coach in Tommy Tuberville. He has really turned the whole program around again. I had the opportunity to be a student coach under him for the 1999 season. I got to spend the whole year with him while I was back in school and I really truly enjoyed being around his staff, which is a very fine staff. I have got a lot of respect for him and his staff. It is a very cohesive group and he is just a normal person. He isn't above himself. He is an excellent people person."

Smith himself was well liked by students, teammates, and coaches during his playing days. He brought energy to the team and seemed to always enjoy what he was doing, something he confirms. "I had a lot of fun playing football," he says. "That kept me going all of the time. Every time I stepped out on the field I was out there to have fun, and that made it interesting."

Chapter 26

PAT SULLIVAN

A LOVE OF THE GAME(S)

Auburn fans have been passionate about football since the sport came to their campus in the 1890s. In nearly 120 years of competition, many Tigers have played the game well enough to excite the fans, but it is doubtful any have been more loved or better respected than 1971 Heisman Trophy winner Pat Sullivan.

Also a favorite of Hall of Fame coach Ralph "Shug" Jordan, Sullivan's sophomore season was one of the most anticipated in Auburn history, as fans couldn't wait to see No. 7 finally throw the football for the varsity after giving an impressive preview of coming attractions as the star of the 1968 freshman team.

The anticipation actually began before his freshman season, dating back to the time the highly recruited John Carroll High star chose the Tigers over Alabama, Georgia, and many others as the most celebrated quarterback in Alabama high school history.

Growing up on the west side of Birmingham, Sullivan was an accomplished athlete who drew large crowds to his high school games to see him play long before he set foot on campus.

"I have been involved in sports ever since I was born," Sullivan says. "That was just something kids did then. From the time I was old enough to remember, what I would get for Christmas would be a new baseball glove, a basketball, a football, or something that pertained to sports. We just played one season after the next. We played in the street. We played in the yard. It was just a way of life."

Sullivan says baseball was probably his favorite sport growing up, and No. 7 of the New York Yankees was the guy he admired the most. "Mickey Mantle was my hero, as he was to most boys of our generation," he says. "In fact, that is why I wore No. 7," adds the quarterback who was honored by Auburn when they retired his jersey.

Sullivan liked other sports, too, particularly football, which came on strong as popular television programming in the 1960s when he was growing up. "When I would watch football, I remember watching the Packers and Bart Starr," he says. "I always thought he was something special, and he is. I tried to emulate some of him."

The future Tiger was also a standout guard in basketball and worked the sport into his busy schedule. "Until my senior year in high school when I didn't have spring football practice, I think there would be maybe one or two days out of the year I would go home after school when I didn't have some form of practice or a game," he says. "It was something I enjoyed doing, something I treasured.

"When I was in high school in the summertime I played baseball. I played on an American Legion team and a team called the Southside 21s, which was like a semi-pro team. I would literally play six or seven days a week and have a job."

Sullivan, the oldest in his family with a brother, Joe, also an Auburn quarterback, and sisters, Karen and Connie, inherited his athleticism from his father, Jerry, who was a star performer at West End High School. Jerry signed a football scholarship with the University of Georgia. However, World War II and service in the Air Force interrupted those plans. After the war he played on the first Howard College (now Samford University) football team in Birmingham, where his son is now head football coach.

"Early on in high school, baseball was probably the sport I was getting more attention in," Sullivan remembers. "Back then, basically freshmen didn't play, but I did. I ended up playing American Legion ball that summer with guys who were 18 who had just graduated high school, and I was the only one who was 15.

"I remember Alabama actually offered me a baseball scholarship when I was a freshman in high school. Coach [Auburn offensive coordinator Gene] Lorendo, when I was a junior, was the first one to offer me a football scholarship. I guess it was actually the first game of my junior year when he came to see [future Auburn receiver] Alvin Bresler play. We were playing

Pat Sullivan won the 1971 Heisman Trophy.
Auburn University Media Relations

Shades Valley. Coach Lorendo came over after the game, introduced himself and talked to me. Of course, at that time all of that was legal."

Sullivan was a three-year starter in football for John Carroll, although he almost missed the opening game of his high school career. After his American Legion team won the state title before his sophomore year, it advanced to the league's world series in Orangeburg, South Carolina.

Sullivan arrived home in time to begin practice two days before the football opener. He started that night at safety. Because he had missed practice time, he didn't play quarterback, but when John Carroll wanted to pass it, he would put the sophomore at running back and let him toss a halfback pass.

RECRUITING VICTORY FOR AUBURN

After a tremendous high school career in all three sports, Sullivan decided that he would concentrate on football in college. He had a long list of suitors.

"Growing up in that area [Birmingham], living in the state, you picked one of the two schools you followed," he says. "I basically picked Auburn. I was fortunate to be recruited by a lot of people, including very strongly by Alabama and Auburn. It was awfully hard to tell coach [Clem] Gryska no. He was at Alabama. With Coach Lorendo and Coach Jordan, I just developed a relationship with them. And then I had some teammates who I played high school ball with, Tom Banks and Dick Schmalz, and they were at Auburn.

"I will never forget that my dad, when it came time to make the decision, we were talking about it as a family and he said, 'I want you to go to school where, if you don't play a down, it is where you want to go to school and get your degree. The football stuff will take care of itself.'

"Auburn is probably where I felt most comfortable," Sullivan says. "Back then recruiting was so different than it is today. You had unlimited visits. I ended up visiting Notre Dame, but I couldn't see myself going that far away from my family. It was impressive. I saw Notre Dame and Southern Cal play for a national championship on a visit.

"[Georgia head coach Vince] Dooley is somebody I had gotten close to, and Billy Payne, who today is head of Augusta [National Golf Club] and was also the head of Olympics in Atlanta, he was a senior then and actually recruited me for Georgia. I got real close to Billy and had a trust with him. Probably the three schools were Auburn, Georgia, and Alabama."

Much to the delight of Jordan and Auburn fans, Sullivan chose the Tigers and word spread of the promising young quarterback on his way to the Plains. If freshmen had been eligible in that era, fans would have been counting down the days until Sullivan lined up for the Tigers. Instead, larger than normal crowds turned out for freshman games to get a glimpse of the QB.

He lived up to advance billing and added even more interest to the Sullivan watch by teaming up with future All-America receiver Terry Beasley to lead the Tigers to a thrilling come from behind victory over the Alabama freshmen.

"I think the transition to college was great," he says. "Freshmen were not eligible when we came in, so there were more numbers than what comes in today. It seems like there were five or six quarterbacks and there were probably 50 of us coming in on scholarship. We were the scout team and we kind of formed our own bond. It was a group that was close.

"I also knew a lot of the older players. They made you feel welcome and feel a part of it. There was hazing back in that time. You had to sing songs and all of that. Once you went through the initiation part of it, you kind of felt a part of it."

As expected, Sullivan opened his sophomore year as the starting quarterback. It didn't take college football long to see what the excitement was about as he led the Tigers to a 57-0 victory over Wake Forest on opening day of the 1969 season.

Before he moved on to the NFL, Sullivan set school records for passing yardage (6,284), touchdown passes (53), and total TDs (71) as he led the Tigers to three bowl games, winning MVP honors in two of them. Also a threat to run the ball, he netted 559 yards and 18 touchdowns and set an NCAA record as a junior, averaging 8.57 yards per play while leading the nation in total offense with 2,856 yards.

As a junior and senior he was named SEC Player of the Year and a first-team All-American. He could have put up even bigger numbers, but the Tigers won many games by such large margins in the Sullivan era he often spent fourth quarters watching his backups run the offense.

His junior season, in which he passed for 2,586 yards and 17 touchdowns while rushing for nine more averaging 5.1 yards per rush, is still probably the best all-around season by an Auburn quarterback.

Sullivan had so many impressive games that it is difficult to single out one as the best. One of the most memorable was the 1971 showdown at Athens between unbeaten Auburn and unbeaten Georgia in one of the most highly anticipated games in SEC history. Sullivan put on a show, leading the Tigers to a 35-20 victory in a super-charged atmosphere at Sanford Stadium as he threw four touchdown passes against a highly regarded defense—a performance that likely put him over the top in the balloting for the 1971 Heisman Trophy.

When Sullivan won the award, it set off a big celebration in Auburn, something he was able to be a part of. "The Heisman ceremony, which everybody sees now, is an announcement on television from New York, and the players have four or five people there with them—maybe their mom and dad, along with their coach," Sullivan notes. "When I won it, it was announced at halftime of the Georgia-Georgia Tech game and I watched it on TV in Auburn just like everybody else did.

"When it was over, I was able to go to the coliseum to the football offices and all of my teammates, my coaches, the Auburn family, [AU president Dr. Harry] Philpott, and other people were there. They could share in that moment with me and I could share it with them. That was something that was special. I think as time goes on, I am sure it meant a lot to the teammates to be there and be a part of it, because they certainly were a part of it."

THE GAME OF MY LIFE
PAT SULLIVAN

We were so fortunate to play so many big games. Obviously, my senior game in Athens was special. I still don't know if I have been in a better atmosphere. You had the sixth-ranked and seventh-ranked teams in the country and there was no TV, so tickets were hard to get. The interest was at an all-time high. It was the first time in the history of both schools that they were both unbeaten at that time of the season.

I guess, selfishly, my favorite is the first Auburn-Alabama game I played in 1969. Being from Birmingham, I sold Cokes in the east stands as a kid growing up, dreaming of one day having an opportunity to play in that game. There it was. You were right in the middle of that big crowd in that scene.

To play in that Auburn-Alabama game, that was something that was special. I will always treasure that.

There were a lot of big moments in that game. I think the big turning point was right before the half. We got the ball back with about a minute and 20 seconds to go. I think Alabama had been leading at that time and we took it right down and scored (on a three-yard run by Wallace Clark) just as the half was ending. I don't think Auburn had won in six years against Alabama, and that touchdown gave us a lot of confidence. We were the better football team and we should have won that day.

MORE FOOTBALL FOR SULLIVAN

Sullivan, a poised, polite, and polished person off the field, was a fierce competitor when a game was on the line. He was a big reason the Tigers posted a 27-7 record during his three seasons. Throughout that time, and even after he graduated and played for the NFL's lowly Atlanta Falcons for four seasons before finishing with the Washington Redskins, Sullivan maintained a close relationship with his college coach.

"As time wore on, Coach Jordan and I got very close," he says. "I can remember, towards the end of my career and after I got through playing, countless times going over to his house sitting in his backyard. We talked and shared things. We developed quite a relationship. There is no doubt that he had a big influence on my life."

Sullivan points out the time he spent with Jordan helped send him on a career path toward coaching. "You learn from people you are around and you want to be with," he says. "Coaching is something that I thought I always wanted to do. We talked about that in his backyard at times.

"When I was playing ball and he passed away, and as things were developing and I was in business before I decided to go into coaching—and throughout my coaching career—I missed talking to Coach Jordan because I really didn't have someone who was a mentor, so to speak."

Also an Academic All-American, Sullivan put his business degree to use before he began coaching. First, he went into the insurance field and then became a tire company executive before the football bug bit him again. He accepted a post on Pat Dye's Auburn staff in 1986 and coached quarterbacks before taking a head coaching job in 1992 at TCU.

Sullivan became Southwest Conference Coach of the Year and was offered the job as head coach at LSU. He was interested in returning to the SEC, but there was a problem buying out his contract, and he stayed in Fort Worth through the 1998 season before resigning there. However, he wasn't finished with football and took a post as offensive coordinator at UAB in his hometown.

He helped the Blazers put together their best offensive seasons before facing the challenge of his life in 2003, when he was diagnosed with throat cancer, requiring chemotherapy and radiation treatments. "I don't think there is any doubt it changed my life in a major way," he says.

"When that doctor tells you that you have a 40-percent to 50-percent chance to live, stark reality comes in. Your priorities change. You want to cherish every day. You want to make sure you have a great relationship with the man upstairs and with your family."

With the help of lots of love and support from his large circle of family and friends, including his wife, Jean, and their children, Kim, Kelly, and Patrick, Sullivan showed the same toughness in his battle to survive that he had displayed as an athlete. Despite some very rough days in the hospital as he battled pneumonia in addition to cancer, the always tough competitor pulled through.

He returned to coaching at UAB and on December 1, 2006, was named head football coach at Samford University and given the assignment of rebuilding a program that is moving into the highly competitive Southern Conference. Sullivan says his goals are "to cherish every day" as head coach of the Bulldogs with the opportunity to live close to family and friends and to be "just as competitive as I was as a youngster at Auburn."

Sullivan set numerous records and won countless awards in sports, but that isn't what stands out to him.

"I think what you get out of athletics, when it is all said and done, are the relationships that last for a lifetime," he says. "That is what I cherish about my career—my relationships with my teammates, coaches, and all of the people. There is obviously not a day that goes by or a service station I go in that somebody doesn't bring it up."

That's not surprising, because, although it has been a long time since he threw a pass or ran past a linebacker, Auburn fans still love Pat Sullivan.

Chapter 27

BEN TAMBURELLO

LATE BLOOMER

A willingness to work harder and longer than many athletes paid dividends for Ben Tamburello, who, as an undersized offensive lineman at Shades Valley High School, got no love from college recruiters.

For the Auburn football program, it turned out to be a good thing that the future All-America center was not easily discouraged.

"I tried a lot of different sports when I was young and I don't think I was any good at anything," Tamburello says. "Then I got a little older and got a little size and started getting a little better, and I found that I just kind of fit in on the offensive line. I felt like it was something I could work hard at and see some results.

"Football just became a natural sport for me. The harder I worked, although it wasn't a glamour position, the more I felt like I could do well at it."

Tamburello's work paid off with a starting assignment his junior and senior high school years. He was a good center, but at 215 pounds, he was not big enough to draw college scouts' interest. "I wasn't recruited by anybody," he remembers. "The rules were a lot different than they are now. I was able to go to a postgraduate school, Tennessee Military Institute, after I graduated from high school. We played college junior varsity teams. We played Georgia, Tennessee, Notre Dame, UTC, South Carolina. We would play their freshmen and sophomores in a game-type atmosphere.

"What going to TMI did was give you exposure to colleges. If you played well against their teams, it got you noticed by the coaches and it also gave you an extra year to play without giving up any eligibility."

Tamburello, who began his senior year of high school as a 17-year-old, figured he was going to get bigger. "Going to TMI gave me an extra year to grow," he says. "I was maturing and with that, I put on weight and got stronger while getting to play an extra year.

"From the time I finished my high school season I knew I was going to TMI, so I began working out immediately and eating to try to put on weight. I was eating protein powder and working out six days a week."

The combination of an extra year, the diet, and the workout regime made a big difference. He grew into a 250-pounder in prep school and became a dominating center. After that, it didn't take long for college coaches to start calling.

"I began being recruited by coach [Bear] Bryant at Alabama, Jerry Stovall at LSU, Johnny Majors at Tennessee, and Jerry Claiborne at Kentucky," Tamburello recalls. "It was a pretty neat thing for me. That is when I started thinking, 'I may be able to play in the SEC and, who knows, maybe one day I will be able to play in the pros.'"

The fall of 1982, when Tamburello attended prep school, was Pat Dye's second season at Auburn. Dye got into the recruiting battle and came away a winner.

"Coach Dye was a salesman about himself and the program," Tamburello notes. "He had a lot of energy and he knew that he had it on the right track and was going to be a winner.

"I grew up in Birmingham, an Alabama fan and a Bear Bryant fan, and I had been recruited by Coach Bryant. I felt like, during the season, that is probably where I would end up going, but toward the end of that season, which was Bryant's last, I took my visit to Tuscaloosa. They were playing Southern Miss for homecoming and got beat. During that trip, I didn't get to spend too much time with Coach Bryant.

"When I went to Auburn, I spent a great deal of time with Coach Dye, who also spent a lot of time with my parents. That meant a lot to me, that he was willing to spend a lot of time recruiting me. I felt like I would have a better chance of him being around and spending time with me when I needed it as a player there in Auburn. Just the fact that I watched practice with him and the type of players he was recruiting and the type of practices with the discipline and all of that, I felt like it was an atmosphere I might be able to do well in.

Ben Tamburello was a four-year starter for AU and an NFL lineman.
Auburn University Media Relations

"Coach Dye is an impressive guy," Tamburello adds. "Sitting there in front of him talking about what his plans were for Auburn and some of the people who were coming and what the plans were for me, that was exciting. Looking at Alabama, there were a lot of questions there. We didn't know if Coach Bryant was going to be around or what his health was like. They kind of had a tough year his last year. They lost to Auburn at the end of the year and it kind of looked like the balance was shifting to Auburn. All of those things came into play in me deciding to go to Auburn."

INSTANT IMPACT

On January 5, 1983, Tamburello enrolled at Auburn and participated in winter workouts and then spring training. He fit in quickly and showed the decision to sign him was a wise one. As a freshman, he opened the season starting at center and stayed there for every game of his college career. He played a key role in '83, as the Tigers won their first SEC Championship under Dye.

Tamburello made his first All-SEC and All-America teams as a junior and was a consensus All-American as a senior, playing a major role in Auburn's success running the football. He also adjusted to college quickly in the classroom and earned Academic All-SEC honors.

"I was very fortunate to have started all four years," he says. "My two biggest memories my freshman year were starting in the Alabama game— the Iron Bowl at Legion Field I grew up watching—and starting in the Sugar Bowl, which meant so much to us.

"My biggest memory, period, of my freshman year was sitting on the bus after we won the Sugar Bowl game. We were going back to the hotel and hearing Nebraska, who was No. 1, getting beat. Also, that same day Georgia beat Texas, which was ranked No. 2. We were No. 3 and won, so I am sitting there thinking, 'We just won the national championship!' It didn't end up working out that way because Miami ended up going from fourth to one. I think Nebraska stayed at two and we stayed at three.

"That was the most talented college football team that I have ever been around," Tamburello says. "We had great guys and great leadership. If there was ever a team that should have won a national championship, that would have been the one, with the schedule that we played and finishing 11-1. That was some kind of special year."

Tamburello notes that he enjoyed his time in college and says it was fun to be around great athletes. "When I was at Auburn, I played with three people who dominated their sport, with Bo Jackson in football, Charles Barkley in basketball, and Frank Thomas in baseball. At one time, those three guys were at the top of their respective sports. I played with a Heisman Trophy winner [Jackson] and a Lombardi and Outland winner, Tracy Rocker. We won an SEC Championship. There were so many things that happened that you look back on and think, 'That is really something unique and special.' The most important thing, though, is the friendships you still have."

Tamburello notes the most important person he met as a college student was his wife, Katy. That happened on Halloween of 1986, the same night as one of the most gut-wrenching losses during the Dye era.

The unbeaten Tigers blew a 17-0 lead in Gainesville to an inferior Florida team and fell 18-17. The day started out badly when the bus wrecked on the way to the stadium, but it finished spectacularly for Tamburello.

"That was a tough loss, obviously, because it was a game we should have won, but it was a great day for me," he says. "I remember that night after we flew back to Montgomery and took the bus back to Auburn, it was about midnight. My teammates Kurt Crain, Rob Selby, and John Hudson and I didn't really have any place to go. We ended up going to the War Eagle Supper Club, which is open late. I liked my odds hanging around those guys as far as being able to find a nice lady I could talk to. That was the night I met Katy."

Tamburello says in hindsight he is glad he made the decision to play for the Tigers. "A lot of being successful has a lot to do with being in the right place at the right time," he says. "I could have gone to another school and maybe never played a down. At Auburn I was very fortunate to play for a bunch of good coaches, like Neil Callaway and James Daniel. I am thankful for the choice I made to come to Auburn."

THE GAME OF MY LIFE
BY BEN TAMBURELLO

The Alabama game my senior year, which was 1986, is a game I remember like it was yesterday. We only had a handful of seniors and we weren't expected to do a lot. The expectations for our team that year weren't that great. We ended up going 10-2 and we finished the regular season beating Alabama. Then we went to the Citrus Bowl and beat USC. It was just a terrific year.

Winning that Alabama game was great, especially with all of the adversity we had on our last drive. We were able to find a way to go ahead and win it. That made it more special. I remember Trey Gainous catching a pass on fourth and two from Jeff Burger to continue the drive. I remember Brent Fullwood had a great run and got us close to the goal line. Then we ran the reverse and (wide receiver) Scott Bolton was supposed to be in the game, but Lawyer Tillman was in there. We ran it anyway and we scored. It just capped off a year when we weren't expected to do much and we did.

I think that year was a springboard for the success that Auburn and Coach Dye had in the next three years when they won three consecutive SEC Championships, and there were so many great players on those teams. The year before, we had a tough year and had gotten beat at the Cotton Bowl to end the season. I think that 1986 season turned things around and made it possible to have the success the team had in the late 1980s.

I remember I was the captain for the Alabama game my senior year and I called the coin toss. I was a nervous wreck. The night before the game, I was thinking about whether I was going to call heads or tails and walking out on that field to represent my team at Legion Field against Alabama.

We wore white that year and they wore red. I had grown up watching the Tide play and now I was out there representing Auburn. We won the coin toss and I remember the whole pageantry of the game. It was so important to us and to win the way we did in the last minute, coming from behind, was a terrific experience. It is something I will never forget.

PHILLY FAN

The All-American wasn't done with football after the bowl victory over Southern Cal. He was selected in the third round of the NFL Draft by the Eagles and, just like in college, he impressed the coaches with his toughness and talent.

"I played with Philadelphia for five seasons, and I was fortunate that I was never traded and was able to play for two contracts with Philly," says Tamburello, who played center, guard, and snapped for field goals as a pro. "Playing through my fifth year, I decided that was about all I could do.

"I was very lucky. We went to the playoffs three of the five years I was there. I played with Reggie White and Randall Cunningham. I played for Buddy Ryan and I played in some of the best games. I was part of the Fog Bowl when we played Chicago. I was part of the rivalries with the Cowboys, the New York Giants, and the Washington Redskins in the NFC East. I saw some great football in some great arenas.

"Philly is such a unique place with all of its personality. Recently we have seen so much of that with the movie about Vince Papale and *Rocky VI*. It shows you what kind of neat place Philly is. It is a great place to play pro football.

"We had Jeff Fisher on our staff as defensive backs coach. He has been the Tennessee Titans' coach for 15 years. Reggie White was probably the greatest defensive lineman and Randall Cunningham was one of the great athletes I have seen, along with Bo Jackson. I just ran across some really unique people. It was a great experience."

Reflecting on his years in college, the lineman says, "The people I met and the friends and the relationships I built at Auburn are still special to me. Every day I talk to guys who I played with at Auburn. I was fortunate enough to finish and get my degree and meet my wife at Auburn. We have three kids now who are all Auburn through and through, and my goal in life is to get all three to Auburn and get them through with a degree.

"When you are 18 years old, you don't always understand how important some decisions are going to be, but for me that was an important one and a great one. Playing for Auburn and Coach Dye was a great experience. It is something that I would never change or trade."

Chapter 28

WILLIE WHITEHEAD

POWER OF PERSISTENCE, PART I

As a young boy, Willie Whitehead dreamed of putting on an Auburn football uniform and stepping onto the field at Jordan-Hare Stadium to play for the Tigers. He tenaciously held onto that dream despite finishing high school without a single scholarship offer from a major college program.

"Growing up in Tuskegee, I played other sports, but football was always my love," Whitehead says. "I was probably about eight years old when I started getting interested in sports. I got involved in Little League, and that was about the time my father started taking me to games at Auburn. I used to go up to see the stadium and I dreamed about one day playing there."

Known as "Sarge," Willie Whitehead Sr. retired from the military just about the time Willie Jr. was born in Montgomery.

"My dad didn't play any sports," the defensive end says. "He was in the military the majority of his life and he didn't have an opportunity to do that, but he exposed me to those opportunities. His taking me to Auburn really shaped my desire to play football."

Whitehead was a good all-around athlete. He competed in all three sports his high school offered—football, basketball, plus track and field. In football, he broke into the starting lineup as a junior. "I was an outside linebacker and a tight end that season," he recalls. "We didn't have enough players on our team, so everybody had to play both ways. I had trouble catching the ball, so I moved to the offensive line and played guard."

227

Whitehead developed into an excellent high school player, but as a skinny senior he was an under-the-radar recruit. His only scholarship offer came from hometown Tuskegee University, a Division II program.

"I really got my growth in college," he says. "When I was in high school I probably weighed about 185 pounds. Once I got through my senior year, going into my freshman year in college I had a growth spurt, and that is when I was able to start putting on weight. I was able to get on a plan and work on it."

An NFL assistant coach, James Daniel, helped Whitehead get to Auburn. A member of Pat Dye's original Auburn staff formed in 1981, Daniel's brother was coaching at Tuskegee Institute High, so he gave Auburn assistant coach Joe Whitt a tip on Whitehead's potential.

Whitt personally checked out the defensive end in a game. He was impressed, but the Tigers didn't have a scholarship available. However, that didn't discourage Whitehead, especially after he heard that Whitt could bring him to Auburn as an invited walk-on who would get an immediate chance to show the coaches what he could do. "After they told me that, I let them know I was on my way," Whitehead says.

CHASING THE DREAM

The Tigers had just won a third consecutive SEC Championship when Whitehead enrolled for classes in 1990. He immediately went to work in the weight room and at the training table. It didn't take long to add muscle and size. As a redshirt, he gained 35 pounds his first year on campus. By the time he graduated, he was close to 80 pounds bigger than he was when he arrived.

An honor student in high school, Whitehead had no trouble making the adjustment off the field. On the field he did well, too, earning praise from the coaches for his desire to succeed.

Whitehead saw his first game action in 1991 as a redshirt freshman. "I didn't play a whole lot that season, but the times I did get in there, I made plays and I know that Coach Whitt and the other coaches noticed that," he says. "I think they saw that this kid makes plays, and they were thinking, 'We are going to continue to look at him.' I continued to work hard, I continued to push myself, and ended up eventually earning a starting spot."

Whitehead arrived with the confidence he could play at the SEC level, which became obvious to even casual observers who attended the A-Day spring game prior to his sophomore season. "I had a great game and I knew I was going to make it after that," he says. "I knew then I could play with

Willie Whitehead went from being a college walk-on to an NFL starter.
Draughon Library Archives

these guys. I made a lot of plays and took the notice of Coach Whitt and the players. They were saying, 'This guy is something special.'"

Whitt, who instructed ends and linebackers with the Tigers from 1981 through 2005, says that Whitehead and another walk-on who had a long NFL career, Kevin Greene, are the hardest workers he's coached.

Whitehead's effort and steady improvement got Dye's attention, and the head coach put him on scholarship as a sophomore. "When that happened I felt like I had made it," Whitehead says. "Back then the walk-ons couldn't even go through the Tiger Walk. You had to go down to the stadium and dress early.

"That was a really exciting time to have that feeling that I had arrived, I had made it on the Auburn team. It was always my dream to play for Auburn and to play in that stadium." Whitehead saw extensive action as a redshirt sophomore and performed well. He broke into the starting lineup on a full-time basis as a junior and stayed there, developing into one of the best ends in the SEC.

Whitehead says he thoroughly enjoyed his time in college and still has strong relationships with many of his teammates. One of his favorite memories was being a part of the 11-0 Tigers his junior season.

"I knew that with the nucleus of the team coming back, we were going to be special in 1993," he says. "I think that year we were the best team in the country. We also had a good team my senior season."

THE GAME OF MY LIFE
BY WILLIE WHITEHEAD

I would have to say our game against LSU my senior year was the most memorable. We played in a really big game that season. We won down at Florida when they were ranked No. 1 in the country, but the LSU game really stands out because we were behind three touchdowns and we came back and won it.

I was getting pressure on their quarterback that day. I hit [Jamie Howard] a couple of times and I got a sack on him, and I remember Brian Robinson intercepting his passes. We had back-to-back interceptions that were run back for touchdowns in the fourth quarter. That was the most remarkable game I ever played in.

LSU kept calling pass plays in the fourth quarter, and we intercepted three and kept running them back for touchdowns. It was something I had never seen in my life. I couldn't believe they kept passing. It was a remarkable thing. We played well on defense that day and we shut down their running game. I don't know why they did it, but they kept passing and we took advantage of it. It turned out big for us.

We had some great guys on the defense. I played with guys like Gary Walker and Alonzo Etheridge at the ends. We had Mike Pelton at linebacker, and in the secondary we had Brian Robinson, Calvin Jackson, and Chris Shelling back there intercepting passes. We had a lot of great athletes and a lot of those guys ended up going to the pros. They were a big part of us going 11-0 our junior year. We also had a good offense, too, although we didn't have a good game on offense against LSU that day.

POWER OF PERSISTENCE, PART II

Although he wasn't selected in the NFL Draft, Whitehead still had a passion for the game and decided to see if he could make a living playing football. It was sort of like walking on again, but without the positive feedback.

He signed a free agent deal with the '49ers, but didn't make it past mini-camp. Not ready to throw in the towel, he got a call from his agent about an expansion Canadian Football League team tryout in Baltimore. He decided to give it a shot, but spent the entire season on the Stallions' practice squad as his team won the league championship Grey Cup.

The CFL's experiment of entering the U.S. market ended the next season and Whitehead's team relocated to Montreal. After playing very well in the preseason, he expected to challenge for a starting job, but when he found out he was again assigned to the practice roster, which barely paid him enough to eat, Whitehead headed home to Tuskegee and found a job. In the meantime, however, he got an offer to play for another CFL team, the Hamilton Tiger-Cats, and decided to give it a shot. Not only did he get to play this time, but he developed into a star at outside linebacker and made 13 sacks, second in the CFL.

That drew the attention of the NFL's Detroit Lions, who brought Whitehead to training camp the following season. He stayed with the Lions until the final cut. Even though the CFL season was almost halfway done, the Tiger-Cats wanted him back, so Whitehead played more football north of the border. An NFL team again noticed his performance, and in 1999 he got a tryout with the New Orleans Saints. This time he stuck, although Coach Mike Ditka told the 26-year-old rookie, who was up to 6-foot-3 and 285 pounds, that he was too big to play outside linebacker and would need to make the team as an end.

Whitehead then got a break when a projected starting end was lost for the season with a knee injury. Once the former Tiger got in games and showed what he could do, he made the regular playing rotation and has remained a key member either in a starting role or as a reserve on the Saints' defense since.

Whitehead notes that he is thoroughly enjoying his time in the NFL and being a part of the Saints. He says that the strong run New Orleans made in the playoffs, coming up a game short of reaching the 2007 Super Bowl, was incredibly important to the community. "After what happened with Hurricane Katrina, the people of New Orleans needed some hope and I think we gave it to them. It was a real special feeling to be playing for something bigger than yourself and your team. I think we made a positive difference."

On the field, Whitehead is also contributing and expects to continue to do so. "I still feel like I am in the prime of my career. I have played pro football for eight years and have gained a lot of experience. I still have a lot of years left."

Whitehead, who maintains homes in New Orleans and Atlanta, is still a big Auburn fan. "I have good memories of my time there. There were a lot of great times and I played with a lot of great guys," adds Whitehead, who is proof that dreams can come true for people willing to work hard enough to make them happen.